Meditation from Sinai

Shabbat as the
Tabernacle inside
of us.

Cover Art: *Revelation at Sinai*, Lesley Friedmann, 2017, acrylic on board, British Columbia, Canada

Printed in the United States of America
© Copyrighted and Published 2022
by The Rohr Jewish Learning Institute
832 Eastern Parkway, Brooklyn, NY 11213

718-221-6900
WWW.MYJLI.COM

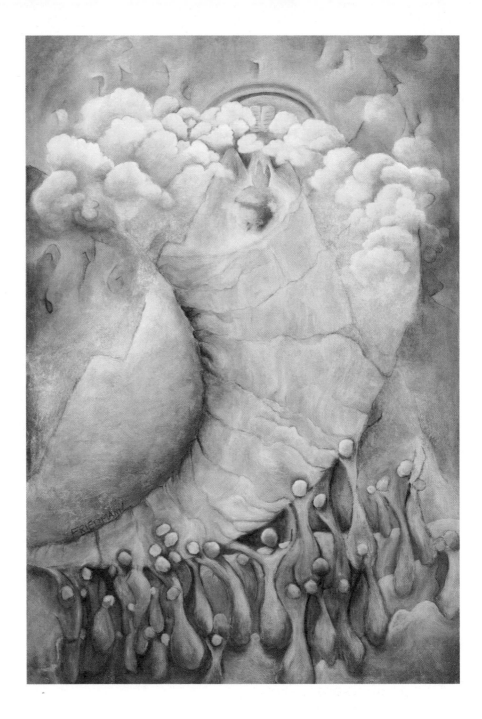

Meditation from Sinai

STUDENT
TEXTBOOK

Mindful awareness and Divine
spirituality to help you think,
feel, and live more deeply

The Rohr Jewish Learning Institute gratefully acknowledges the pioneering and ongoing support of

George and Pamela Rohr

Since its inception, the Rohr JLI has been a beneficiary of the vision, generosity, care, and concern of the Rohr family.

In the merit of the tens of thousands of hours of Torah study by JLI students worldwide, may they be blessed with health, *Yiddishe nachas* from all their loved ones, and extraordinary success in all their endeavors.

Citation Types

SCRIPTURE

The icon for Scripture is based on the images of a scroll and a spiral. The scroll is a literal reference; the spiral symbolizes Scripture's role as the singular source from which all subsequent Torah knowledge emanates.

SCRIPTURAL COMMENTARY

Throughout the ages, Jews scrutinized the Torah's text, generating many commentaries.

TALMUD AND MIDRASH

The Talmud and Midrash record the teachings of the sages—fundamental links in the unbroken chain of the Torah's transmission going back to Mount Sinai.

TALMUDIC COMMENTARY

The layers of Talmudic teaching have been rigorously excavated in each era, resulting in a library of insightful commentaries.

JEWISH MYSTICISM

The mystics explore the inner, esoteric depths. The icon for mystical texts reflects the *"sefirot* tree" commonly present in kabbalistic charts.

JEWISH PHILOSOPHY

Jewish philosophic texts shed light on all of life's big questions. They often demonstrate the relevance of Jewish teachings even as the sands of societal values continuously shift.

JEWISH LAW AND CUSTOM

The guidance that emerges from Scripture and the Talmud finds practical expression in Jewish law, known as *halachah* ("the way"), alongside customs adopted by Jewish communities through the generations.

CHASIDUT

Chasidism's advent in the eighteenth century brought major, encouraging changes to Jewish life and outlook. Its teachings are akin to refreshing, life-sustaining waters from a continuously flowing well of the profoundest insights.

PERSPECTIVES

Personal, professional, and academic perspectives, expressed in essays, research papers, diaries, and other works, can often enhance appreciation for Torah ideas and the totality of the Jewish experience.

Contents

Foreword

Welcome to *Meditation from Sinai*, a fresh and mentally stimulating course that clarifies the Jewish view of the ancient art of meditation and advances its practice.

The course title may sound like a misnomer: When the average person mentions meditation, the last thing that springs to mind is the Sinaitic tradition delivered by Moses. It is often assumed that meditation is a product of Eastern cultures, and that mindfulness is utterly alien to Judaism.

The reality is that meditational practices have been intrinsic to Judaism for millennia, from its earliest origins. The patriarchs of the Jewish people—Abraham and his immediate family—spent the majority of their days in secluded meditation, and ever since, our ancient and rich religious heritage nurtured mindfulness as an integral component to attaining its goal of injecting meaningfulness and purpose into life's everyday practices and routines, for our greater spiritual and material health and success.

Jewish meditation builds on Judaism's classic themes and it's unique takes on topics such as Divine providence and G-d's omnipresence within the material universe. It calls for deep contemplation and facilitates profound realizations.

Meditation from Sinai is developed through six insightful lessons that cover a colorful variety of concepts within the conversation of Jewish meditation. It explores the argument that meditation is rightly and profoundly a Jewish practice with ancient roots, and it delves into the purposes and goals of Jewish meditation. These include immediate goals such as improving overall well-being, banishing negative thoughts, and steering the mind toward positive and spiritual reality. Beyond those, its more primary goal is to deepen our spiritual perspective of ourselves, the world around us, and G-d.

An overarching distinction between Jewish meditation and that of several other cultures is that the latter employ mindfulness techniques as tools of escape that allow a person to break free of the mundane—and they therefore lean heavily on terms such as "transcendence." By contrast, Jewish thought and practice embrace mindfulness and meditation to achieve the very opposite: to inject meaning and purpose into the everyday—into the decidedly non-transcendent, material, and corporeal, and even into the downright boring.

Meditation from Sinai is a journey. Successive focused meditations, featuring a variety of practical meditation types, allow participants to peel back layers of externality and discover the depths of wonder and meaning hiding in plain sight all around us. They also uncover that wonder already existing within each individual, buried but blazing silently in the depths of our souls.

Even while it supplies meditations, Judaism frowns on leaving ideas in the abstract. Just as Moses received G-d's word atop Mount Sinai but then descended the mountain to its very base in order to transmit G-d's message, every lofty realization must be translated into practicality, to impact our daily living. To that end, the course provides meditative thought patterns and techniques designed to infuse spiritual understandings into matters as mundane as the food we eat and the work we do. The result is a fresh and empowering view of our world, and a practical toolkit for dramatically improving our material and spiritual well-being.

Continuing Education Credits

The *Meditation from Sinai* series is cosponsored by The Wellness Institute and The Rohr Jewish Learning Institute to provide psychologists and mental health providers with an introductory cultural sensitivity to Jewish spirituality and mindful awareness practices that contribute to happiness, well-being, and emotional and behavioral regulation.

ACCREDITATION STATEMENT

The Wellness Institute is approved by the **American Psychological Association** to sponsor continuing education for psychologists. The Wellness Institute maintains responsibility for this program and its content.

CREDITS PER SESSION: 1.5

BEHAVIORAL LEARNING OBJECTIVES FOR PSYCHOLOGISTS

LESSON 1

Identify why mind-based therapies such as ACT, DBT, MBSR, etc., are effective in regulating emotions and behavior.

LESSON 2

List the benefits of spirituality to a person's happiness and well-being and discuss how their beliefs can contribute to it.

LESSON 3

Identify the psychological benefits religious people derive from believing in an omniscient and omnipotent being that purposefully directs the world.

LESSON 4

Describe and explain the facets of mindfulness and how it allows for better self-regulation, decision-making, and tolerance of negativity.

LESSON 5

Discuss why pursuing meaning in life positively correlates with the overall quality of life, happiness, hope, and life satisfaction, and the evidence that supports it.

LESSON 6

Describe mindful awareness practices and how they help regulate emotions and behavior.

DISCLOSURE OF COMMERCIAL SUPPORT

These activities are receiving NO commercial support.

DISCLOSURES: No member of the planning committee and no member of the faculty for this event has a financial interest or other relationship with any commercial product.

The members of the Planning Committee are:

Sigrid Pechenik, PsyD—Planner
Chief Clinical Advisor
The Wellness Institute

Edward I. Reichman, M.D.—Reviewer
Professor of Emergency Medicine and Epidemiology & Population Health
Albert Einstein College of Medicine

Mindy Wallach – Planner
Administrator, Continuing Education
The Wellness Institute

AMERICAN DISABILITY ACT STATEMENT

The Wellness Institute fully complies with the legal requirements of the Americans with Disabilities Act. If you require special assistance, please submit your request in writing thirty (30) days in advance of the activity to **continuingeducation@myjli.com.**

1

DO YOU MIND?

The Surprising Powers of Jewish Meditation

Often associated with other religions, meditation is an authentic Jewish practice that plays a key role in Jewish life and spirituality. This lesson delves into the foundational underpinnings of Jewish meditation to discover how it can be harnessed as a mindfulness practice to overcome negative feelings and produce positive ones. Taking this a step further, it promotes the power of positive meditation to shape reality.

I. COURSE INTRODUCTION

The term "meditation" has many meanings, but in this course it is defined in its broad sense of the deliberate focus of one's mind to achieve a desired result. Specifically, this study explores the uniquely Jewish role of meditation in Jewish life and in the practice of Judaism.

EXERCISE 1.1

Record three things you hope to gain through this study:

1

2

3

EXERCISE 1.2

In your mind's eye, envision a person meditating.
Now sketch that image on paper.

II. JEWISH MEDITATION

Meditation is organic to Judaism, serving a sizeable role in Jewish life and practice. It can be traced back to the patriarchs of our people and religion, who spent most of their days in meditation, and it is ritualized in Judaism as part of the formal practice of daily prayer. In addition, meditation appears in multiple forms to fill a variety of roles in Jewish life.

TEXT 1

Career Meditators

Rabbi Eliyahu Hakohen Ha'Itamari, *Midrash Talpiyot*, entry *Avot*

טַעַם הָאָבוֹת שֶׁהָיוּ רוֹעִים, כְּדֵי לְהִתְבּוֹדֵד עַצְמָם בְּעִנְיָן אֱלוֹקוּת, שֶׁאֲוִיר הַמִּדְבָּרוֹת זַךְ וְנָקִי וְהָיוּ נִפְרָשִׁים שָׁם מִבְּנֵי אָדָם.

The patriarchs chose to be shepherds so that they could be alone in the wilderness—where the air is clean and pure and they would be far from other people—for the sake of secluding themselves in Divine meditation.

The North French Hebrew Miscellany is more a library than a book. Produced on parchment during the last quarter of the 13th century, it consists of 84 different groups of Hebrew texts, with many of its pages decorated with fine art. There are 36 full-page miniatures like this one depicting King David, a shepherd in his youth, playing an instrument. (British Museum [MS 11639], London)

RABBI ELIYAHU HAKOHEN HA'ITAMARI C. 1659-1729

Preacher and ethicist. Born in Izmir, Turkey, Rabbi Eliyahu Hakohen Ha'Itamari served as a judge on the local rabbinic court and was a popular preacher and author. He is best known for *Shevet Musar*, an ethical work divided into 52 chapters corresponding to the weeks of the year, which has been translated into a number of languages.

FIGURE 1.1

Prayer

PRAYER—תְּפִילָה	
אִם יֶחֱטָא אִישׁ לְאִישׁ **וּפִלְלוֹ** אֱלֹקִים (שְׁמוּאֵל א ב, כה)	הַ**טּוֹפֵל** כְּלֵי חֶרֶס (מִשְׁנָה כֵּלִים ג, ה)
If one commits a crime against another, he will be **judged** by a judge.	One who **glues** an earthenware vessel
An introspective exercise of self-judgment	*A contemplative practice of cementing a relationship with the Divine*

The Forli Siddur (prayer book) for the entire year in the Italian rite was created in Central Italy in 1383 CE. The Hebrew script and illumination were done by Moses ben Jekutiel Hefetz of the Tzifroni family. Additional textual illustrations were later added in the 2nd or 3rd quarter of the 15th century. The page shown here marks the beginning of the Maariv evening prayer. (British Museum [MS 26968], London)

TEXT 2

Meditative Prayer

Mishnah, Berachot 5:1

אֵין עוֹמְדִין לְהִתְפַּלֵּל אֶלָּא מִתּוֹךְ כֹּבֶד רֹאשׁ. חֲסִידִים הָרִאשׁוֹנִים הָיוּ שׁוֹהִים שָׁעָה אַחַת וּמִתְפַּלְלִים, כְּדֵי שֶׁיְּכַוְּנוּ אֶת לִבָּם לַמָּקוֹם.

We must approach prayer with reverence. The early pious sages would pause [in thought] for one hour—so that they could focus their hearts on G-d*—and [only then] pray.

THERE'S MORE...

An assortment of insights into the nature of the sages' meditation—corresponding to the three general meditation categories outlined further below—appears in Appendix A (p. 25).

MISHNAH

The first authoritative work of Jewish law that was codified in writing. The Mishnah contains the oral traditions that were passed down from teacher to student; it supplements, clarifies, and systematizes the commandments of the Torah. Due to the continual persecution of the Jewish people, it became increasingly difficult to guarantee that these traditions would not be forgotten. Rabbi Yehudah Hanasi therefore redacted the Mishnah at the end of the 2nd century. It serves as the foundation for the Talmud.

Rabbi Pinchas Taylor discusses the history of Jewish meditation: **myjli.com/meditation**

*Throughout this book, "G-d" and "L-rd" are written with a hyphen instead of an "o" (both in our own translations and when quoting others). This is one way we accord reverence to the sacred Divine name. This also reminds us that, even as we seek G-d, He transcends any human effort to describe His reality.

Can you think of several ways in which meditation might advance Jewish goals?

FIGURE 1.2

Meditation

HEBREW TERM	TRANSLATION	MEDITATION PRACTICE
הִתְבּוֹדְדוּת *hitbodedut*	**seclusion**	transcendence meditation
הִתְבּוֹנְנוּת *hitbonenut*	**contemplation**	contemplative meditation
כַּוָּנָה *kavanah*	**focus**	mindful awareness or intention meditation

III. THE JEWISH "RELAXATION RESPONSE"

Jewish meditation is primarily focused on providing religious depth, but it also offers the tools to healthier living. We all struggle with negative feelings and experiences, such as anxiety, anger, and self-doubt. Judaism insists that we can overcome these unwanted experiences, and it is eager to offer effective methods of achieving that goal.

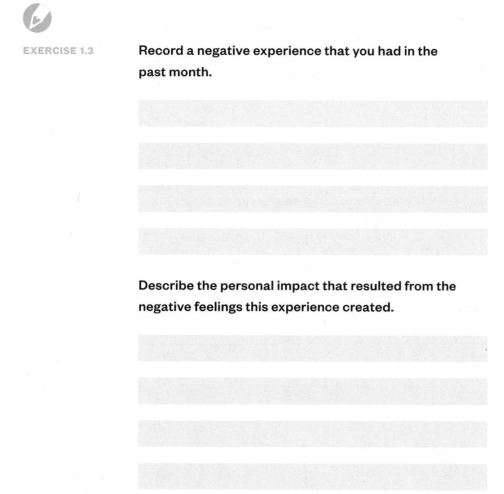

EXERCISE 1.3

Record a negative experience that you had in the past month.

Describe the personal impact that resulted from the negative feelings this experience created.

TEXT 3

Conquering Fear

Deuteronomy 20:2–3

וְהָיָה כְּקָרָבְכֶם אֶל הַמִּלְחָמָה, וְנִגַּשׁ הַכֹּהֵן וְדִבֶּר אֶל הָעָם.
וְאָמַר אֲלֵהֶם שְׁמַע יִשְׂרָאֵל, אַתֶּם קְרֵבִים הַיּוֹם לַמִּלְחָמָה עַל אֹיְבֵיכֶם,
אַל יֵרַךְ לְבַבְכֶם, אַל תִּירְאוּ וְאַל תַּחְפְּזוּ וְאַל תַּעַרְצוּ מִפְּנֵיהֶם.

As you approach the battle, the *Kohen* shall
come near and speak to the people. He shall
say to them: "Hear, Israel! Today you are
approaching the battle against your enemies.
Do not be discouraged! Do not be afraid! Do
not be alarmed or terrified because of them!"

QUESTION

**List some of the methods you personally employ to
overcome negative feelings and emotions.**

IV. THE KABBALAH OF CONSCIOUSNESS

Key to appreciating the mindfulness practice presented in this study is awareness of the spiritual technology that makes it tick. That mechanism can be discovered only by peeking beneath the hood of our souls:

Human souls are equipped with intellect first and emotion second. We therefore process experiences in that precise order. It is our cognitive judgment that triggers our emotions. This soul process operates on the platform of three soul garments, three distinct modes of active consciousness that the soul dons for the sake of processing and interacting with entities and experiences beyond itself in this world.

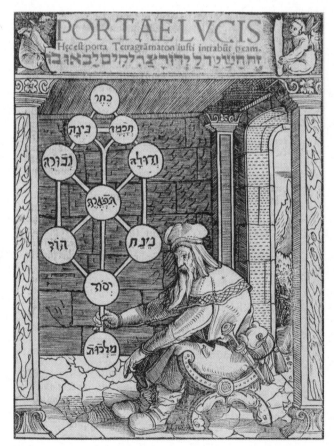

Cover of a copy of an influential kabbalistic work by Rabbi Yosef ben Avraham Gikatilla, a Spanish kabbalist who lived in the mid-13th century. The book is titled *Shaarei Orah—Gates of Light.* This Latin edition was printed in Augsburg in 1516.

FIGURE 1.3   Soul Map

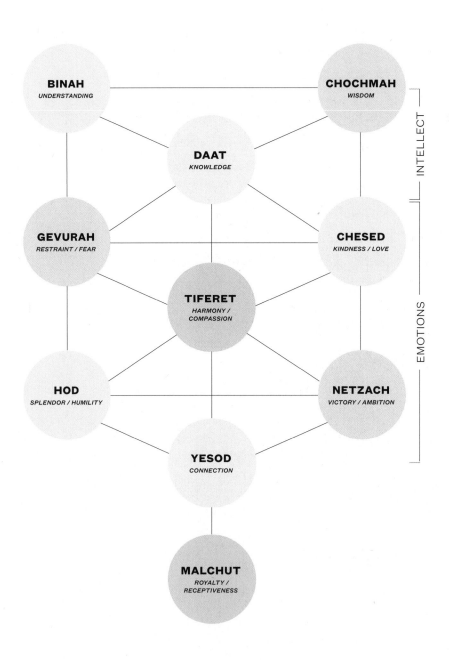

TEXT 4

The Root of Emotion

Rabbi Shneur Zalman of Liadi, *Tanya*, *Likutei Amarim*, ch. 3

וְכָךְ בְּנֶפֶשׁ הָאָדָם, שֶׁנֶּחְלֶקֶת לִשְׁתַּיִם:
שֵׂכֶל וּמִדּוֹת . . . וְחָכְמָה בִּינָה דַעַת נִקְרְאוּ אִמּוֹת וּמָקוֹר
לַמִּדּוֹת, כִּי הַמִּדּוֹת הֵן תּוֹלְדוֹת חָכְמָה בִּינָה דַעַת.

The human soul is divided into two categories: intelligence and emotion. . . . [The intellectual faculties, namely,] *chochmah* [wisdom], *binah* [understanding], and *daat* [knowledge] are referred to as the mothers and the source of the emotions, for the emotions are the offspring of the intelligence.

RABBI SHNEUR ZALMAN OF LIADI (ALTER REBBE) 1745–1812

 Chasidic rebbe, halachic authority, and founder of the Chabad movement. The Alter Rebbe was born in Liozna, Belarus, and was among the principal students of the Magid of Mezeritch. His numerous works include the *Tanya*, an early classic containing the fundamentals of Chabad Chasidism; and *Shulchan Aruch Harav*, an expanded and reworked code of Jewish law.

FIGURE 1.4

Three Soul Garments

	machshavah	thinking	מַחְשָׁבָה
	dibur	speaking	דִבּוּר
	maaseh	doing	מַעֲשֶׂה

FIGURE 1.5

Regular Soul Process

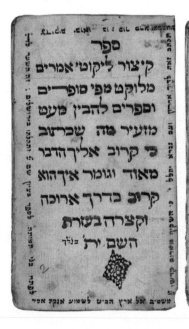

A manuscript of the *Tanya* written in the late 18th century. This handwritten copy predates the first edition printed in Slavuta in 1796 CE. It contains a letter captioned "A letter from my master and teacher" that was eventually used as the introduction to the printed *Tanya*. (British Library [OR 10456], London)

V. INTENTIONAL THINKING

Being aware of the process that produced our negative feelings permits us to identify methods of taming them. Our simplest method is to pull out the rug from under these feelings by shifting our thoughts to something positive.

Firstly, depriving our intellectual attention of negativity prevents our swirling mental judgments from developing funnel clouds of negative emotion. Secondly, we can actively insert a positive focus in its place, feeding positivity to our intellectual palates, to produce offspring of pleasantly positive emotions.

TEXT 5

You Are in Control

Rabbi Shneur Zalman of Liadi, *Tanya, Likutei Amarim*, ch. 12

כִּי הַמֹּחַ שַׁלִּיט עַל הַלֵּב בְּתוֹלַדְתּוֹ וְטֶבַע יְצִירָתוֹ, שֶׁכָּךְ נוֹצַר הָאָדָם בְּתוֹלַדְתּוֹ, שֶׁכָּל אָדָם יָכוֹל בִּרְצוֹנוֹ שֶׁבְּמוֹחוֹ לְהִתְאַפֵּק וְלִמְשׁוֹל בְּרוּחַ תַּאֲוָתוֹ שֶׁבְּלִבּוֹ, שֶׁלֹּא לְמַלְּאות מִשְׁאֲלוֹת לִבּוֹ בְּמַעֲשֶׂה דִבּוּר וּמַחֲשָׁבָה, וּלְהַסִּיחַ דַּעְתּוֹ לְגַמְרֵי מִתַּאֲוַת לִבּוֹ אֶל הַהֵפֶךְ לְגַמְרֵי.

The mind naturally controls the heart. Humans were created from birth with the ability to exercise willpower to control the drives of our hearts, so that they not be expressed in our behavior, speech, or thought. We are able to divert our attention completely from things our hearts crave to something entirely different.

THERE'S MORE...

A practical tool for becoming more consciously aware of our thoughts, using a breathing technique, is provided in Appendix B (p. 28).

TEXT 6

Dissolving Anxiety by Distraction

Rabbi Menachem Mendel of Lubavitch, *Igrot Kodesh*, p. 19

וְאַף אִם מְפַחֵד בְּלִבּוֹ, יוּכַל לְסַלֵּק הַמַּחֲשָׁבָה דִּיבּוּר וּמַעֲשֶׂה. וְהָעִיקָר שֶׁלֹּא לַחֲשׁוֹב וּלְדַבֵּר מִזֶּה כְּלָל, אֶלָּא לְצַד הַהִיפּוּךְ . . .

וּמִיָּד שֶׁלֹּא יַחֲשׁוֹב בָּזֶה כְּלָל, מִמֵּילָא יִתְבַּטֵּל גַּם הַפַּחַד שֶׁבַּלֵּב. וְעַל כָּל פָּנִים, מִיָּד יִהְיֶה הַפַּחַד כְּאִלּוּ הוּא יָשֵׁן וְאֵינוֹ נִרְגָּשׁ בַּגּוּף, וּבְמֶשֶׁךְ יָמִים אֲחָדִים יִתְבַּטֵּל לְגַמְרֵי עַד שֶׁלֹּא יִפּוֹל בְּמוֹחוֹ כְּלָל . . .

וְהַטַּעַם לָזֶה שֶׁעַל יְדֵי סִילוּק הַמַּחֲשָׁבָה יִתְבַּטֵּל הַפַּחַד הוּא, לְפִי שֶׁכָּל הַמִּדּוֹת קַיָּמָן מֵהַדַּעַת . . . עַל יְדֵי אֶמְצָעוּת הַמַּחֲשָׁבָה. וְלָכֵן עַל יְדֵי סִילוּק הַמַּחֲשָׁבָה, הֲרֵי זֶה מְמֵילָא הֶסֵּחַ הַדַּעַת מֵהַמִּדָּה, וְאָז אֵין הַמִּדָּה מִתְעוֹרֶרֶת . . .

וְהִנֵּה רָאוּי לְמַעֲלָתוֹ לִלְמוֹד אֶת עַצְמוֹ מִכָּל מָרָה שְׁחוֹרָה, שֶׁיֵּשׁ לָאָדָם לְסַלֵּק הַפַּחַד מִלִּבּוֹ אַף בְּמָקוֹם שֶׁיֵּשׁ מִמַּה לְפָחֵד, כְּמוֹ שֶׁכָּתַבְתִּי. וְכָל שֶׁכֵּן בְּנִדּוֹן דְּמַעֲלָתוֹ, שֶׁבָּרוּךְ הַשֵּׁם אֵין לוֹ מִמַּה לְפַחֵד כְּלָל וּכְלָל, בֵּין בִּבְרִיאוּת הַגּוּף וּבֵין בְּמָמוֹנוֹ.

Even if we are emotionally afraid, we are able to divorce our thought, speech, and action from that emotion. The essential thing is not to contemplate or discuss the fear at all, but to do the perfect opposite. . . .

Immediately upon letting go of the thought entirely, the fear will dissolve on its own. At the very least,

RABBI MENACHEM MENDEL OF LUBAVITCH (TZEMACH TZEDEK) 1789–1866

Chasidic rebbe and noted author. The *Tzemach Tzedek* was the third leader of the Chabad Chasidic movement and a noted authority on Jewish law. His numerous works include halachic responsa, Chasidic discourses, and kabbalistic writings. Active in the communal affairs of Russian Jewry, he worked to alleviate the plight of the cantonists, Jewish children kidnapped to serve in the Czar's army. He passed away in Lubavitch, leaving seven sons and two daughters.

it will become instantly dormant and not felt in the body. Then, over the course of several days, it will completely dissolve, to the point that it will not enter our mind at all. . . .

Removal of the thought leads to dissipation of the fear because emotions are entirely reliant upon intellectual focus (*daat*) for their existence . . . which requires active thought. Therefore, by removing our thought from the matter, the intellectual power (*daat*) is withdrawn from the emotion, with the result that the emotion ceases to be activated. . . .

It is worth training yourself to remove all negativity, for we must rid ourselves from all fear, including justifiable fear, as I wrote. This is certainly true in your case, where there is nothing to worry about whatsoever—thank G-d!—in terms of your health and financial situation.

REBBE IN FOREST
Zalman Kleinman (1933–1995)

TEXT 7

Positive Distraction

Rabbi Menachem Mendel of Lubavitch, Ibid., p. 21

אַךְ עִיקַר הֶיסַח הַדַעַת וְהַמַחֲשָׁבָה הוּא עַל יְדֵי שֶׁיִשְׁמוֹר
מַחֲשַׁבְתוֹ לְהַלְבִּישָׁהּ בְּעִנְיָנִים אֲחֵרִים, דְהַיְינוּ אֲפִילוּ בְּעִנְיָנִים
דְהַאי עָלְמָא הַנִצְרָכִים וּמְשַׂמְחִים, וּבְתוֹרַת ה' הַמְשַׂמְחִים לֵב
דְבַר יוֹם בְּיוֹם בִּקְבִיעוּת עִתִּים לְתוֹרָה, וּבִפְרָט עִם עוֹד אֶחָד.

The primary method of removing worrying
thoughts from your mind is by redirecting
your mind toward other matters. You can
replace them with thoughts of necessary
material matters that bring you joy, and you can
contemplate G-d's Torah that delights the heart.
The latter is best achieved through creating a
fixed schedule of daily Torah study, which is
particularly effective with a study partner.

Need something positive to think about

FIGURE 1.6

Thought-Induced Soul Process

Thought ► Judgment/Understanding ► Emotion

Neuroscientist
Dr. Michael Merzenich
on the brain's amazing
ability to change:
myjli.com/meditation

VI. THE POWER OF POSITIVITY

Positive meditation is more than a psychological life hack. The mystics reveal that thinking positively actually shifts reality. Our thoughts place us into a mental space that allows us to align with a specific flow of Divine energy and channel it into our world. Meditating on something positive directs a positive flow of energy, which has a positive impact on reality.

TEXT 8

Real Impact

Rabbi Menachem Mendel of Lubavitch, Ibid., p. 21

אַדְרַבָּה לְדַבֵּר וְלַעֲשׂוֹת כַּנַּ"ל, וְאָז יָקָבְעוּ כֵּן הַמִּדּוֹת בְּנַפְשׁוֹ, וְכָכָה יַעֲרֶה עָלָיו רוּחַ מִמָּרוֹם בְּשִׂמְחָה וּבְטוּב לֵבָב. וְכֵן שָׁמַעְתִּי מֵאַאַזְמוּ"ר ז"ל, שֶׁכָּךְ הָיָה הָרַב הַמַּגִּיד נ"ע אוֹמֵר עַל פָּסוּק (יְחֶזְקֵאל א, כו) "כְּמַרְאֵה אָדָם עָלָיו מִלְמָעְלָה", שֶׁכְּפִי הַמִּדָּה שֶׁהָאָדָם מַרְאֶה מִלְּמַטָּה, כָּךְ מַרְאִין לוֹ מִלְמַעְלָה. וְלָכֵן מָנַע אוֹתִי מִלְשׁוֹרֵר נִגּוּן שֶׁיֵּשׁ בּוֹ מָרָה שְׁחֹרָה בִּתְפִלַּת עַרְבִית, וְהִמְתִּין לִי עַד שֶׁסִּיַּמְתִּי אֶת תְּפִלָּתִי, וְאַחַר כָּךְ אָמַר לִי בְּשֵׁם הָרַב הַמַּגִּיד ז"ל.

To the contrary, you should speak and act [in a manner that projects positivity,] as described above, so that these positive emotions will be established within you. In this way, a spirit of joy and good-heartedness will descend upon you from Above. I say this on the basis of a teaching I received from my holy grandfather, of blessed memory, who shared an insight—authored by Rabbi DovBer, the Magid of Mezeritch—into the verse, "Like a person's appearance upon it—from above" (EZEKIEL 1:26).

The Magid would read the verse [this way]: According to the feelings a person displays down here in this world ("Like a person's appearance"), so is the nature of that which rests upon the person from Above ("upon it from above"). In light of this teaching, my grandfather, Rabbi Shneur Zalman of Liadi, did not permit me to sing a melancholy tune during the evening prayer. After I had completed the prayer, he explained his reasoning [for objecting to my choice of melody], and shared the above insight in the name of the Magid, of blessed memory.

A page from the second volume of a Tanach copied and illuminated on parchment in Italy, in the last quarter of the 13th century. This decorated panel is the beginning of the Book of Ezekiel. (British Museum [Harley MS 5711], London)

TEXT 9

A Balanced World

Midrash, *Bereshit Rabah* 12:15

לְמֶלֶךְ שֶׁהָיוּ לוֹ כּוֹסוֹת רֵיקִים, אָמַר הַמֶּלֶךְ, אִם אֲנִי נוֹתֵן לְתוֹכָן חַמִּין, הֵם מִתְבַּקְעִין. צוֹנֵן, הֵם מַקְרִיסִין. וּמָה עָשָׂה הַמֶּלֶךְ? עֵרַב חַמִּין בְּצוֹנֵן וְנָתַן בָּהֶם וְעָמְדוּ. כָּךְ אָמַר הַקָּדוֹשׁ בָּרוּךְ הוּא, אִם בּוֹרֵא אֲנִי אֶת הָעוֹלָם בְּמִדַּת הָרַחֲמִים, הֲוֵי חֲטָיֵיהּ סַגִּיאִין. בְּמִדַּת הַדִּין, הָאֵיךְ הָעוֹלָם יָכוֹל לַעֲמֹד?! אֶלָּא הֲרֵי אֲנִי בּוֹרֵא אוֹתוֹ בְּמִדַּת הַדִּין וּבְמִדַּת הָרַחֲמִים, וְהַלְוַאי יַעֲמֹד.

This is analogous to a king who had empty glasses. The king told himself, "If I pour hot water in them, they will burst. If I pour freezing water in them, they will crack." What did the king do? He mixed hot water with frigid water and poured the blend into the glasses.

Similarly, G-d said: "If I create the world with the attribute of compassion [alone], people will be unconcerned with the consequences of their actions. If I use the attribute of judgment [alone], the world will not survive [the judgment of honest scrutiny]. Rather, I will create it with [a blend of] the attribute of judgment and the attribute of compassion, and I hope that it will endure."

BERESHIT RABAH

An early rabbinic commentary on the Book of Genesis. This Midrash bears the name of Rabbi Oshiya Rabah (Rabbi Oshiya "the Great"), whose teaching opens this work. This Midrash provides textual exegeses and stories, expounds upon the biblical narrative, and develops and illustrates moral principles. Produced by the sages of the Talmud in the Land of Israel, its use of Aramaic closely resembles that of the Jerusalem Talmud. It was first printed in Constantinople in 1512 together with 4 other Midrashic works on the other 4 books of the Pentateuch.

TEXT 10

The World Is in Our Hands

Zohar, vol. 2, 179b

תָּא חֲזֵי: עָלְמָא תַּתָּאָה קַיְמָא לְקַבָּלָא תָּדִיר . . .

וְעָלְמָא עִלָּאָה לֹא יָהִיב לֵיה אֶלָּא כְּגַוְנָא דְּאִיהוּ קַיְמָא, אִי אִיהוּ קַיְמָא בִּנְהִירוּ דְּאַנְפִּין מִתַּתָּא, כְּדֵין הָכִי נַהֲרִין לֵיה מֵעֵילָּא. וְאִי אִיהוּ קַיְמָא בַּעֲצִיבוּ, יָהֲבִין לֵיה דִּינָא בְּקַבְלֵיה.

כְּגַוְנָא דָא (תְּהִלִּים ק, ב) "עִבְדוּ אֶת ה' בְּשִׂמְחָה", חֶדְוָה דְּבַר נַשׁ מָשִׁיךְ לְגַבֵּיה חֶדְוָה אַחֲרָא עִלָּאָה.

Come and observe! Our world is always ready to receive [the spiritual flow that emanates from Above]. . . .

The Upper World provides in accordance with the [emotional] state below [in this world]: if the state below is joyous, then, correspondingly, abundance flows from Above; but if the state below is one of sadness, then, correspondingly, the flow of blessing is constricted.

We are therefore directed, "Serve G-d with joy" (PSALMS 100:2), because mortal joy elicits corresponding supernal joy.

ZOHAR

The seminal work of kabbalah, Jewish mysticism. The *Zohar* is a mystical commentary on the Torah, written in Aramaic and Hebrew. According to the Arizal, the *Zohar* contains the teachings of Rabbi Shimon bar Yocha'i, who lived in the Land of Israel during the 2nd century. The *Zohar* has become one of the indispensable texts of traditional Judaism, alongside and nearly equal in stature to the Mishnah and Talmud.

Mrs. Sara Esther Crispe explores the power of our thoughts and the power we have over them: **myjli.com/meditation**

TEXT 11

You Are What You Think

Rabbi Yisrael Baal Shem Tov, *Keter Shem Tov* 230

**RABBI YISRAEL
BAAL SHEM TOV
(BESHT)
1698–1760**

Founder of the Chasidic
movement. Born in
Slutsk, Belarus, the Baal
Shem Tov was orphaned
as a child. He served as a
teacher's assistant and
clay digger before
founding the Chasidic
movement and
revolutionizing the
Jewish world with his
emphasis on prayer, joy,
and love for every Jew,
regardless of his or her
level of Torah knowledge.

"הַבּוֹטֵחַ בַּה' חֶסֶד יְסוֹבְבֶנּוּ" (תְּהִלִּים לב, י). וּמִי שֶׁהוּא לְהֵפֶךְ וּמִתְיָרֵא תָּמִיד מֵהָעֹנֶשׁ, הוּא מְדַבֵּק עַצְמוֹ בְּדִינִים, וְחַס וְשָׁלוֹם שֶׁלֹּא תָּבוֹא לוֹ רָעָה, כְּמוֹ שֶׁכָּתוּב "וּמְגוּרֹתָם הֵבִיא לָהֶם" (יְשַׁעְיָהוּ סו, ד).

כִּי בְּכָל עִנְיָן שֶׁאָדָם חוֹשֵׁב עָלָיו, הוּא נִדְבָּק בּוֹ, וְאִם הוּא חוֹשֵׁב עַל הַדִּין - הוּא נִדְבָּק בַּדִּין, וְאִם הוּא בּוֹטֵחַ בְּחֶסֶד - שָׁם תִּדְבַּק נִשְׁמָתוֹ, "חֶסֶד יְסוֹבְבֶנּוּ".

The psalmist states that "one who trusts in G-d will be enveloped in kindness" (PSALMS: 32:10). We can infer the reverse as well: one who is constantly anxious of punishment associates themselves with strict judgment that can lead to negative consequences (G-d forbid!), in line with the verse (ISAIAH 66:4), "Their fears I will bring to them."

We become attached to whatever we contemplate. If we contemplate matters associated with severity, we become attached to judgment. If we trust in G-d's kindness, our souls will become attached to that kindness, and we will indeed "be enveloped in kindness."

FIGURE 1.7

Mind over Matter: Contemporary Intervention Techniques

The mind possesses tremendous power, capable of controlling and regulating so much of our lives. Indeed, many therapies have been developed on this basic premise: your mind can regulate your emotions.

TABLE 1

Glossary of intervention techniques

Summary of mindfulness-based interventions (MBIs) and main evidence-based targeted conditions.

MBI	Main conditions with evidence support for MBI
MBSR	Stress, burnout (health professions) Chronic pain (low-back pain, fibromyalgia) Cancer
MBCT	Manic depressive disorder (relapse prevention and acute treatment), bipolar disorder
MBRP	Substance use disorders (relapse prevention)
ACT	Chronic pain, anxiety, and depressive disorders
DBT	Borderline personality disorder, substance use disorder

MBSR
"MINDFULNESS-BASED STRESS REDUCTION"

An intensive training regimen focused on developing mindfulness techniques, originally developed in the late 1970s by Dr. Jon Kabat-Zinn. The training includes formal meditation techniques (such as sitting meditation) as well as informal meditation techniques (such as mindfulness while eating or conducting routine activities). The goal of this training is for participants to cultivate "a stable and nonreactive present-moment awareness."[1]

MBCT
"MINDFULNESS-BASED COGNITIVE THERAPY"

Developed in the 1990s by a group of research psychologists to target depression, this approach combines MBSR with cognitive behavioral therapy (a form of therapy that attempts to adjust maladaptive patterns of thought and behavior).[2] Like MBSR, this therapy usually consists of intensive training in formal and informal meditation techniques, but also includes training for identifying and diffusing negative patterns of thought.[3]

MBRP
"MINDFULNESS-BASED RELAPSE PREVENTION"

Designed to prevent relapse in patients recovering from addictive behaviors, this program was engineered by a group of addiction specialists in the early 2000s. Like MBCT, it combines mindfulness with cognitive behavioral therapy techniques, training participants in both. Together, these techniques help individuals identify their personal triggers for addictive behavior, notice when they have become triggered, and respond to addictive triggering in adaptive ways.[4]

ACT
"ACCEPTANCE AND COMMITMENT THERAPY"

This therapy uses a combination of mindfulness and psychotherapy techniques to help participants accept potentially painful psychological experiences. The aim is to thereby enhance the patient's "psychological flexibility": the ability to fully engage the present moment and act on it in accordance with one's chosen values.

DBT
"DIALECTICAL BEHAVIORAL THERAPY"

Originally developed in the early 1990s by Dr. Marsha Linehan for treating borderline personality disorder, this therapy has since been expanded to treat a wide range of psychopathologies, including eating disorders, mood disorders, substance abuse disorders, and post-traumatic stress disorder. The core of its therapy is mindfulness training, which is then used as a foundation for teaching skills in maintaining healthy relationships, effectively controlling one's emotions, and coping with psychological distress. Therapy typically lasts for approximately six months.[5]

1. John J. Miller, et al., "Three-Year Follow-Up and Clinical Implications of a Mindfulness Meditation-Based Stress Reduction Intervention in the Treatment of Anxiety Disorders," *General Hospital Psychiatry*, Volume 17, Issue 3, 1995, p. 193, ISSN 0163-8343, https://doi.org/10.1016/0163-8343(95)00025-M.

2. Segal, Z. V., et al. *Mindfulness-Based Cognitive Behavior Therapy for Depression: A New Approach to Preventing Relapse* (New York, N.Y.: Guilford Press, 2002).

3. Eisendrath, S. J., "Mindfulness-Based Cognitive Therapy: Theory and Practice," *The Canadian Journal of Psychiatry*, 57(2), 2012: pp. 63–69. doi:10.1177/070674371205700202.

4. Bowen, S., et al., *Mindfulness-Based Relapse Prevention for Addictive Behaviors: a Clinician's Guide.* (New York, N.Y.: Guilford Press, 2010).

5. May, Jennifer M., et al., "Dialectical Behavior Therapy as Treatment for Borderline Personality Disorder," *Mental Health Clinician*, 6 (2), 1 March 2016: pp. 62–67. https://doi.org/10.9740/mhc.2016.03.62.

KEY POINTS

1   Meditation is an authentic Jewish practice
     that plays a large role in Jewish life.

2   We have control over our feelings and have the capacity
     to overcome negative feelings and experiences.

3   We have the ability to be in control of our thoughts and
     can choose what we think about at any given moment.

4   Our thinking feeds our emotions. By getting rid of
     negative thoughts, we cut off negative feelings.

5   Meditating on positive thoughts develops a
     positive mindset and positive emotions.

6   Positive meditation actually impacts the world
     around us and elicits a positive response from
     G-d, which shapes reality for the good.

APPENDIX A

Earlier (in Text 2), we learned about a meditation that the rabbis would practice before prayer: "The early pious sages would pause [in thought] for one hour—so that they could focus their hearts on G-d—and [only then] pray" (Mishnah, Berachot 5:1). Here is an assortment of insights into the nature of their meditation.

TEXT 12

Focus Meditation

Maimonides, Berachot 5:1

וּפֵרוּשׁ שׁוֹהִין - מִתְעַכְּבִין. רוֹצֶה לוֹמַר שֶׁהֵן מִתְעַכְּבִין קֹדֶם הַתְּפִלָּה שָׁעָה אַחַת כְּדֵי לְיַשֵּׁב דַּעְתָּם וּלְהַשְׁקִיט מַחְשְׁבוֹתָם, וְאָז יַתְחִילוּ בִּתְפִלָּה.

The meaning of *shohin* is "waiting." They would pause for an hour before prayer in order to calm their minds and to quiet their thoughts. Only then would they begin to pray.

RABBI MOSHE
BEN MAIMON
(MAIMONIDES, RAMBAM)
1135-1204

Halachist, philosopher, author, and physician. Maimonides was born in Córdoba, Spain. After the conquest of Córdoba by the Almohads, he fled Spain and eventually settled in Cairo, Egypt. There, he became the leader of the Jewish community and served as court physician to the vizier of Egypt. He is most noted for authoring the *Mishneh Torah*, an encyclopedic arrangement of Jewish law; and for his philosophical work, *Guide for the Perplexed*. His rulings on Jewish law are integral to the formation of halachic consensus.

SHACHARIT
Yehoshua Wiseman, Israel

Contemplative Meditation

Rabbi Yonah of Gerona, Berachot 5:1

יֵשׁ מְפָרְשִׁים כְּדֵי שֶׁיְּפַנּוּ טִרְדַּת הַמַּחֲשָׁבוֹת וִיכַוְּנוּ בַּאֲמִירַת הַתְּפִלָּה.
וְאֵין זֶה נִרְאֶה לְמוֹרִי הָרַב נר"ו, דְּאִם כֵּן לֹא הָיָה לוֹ לוֹמַר לַמָּקוֹם,
אֶלָּא לִתְפִלָּתָם . . . אֶלָּא וַדַּאי כָּךְ הוּא הַפֵּרוּשׁ, כְּדֵי שֶׁיְּכַוְּנוּ שֶׁיִּהְיֶה
לִבָּם שָׁלֵם בַּעֲבוֹדַת הַמָּקוֹם, וִיבַטְּלוּ מִלִּבָּם תַּעֲנוּגֵי הָעוֹלָם הַזֶּה
וַהֲנָאוֹתֵיהֶם. כִּי כְּשֶׁיִּטַהֲרוּ לִבָּם מֵהֶבְלֵי הָעוֹלָם הַזֶּה, וְיִהְיֶה כַּוָּנָתָם
בְּרוֹמְמוּת הַשֵּׁם, תִּהְיֶה תְּפִלָּתָם רְצוּיָה וּמְקֻבֶּלֶת לִפְנֵי הַמָּקוֹם.

Some explain that they would pause to
remove mental distractions for the sake
of concentrating on reciting their prayers,
to the exclusion of all other concerns.

However, if that were the case, the Mishnah
would have said, "focus their hearts on their
prayers" instead of "focus their hearts on G-d."

Rather, the meaning is that they intended for their
hearts to be wholesome in their service of G-d by
eradicating any vestige of corporeal or material
desire from their hearts. By emptying their hearts
from the fleeting pleasures and benefits of the
material world and focusing on the greatness of
G-d to the exclusion of material existence, their
prayers would be worthy and accepted by G-d.

RABBI YONAH OF GERONA
C. 1210–C. 1263

Spanish talmudist and
ethicist. A native of
Gerona, Catalonia, Rabbi
Yonah studied with
leading figures of the
Tosafist school in France,
thus combining
Ashkenazic and Sefardic
scholarship. He wrote
biblical and talmudic
commentaries, and he is
best known for his
moralistic works on
repentance and
ethical conduct.

TEXT 14

Mystical Meditation

Rabbi Elazar Azikri, *Sefer Charedim* 65

RABBI ELAZAR BEN MOSHE AZIKRI 1533–1600

וְזֶהוּ שֶׁשָּׁנִינוּ, "חֲסִידִים הָרִאשׁוֹנִים הָיוּ שׁוֹהִין שָׁעָה אַחַת וּמִתְפַּלְלִים, כְּדֵי שֶׁיְּכַוְנוּ לַמָּקוֹם". שֶׁהָיוּ בְּטֵלִים מִלִּמּוּדָם וּמִמְּלַאכְתָּם לְהִתְבּוֹדְדוּת וְהַדְּבֵיקוּת, וּמְדַמִּין אוֹר שְׁכִינָה שֶׁעַל רָאשֵׁיהֶם כְּאִלּוּ מִתְפַּשֵּׁט סְבִיבָם, וְהֵם בְּתוֹךְ הָאוֹר יוֹשְׁבִים.

We have been taught that "the early pious sages would pause [in thought] for one hour—so that they could focus their hearts on G-d—and [only then] pray." They would cease studying and strive to meditate and cleave to G-d. They would picture the light of G-d's presence [*Shechinah*] above their heads as if it were spreading all around them until they were sitting within that light.

Kabbalist, poet, and author, born in Safed to a Sefardic family that settled in the Holy Land after the Expulsion from Spain. Rabbi Elazar studied Torah under Rabbi Yosef Sagis and Rabbi Yaakov Berab and is counted with the greatest rabbis and intellectuals of his time. Rabbi Elazar authored the *Sefer Charedim*, a work focused on ethics, morals, and personality development. It was printed after his death in 1600. He composed the ode "Yedid Nefesh," traditionally sung in many communities before Kabbalat Shabbat and/or at the third Shabbat meal.

KABBALIST
Tommaso Garzoni, 1641, woodcut print on paper. (Deutsche Fotothek of the Saxon State Library/State and University Library Dresden [88967185])

APPENDIX B

TEXT 15

Accessing the Subconscious

Rabbi Aryeh Kaplan, *Jewish Meditation*
(New York: Knopf Doubleday Publishing Group, 2011), pp. 5–6

**RABBI ARYEH KAPLAN
1934–1983**

 American rabbi, author, and physicist. Rabbi Kaplan authored more than 50 volumes on Torah, Talmud, Jewish mysticism, and philosophy, many of which have become modern-day classics. He is best known for his popular translation and elucidation of the Bible, *The Living Torah*; and his translation of the Ladino biblical commentary, *Me'am Lo'ez*.

This explains why so many disciplines use breathing exercises as a meditative device. Breathing usually occurs automatically and is therefore normally under the control of the unconscious mind. Unless you are consciously controlling your breathing, it will mirror your unconscious mood. This is one reason why breathing is one of the indicators in a lie detector test.

Yet, if you wish, you can control your breath, and do so quite easily. Breathing therefore forms a link between the conscious mind and the unconscious. By learning how to concentrate on and control your breath you can go on to learn how to control the unconscious mind. . . .

One learns to use the conscious mind to control mental processes that are usually under the control of the unconscious. Gradually, more and more of the subconscious becomes accessible to the conscious mind, and one gains control of the entire thought process.

Count Your Blessings

A series of blessings customarily recited each morning is collectively known as *Birchat Hashachar*—the Morning Blessings. Each of these calls attention to another element of the daily human experience that is otherwise taken for granted. These daily blessings provide an opportunity to pause and reflect on our good fortune for the basic underpinnings and purpose of life, and they encourage us to express gratitude to G-d for gifting us with the functions and roles described in the blessings.

Taking the time to enter a gratitude mindset each morning is a surefire method of channeling goodness and positivity into your day. All it takes is a little mindfulness and a couple of minutes.

Brief explanations have been added to the following excerpt from the first part of the Morning Blessings:

① THE ROOSTER

בָּרוּךְ אַתָּה ה', אֱלֹקֵינוּ מֶלֶךְ הָעוֹלָם,
הַנּוֹתֵן לַשֶּׂכְוִי בִינָה לְהַבְחִין בֵּין יוֹם וּבֵין לָיְלָה.

Blessed are You, G-d, King of the universe,
Who grants the rooster the understanding
to distinguish between day and night.

Before electrical alarm clocks, people relied on nature's alarm clock—the rooster—to awaken at dawn. This blessing was a way to thank G-d for providing a reliable method of timely arousal from sleep. As we recite the blessing today, we bear in mind (a) whichever of G-d's marvels we use to wake up each morning, and (b) the diverse wonders of nature found in the animal kingdom.

Each prayer offers multiple layers of significance. A deeper insight notes[1] that the text employs a rare Hebrew term for rooster, *sechvi*, which carries an alternate translation, "heart." We thank G-d for granting us the mental and emotional capacity to distinguish between moral day and night—between that which is good, sacred, and worthy, and the opposite. This is a morning blessing, to remind us that throughout our day we will face choices that require a moral compass and an inner strength to embrace the good and distance ourselves from its opposite.

---

1. Rosh, Berachot 9:23.

Count Your Blessings *continued*

❷ VISION

בָּרוּךְ אַתָּה ה׳, אֱלֹקֵינוּ מֶלֶךְ הָעוֹלָם,
פּוֹקֵחַ עִוְרִים.

*Blessed are You, G-d, King of the universe,
Who opens the eyes of the blind.*

The human eye is an astonishing, complex organ. To avoid taking this major miracle for granted, we thank G-d each day for the blessing of sight.

Helen Keller (who was blind) famously said, "Recently I was visited by a very good friend who had just returned from a long walk in the woods, and I asked her what she had observed. 'Nothing in particular,' she replied. I might have been incredulous had I not been accustomed to such responses, for long ago I became convinced that the seeing see little."

A Chasidic deeper insight[2] views this blessing as addressing the gift of being able to see the bigger picture. Poor decisions are often due to shortsightedness or a failure to see beneath the surface. Conversely, positive and Divine choices arrive upon exercising our mental ability to view the larger truth: a truly valuable gift.

❸ STRETCHING THE LIMBS

בָּרוּךְ אַתָּה ה׳, אֱלֹקֵינוּ מֶלֶךְ הָעוֹלָם,
מַתִּיר אֲסוּרִים.

*Blessed are You, G-d, King of the
universe, Who releases the bound.*

Our limbs barely move or stretch as we sleep; we largely appear as if we were bound. Upon awakening we begin to move and stretch, and we thank G-d for the gift of movement.

A deeper insight[3] sees this as a reference to the battle between the two souls within us. Our natural, impulsive soul holds a greater grip on our conscious character and daily choices. By contrast, our pristine, Divine soul is largely a prisoner of the former. The Divine soul longs to find joy in sacred endeavors but is shackled by our animalistic impulses and goals. There are moments, however, when our Divine soul succeeds in breaking free from captivity and it shines through our noble deeds. Our ability to tip the scales in favor of our Divine soul is a gift from G-d. Each morning, we thank G-d for the power to overcome our baser instincts and to act in accordance with our Divine core.

---

2. Rabbi Menachem Mendel of Lubavitch, *Or HaTorah Maamarei Chazal*, p. 306.

---

3. Rabbi DovBer of Lubavitch, *Torat Chayim*, Shemot 1, p. 74c.

④ SITTING UP

בָּרוּךְ אַתָּה ה', אֱלֹקֵינוּ מֶלֶךְ הָעוֹלָם,
זוֹקֵף כְּפוּפִים.

*Blessed are You, G-d, King of the universe,
Who straightens those who are stooped.*

After lying prone in a horizontal position for hours, we thank G-d for the ability to prop our bodies up.

Looking deeper,[4] our head and the rest of our body are of similar altitude while we rest horizontally. We are similar to animals, whose heads are more or less on the same level as their bodies. A feature of human uniqueness is our ability to stand erect, with our head securely above and leading our body. This posture implies that our minds can control our impulses. As we thank G-d for our ability to sit up, we reflect on the Divine gift—the ability to use the mind to regulate emotions, thereby warding off pettiness, anger, and similar destructive emotional forces.

⑤ CLOTHING

בָּרוּךְ אַתָּה ה', אֱלֹקֵינוּ מֶלֶךְ הָעוֹלָם,
מַלְבִּישׁ עֲרֻמִּים.

Blessed are You, G-d, King of the universe, Who clothes the naked.

We thank G-d for the clothing we wear each day. At the dawn of time, G-d personally fashioned clothing for Adam and Eve, who realized their nakedness after committing the first sin. The Torah subsequently commanded us to follow G-d's example, including providing clothing for those in need.

Included in this blessing is a reminder and appreciation for our inherent sense of modesty and decency that, among other things, instinctively compels us to don clothing.

A deeper reflection draws our attention to the clothing of our soul—namely, the *mitzvot*. As clothing and work gear enable us to operate, so do soul-garments allow the soul to function in this world. We thank G-d at the start of each day for the tremendous opportunity to connect with Him through the gift of *mitzvot*.[5]

---

4. See Rabbi Menachem Mendel of Lubavitch, *Or HaTorah, Maamarei Chazal*, p. 306.

---

5. See *Or HaTorah*, Ibid.

Count Your Blessings *continued*

⑥ STRENGTH TO THE WEARY

בָּרוּךְ אַתָּה ה׳, אֱלֹקֵינוּ מֶלֶךְ הָעוֹלָם,
הַנּוֹתֵן לַיָּעֵף כֹּחַ.

*Blessed are You, G-d, King of the universe,
Who gives strength to the weary.*

After awakening, moving, and getting dressed, we begin to internalize that refreshed morning feeling—and thank G-d for our new dose of energy.

Looking deeper, there are moments in our lifelong spiritual journey when fatigue sets in, inspiration runs dry, and we are left feeling lifeless in terms of zeal or motivation. Then, G-d reaches out and awakens us with a jolt—we are reenergized and eternally grateful.[6]

⑦ HABITABLE LAND

בָּרוּךְ אַתָּה ה׳, אֱלֹקֵינוּ מֶלֶךְ הָעוֹלָם,
רוֹקַע הָאָרֶץ עַל הַמָּיִם.

*Blessed are You, G-d, King of the universe,
Who spreads out the earth upon the water.*

As we move to take our first steps of a fresh day, we thank G-d for terra firma. The Torah relates that at the start of Creation, all the earth was covered by deep water, until on the third day of Creation, G-d divided the surface of the globe between oceans and dry land, although water may be present deeper within. We thank G-d for His kindness in providing us with habitable terrain and the ability to maneuver across it.

Digging deeper, the vast ocean symbolizes unlimited aspirations, big ideas. However, without demarcation to ensure a concrete start and end, it all remains a dream. Every vision requires a line in the sand to contain and channel it, like the earth contains and stems the tide of the endless ocean. We thank G-d for our internal oceans—aspirations and visions—and even more so for the land spread upon it: the ability for practical implementation.[7]

---

6. See *Or HaTorah*, Ibid.

7. Rabbi Avraham Yitzchak Hakohen Kook, *Olat Rei'yah*, Morning Blessings.

⑧ THE STEPS OF HUMANKIND

בָּרוּךְ אַתָּה ה', אֱלֹקֵינוּ מֶלֶךְ הָעוֹלָם,
הַמֵּכִין מִצְעֲדֵי גָבֶר.

*Blessed are You, G-d, King of the universe,
Who directs the steps of humanity.*

As parents cheer excitedly for a baby's first step, this blessing reminds us to reflect and experience wonder and gratitude for *each* step we take, each day of our lives. Repetition dulls our attention to the marvel of walking, but a moment of reflection restores it.

From a deeper perspective, we cannot take a single step in life—in the sense of implementing a decision—without Divine direction. Our logical and emotional motivations for making a move exist only because G-d previously ordained that precise move, to serve a purpose of which we may be entirely unaware. All the unique elements of our life story that shape our character and experience are steps guided by G-d, placing us into settings in which we are uniquely outfitted to accomplish in this world.[8]

⑨ PROVIDES ALL MY NEEDS

בָּרוּךְ אַתָּה ה', אֱלֹקֵינוּ מֶלֶךְ הָעוֹלָם,
שֶׁעָשָׂה לִי כָּל צָרְכִּי.

*Blessed are You, G-d, King of the universe,
Who has provided me with all my needs.*

Our sages[9] associate this blessing with tying shoes or securing footgear. The "steps of humanity" (previous blessing) are made easier with protected feet. Indeed, on the two dates in the Jewish calendar (Yom Kippur and the Ninth of Av) on which leather footwear is prohibited, we omit this blessing.

In a mystical sense, "all my needs" includes spiritual requirements. We thank G-d for a universe filled with material and also spiritual potential.[10]

The blessing employs the past tense—"*Who has provided.*" G-d has already allocated our needs and has orchestrated methods of delivering those blessings. The work we do to earn a profit or paycheck is simply a tool to channel those blessings to us—a concept worth recalling before leaving for work, to exchange pressure and panic for positivity and trust.

---

8. See Rabbi Menachem Mendel of Lubavitch, *Or HaTorah, Maamarei Chazal*, p. 307.

9. Talmud, Berachot 60b.

10. Rabbi Avraham Yitzchak Hakohen Kook, *Olat Rei'yah*, Morning Blessings.

Count Your Blessings *continued*

⑩ BELT

בָּרוּךְ אַתָּה ה', אֱלֹקֵינוּ מֶלֶךְ הָעוֹלָם,
אוֹזֵר יִשְׂרָאֵל בִּגְבוּרָה.

Blessed are You, G-d, King of the universe,
Who girds Israel with might.

The Talmud[11] associates this blessing with tying a belt around the waist, the common way of securing the loose robes of antiquity before leaving home. It also carried the connotation of strength—a tight belt supports the torso during strenuous activities— and also power and prestige, for the belt held money pouches and weapons. We thank G-d for our strength as well as any honor G-d provides us.

Looking deeper, the belt is a tool that binds two entities, holding them in a mighty embrace. For a Jew, it symbolizes our close attachment to G-d. We thank G-d for His incredible closeness to us, and we acknowledge that our unique Divine intimacy empowers us to overcome the hardships of our history and the challenges of daily life.

On a more personal note, we bless G-d for girding us with the moral strength to overcome our base impulses.[12]

⑪ HAT

בָּרוּךְ אַתָּה ה', אֱלֹקֵינוּ מֶלֶךְ הָעוֹלָם,
עוֹטֵר יִשְׂרָאֵל בְּתִפְאָרָה.

Blessed are You, G-d, King of the universe,
Who crowns Israel with glory.

Our ancient sages[13] associate this blessing with headgear—no Jew would leave home without it.

For millennia, headgear has been a hallmark feature of a Jewish individual. Males wear a *kipah* or another traditional head covering, and married females wear feminine hair coverings, according to the era and locale. A Jew is forever conscious of the One Above and walks constantly in the presence of the King of the universe. As we don our covering each morning, we thank G-d for the opportunity to maintain such an empowering and transformative consciousness throughout our day.

11. Talmud, Berachot 60b.

12. Rabbi Menachem Mendel of Lubavitch, *Or HaTorah, Maamarei Chazal*, p. 307.

13. Talmud, Berachot 60b.

orit martin ©

LESSON

2

*LEHIT'CHABER LEKEDUSHAH—
TO CONNECT TO HOLINESS
(A KOHEN—PRIEST BLOWS
A SHOFAR DRESSED IN HIS
HOLY TEMPLE UNIFORM)*
Orit Martin

MIND YOURSELF!

Reflecting Inward to Find the Divine

Spirituality is often perceived as distant or irrelevant to daily reality. This lesson explores the innate spiritual sense that our souls possess and demonstrates the means of harnessing it through meditation. This leads us to experience a spiritual depth to reality and to find profound meaning in our every experience.

I. INTRODUCTION

We are corporeal beings trapped in a material world. Consequently, we struggle to relate to spirituality, and we have an even harder time defining and understanding it. Judaism offers ready access to profound spiritual understanding and experience. This lesson serves as a guide to employing Jewish meditation to gain awareness of the spiritual.

EXERCISE 2.1

How would you define spirituality?

How might spirituality be experienced?

WINDOW THOUGHT
Yehoshua Wiseman, Israel

II. INNATE SPIRITUALITY

We are creatures of internal duality due to our unique composition, an unlikely marriage of body and soul: a decidedly corporeal body with material needs, and a powerfully spiritual soul. Our body-consciousness is driven to pursue material needs and wants, whereas our soul-consciousness lives only for a higher purpose and longs constantly for deeper connection with G-d.

The fact that we inhabit a material world causes our body-related consciousness to present as our dominant, default consciousness. Nevertheless, that does not prevent us from developing awareness of our soul and from harnessing its innate spirituality by detaching from our materially-oriented consciousness.

EXERCISE 2.2   **Record as many words as possible to accurately describe *you*.**

Kind	short
generous	older
impatient	
complaining/critical	
funny	

TEXT 1

Composite Creation

Genesis 2:7

וַיִּיצֶר ה' אֱלֹקִים אֶת הָאָדָם עָפָר מִן הָאֲדָמָה,
וַיִּפַּח בְּאַפָּיו נִשְׁמַת חַיִּים.

G-d formed the human from the dust of the ground, and He breathed into the human's nostrils the soul of life.

Essence of your soul is a part of G-d

TEXT 2

Divine Soul

Siddur, Morning Blessings

אֱלֹקַי, נְשָׁמָה שֶׁנָּתַתָּ בִּי, טְהוֹרָה הִיא.
אַתָּה בְרָאתָהּ, אַתָּה יְצַרְתָּהּ, אַתָּה נְפַחְתָּהּ בִּי.

My G-d! The soul that You placed within me is pure. You created it. You formed it. You breathed it into me.

SIDDUR

The siddur is the Jewish prayer book. It was originally developed by the sages of the Great Assembly in the 4th century BCE, and later reconstructed by Rabban Gamliel after the destruction of the Second Temple. Various authorities continued to add prayers, from then until contemporary times. It includes praise of G-d, requests for personal and national needs, selections from the Bible, and much else. Various Jewish communities have slightly different versions of the siddur.

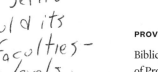

[handwritten note:] Essence of our soul
10 Sefirot – attributes of G-d
Soul & its
faculties –
10 levels

TEXT 3

The Flaming Soul

Proverbs 20:27

נֵר ה' נִשְׁמַת אָדָם.

The human soul is the candle of G-d.

QUESTION

In which ways can you imagine a flame serving as a metaphor for the human soul?

PROVERBS

Biblical book. The book of Proverbs appears in the "Writings" section of the Bible and contains the wise teachings, aphorisms, and parables of King Solomon, who lived in the 9th century BCE. The ethical teachings of Proverbs give counsel about overcoming temptation, extol the value of hard work, laud the pursuit of knowledge, and emphasize loyalty to G-d and His commandments as the foundation of true wisdom.

NESHAMAH (SOUL)
Rivka Cyprys

TEXT 4

The Flickering of the Soul

Rabbi Shneur Zalman of Liadi, *Tanya*, *Likutei Amarim*, ch. 19

RABBI SHNEUR ZALMAN OF LIADI (ALTER REBBE) 1745–1812

Chasidic rebbe, halachic authority, and founder of the Chabad movement. The Alter Rebbe was born in Liozna, Belarus, and was among the principal students of the Magid of Mezeritch. His numerous works include the *Tanya*, an early classic containing the fundamentals of Chabad Chasidism; and *Shulchan Aruch Harav*, an expanded and reworked code of Jewish law.

לְמָשָׁל, כְּאוֹר הַנֵּר שֶׁמִּתְנַעֲנֵעַ תָּמִיד לְמַעְלָה בְּטִבְעוֹ, מִפְּנֵי שֶׁאוֹר הָאֵשׁ חָפֵץ בְּטֶבַע לִיפָּרֵד מֵהַפְּתִילָה וְלִידָּבֵק בְּשָׁרְשׁוֹ לְמַעְלָה . . .

כָּךְ נִשְׁמַת הָאָדָם, וְכֵן בְּחִינַת רוּחַ וָנֶפֶשׁ, חֶפְצָהּ וְחֶשְׁקָהּ בְּטִבְעָהּ לִיפָּרֵד וְלָצֵאת מִן הַגּוּף וְלִידָּבֵק בְּשָׁרְשָׁהּ וּמְקוֹרָהּ - בַּה' חַיֵּי הַחַיִּים, בָּרוּךְ הוּא.

The nature of a flame is to flicker upward, indicating that the flame intrinsically seeks to part from its wick in order to unite with its source above. . . .

Similarly, the human soul naturally desires and yearns to separate itself and escape its body in order to unite with its origin and source in G-d—the blessed Source of all life.

KEMIHAH—LONGING
Orit Martin

[handwritten notes:] Go beyond intellect to seek Truth

Soul is in exile in the body. We have our own personal Egypt.

TEXT 5

The Ideal Practice

Rabbi Avraham ben HaRambam,
Sefer Hamaspik Le'ovdei Hashem, ch. 13

הַהִתְבּוֹדְדוּת הִיא אַחַת הַנִּכְבָּדוֹת
שֶׁבֵּין הַמִּדוֹת הַתִּרוּמִיּוֹת.
וְהִיא דַּרְכָּם שֶׁל גְּדוֹלֵי הַצַּדִיקִים,
וּבְאֶמְצָעוּתָהּ הִגִּיעוּ הַנְּבִיאִים לִידֵי הִתְגַּלּוּת.

Hitbodedut [seclusion] is one of the most superior of all the distinguished practices. It is a practice of the greatest saints and the medium through which the prophets experienced revelation.

RABBI AVRAHAM BEN HARAMBAM
1186–1237

Talmudist and philosopher. Rabbi Avraham, the only son of Maimonides, was born in Cairo, Egypt. Rabbi Avraham studied under his father's tutelage and succeeded him as the leader of the Egyptian Jewish community. Rabbi Avraham authored a commentary to the Torah and a book of ethics, only parts of which are extant. He is best known for his writings in defense of his father, including halachic responsa and *Milchamot Hashem*, a defense of the *Guide for the Perplexed*.

ASCENDING THE LADDER
Zalman Kleinman (1933–1995)

TEXT 6

Finding the Spirit Within

Rabbi Yeshayahu Horowitz, *Shenei Luchot Haberit*,
Yoma, *Ner Mitzvah* 2:80

RABBI YESHAYAHU
HALEVI HOROWITZ
(*SHALAH*)
1565–1630

Kabbalist and author.
Rabbi Horowitz was born
in Prague and served as
rabbi in several
prominent Jewish
communities, including
Frankfurt am Main and
his native Prague. After
the passing of his wife in
1620, he moved to Israel.
In Tiberias, he completed
his *Shenei Luchot
Haberit*, an encyclopedic
compilation of
kabbalistic ideas. He is
buried in Tiberias, next
to Maimonides.

וְגַם בְּכַמָּה חִבּוּרִים מֵהָרִאשׁוֹנִים נִמְצָא, שֶׁהַהִתְבּוֹדְדוּת וְהַפְּרִישׁוּת
וְהַדְּבֵקוּת הָיוּ נוֹהֲגִין בָּהּ חֲסִידֵי יִשְׂרָאֵל. הַיְנוּ, שֶׁבִּהְיוֹתָם לְבַדָּם,
מַפְרִישִׁים מִדַּעְתָּם עִנְיְנֵי הָעוֹלָם, וּמְקַשְּׁרִים מַחְשְׁבוֹתָם עִם אֲדוֹן הַכֹּל.

וְכָךְ לִמֵּד מוֹרִי הָרַב יִצְחָק הַמְקֻבָּל הַנִּזְכָּר (הָאֲרִיזַ"ל), שֶׁזֶּה
מוֹעִיל לַנֶּפֶשׁ שִׁבְעָתַיִם מֵהַלִּמּוּד. וּלְפִי כֹּחַ וִיכֹלֶת הָאָדָם
יִפְרֹשׁ וְיִתְבּוֹדֵד יוֹם אֶחָד מִן הַשָּׁבוּעַ, אוֹ יוֹם אֶחָד בַּחֲמִשָּׁה
עָשָׂר יוֹם, אוֹ יוֹם אֶחָד בְּחֹדֶשׁ, וְלֹא יִפְחֹת מִזֶּה.

It is recorded in many of the works of the medieval
rabbis that seclusion [*hitbodedut*], separation
[from everything mundane: *perishut*], and
devotional clinging [*devekut*] were practiced
by the pious Jews. This is to say that when they
were alone, they would empty their minds
of all worldly concerns and connect their
minds with the Master of All [Existence].

The famed kabbalist, the Arizal, taught that
this practice is far more beneficial for the
soul than study, and that every person should
practice this seclusion meditation according
to their ability, either once a week, once a
fortnight, or, at the very least, once a month.

Rabbi Tzvi Freeman
illustrates how to control
the mind and emotions:
myjli.com/meditation

THERE'S MORE...

Hitbodedut meditation has evolved and been practiced in various forms in more contemporary times. For more details, see Appendix A.

TEXT 7

Mystical Meanderings

Rav Hai Ga'on, _Otzar Hage'onim_, Chagigah 14b

RAV HAI GA'ON
939–1038

וְשֶׁמָּא אַתָּה יוֹדֵעַ, כִּי הַרְבֵּה מִן הַחֲכָמִים הָיוּ סוֹבְרִים כִּי מִי שֶׁהוּא הָגוּן בְּכַמָּה מִדּוֹת זְכוּרוֹת וּמְבֹאָרוֹת, כְּשֶׁמְּבַקֵּשׁ לִצְפּוֹת בַּמֶּרְכָּבָה וּלְהָצִיץ בְּהֵיכָלוֹת שֶׁל מַלְאֲכֵי מָרוֹם, יֵשׁ לוֹ דְּרָכִים לַעֲשׂוֹת: שֶׁיֵּשֵׁב בְּתַעֲנִית יָמִים יְדוּעִים, וּמַנִּיחַ רֹאשׁוֹ בֵּין בִּרְכָּיו, וְלוֹחֵשׁ לָאָרֶץ שִׁירוֹת וְתִשְׁבָּחוֹת הַרְבֵּה שֶׁהֵן מְפֹרָשׁוֹת, וּבְכֵן מֵצִיץ בִּפְנִימָיו וּבַחֲדָרָיו כְּמִי שֶׁהוּא רוֹאֶה בְּעֵינָיו הֵיכָלוֹת שִׁבְעָה, וְצוֹפֶה כְּאִלּוּ הוּא נִכְנָס מֵהֵיכָל לְהֵיכָל וְרוֹאֶה מַה שֶּׁיֵּשׁ בּוֹ.

וְיֵשׁ שְׁתֵּי מִשְׁנָיוֹת שֶׁהַתַּנָּאִים שׁוֹנִין אוֹתָן בְּדָבָר זֶה, וְנִקְרָא הֵיכָלוֹת רַבָּתֵי וְהֵיכָלוֹת זוּטְרָתֵי, וְדָבָר זֶה מְפֻרְסָם וְיָדוּעַ . . . וְדַע, כִּי דָבָר זֶה הָיָה מְקֻבָּל אֵצֶל הָרִאשׁוֹנִים כֻּלָּן יַחְדָּיו, וְלֹא הָיָה אֶחָד מֵהֶם מְכַחֵשׁ, כִּי אוֹמְרִים הָיוּ כִּי הַקָּדוֹשׁ בָּרוּךְ הוּא עוֹשֶׂה אוֹתוֹת וְנוֹרָאוֹת עַל יְדֵי הַצַּדִּיקִים כְּמוֹ שֶׁהוּא עוֹשֶׂה עַל יְדֵי הַנְּבִיאִים, וּמַרְאֶה אֶת הַצַּדִּיקִים מַרְאוֹת נוֹרָאוֹת כְּדֶרֶךְ שֶׁהוּא מַרְאֶה אֶת הַנְּבִיאִים.

You may be aware that in the view of many of our great sages, there is a technique for individuals of extremely advanced character to experience the mystical visions of the Divine chariot [the angels in Heaven surrounding G-d's throne, as revealed to Ezekiel and others] and to gaze into the spiritual chambers of angels and the like. They would fast for a designated amount of days, then

Rabbi, author, and poet. Born to a distinguished family that included amongst its ancestors exilarchs and heads of yeshiva, Rav Hai succeeded his aged father, Sherira, as _ga'on_ of Pumpedita (in modern-day Iraq). As head of the rabbinical court and later as head of the yeshiva, Rav Hai was seen as the leader of world Jewry, which is evident in his correspondence, some of which is still extant, with Jewish communities worldwide. He authored works on Jewish law, Talmud, the Hebrew language, poetry, and Tanach, most of which has not been preserved. With his passing at the ripe age of 99, the epoch of the _ge'onim_ came to a close.

place their head between their knees and whisper copious songs of praise to G-d with their faces toward the earth. This opened them to mystical visions and allowed them to experience roaming the Heavens and exploring its supernal chambers with clarity.

There are two works of the mishnaic sages regarding this, entitled *Heichalot Rabati* [The Great Chambers] and *Heichalot Zutrati* [The Minor Chambers]. This is all very well-known and was regarded by all of the sages as authentic. They insisted that G-d performs miracles and wonders through saintly individuals [*tzadikim*] just as He did with the prophets, and that G-d shows them awesome visions just as he showed the prophets.

HEICHAL SHEL MAALAH
Yoram Raanan

THERE'S MORE...

For an overview of diverse forms of transcendent mystical meditation throughout Jewish history, see Appendix B.

TEXT 8

Entering the Orchard

Talmud, Chagigah 14b

תָּנוּ רַבָּנָן, אַרְבָּעָה נִכְנְסוּ בַּפַּרְדֵּס, וְאֵלּוּ הֵן: בֶּן עַזַאי, וּבֶן זוֹמָא, אַחֵר וְרַבִּי עֲקִיבָא...

בֶּן עַזַאי הֵצִיץ וָמֵת... בֶּן זוֹמָא הֵצִיץ וְנִפְגַּע... אַחֵר קִצֵּץ בִּנְטִיעוֹת, רַבִּי עֲקִיבָא יָצָא בְּשָׁלוֹם.

Four individuals entered the orchard [*pardes*; they explored the Torah's mystical secrets]. They are: Ben Azai, Ben Zoma, Acher, and Rabbi Akiva. . . .

Ben Azai gazed at the Divine Presence and died. . . . Ben Zoma gazed at the Divine Presence and became crazed. . . . Acher gazed and chopped down the shoots of saplings [i.e., he became a heretic], and Rabbi Akiva emerged safely.

BABYLONIAN TALMUD

A literary work of monumental proportions that draws upon the legal, spiritual, intellectual, ethical, and historical traditions of Judaism. The 37 tractates of the Babylonian Talmud contain the teachings of the Jewish sages from the period after the destruction of the 2nd Temple through the 5th century CE. It has served as the primary vehicle for the transmission of the Oral Law and the education of Jews over the centuries; it is the entry point for all subsequent legal, ethical, and theological Jewish scholarship.

Rabbi Shais Taub
uses hands-on science experiments to explain the deepest secrets of the universe:
myjli.com/meditation

HE CAST A LOOK AND WENT MAD

Maurycy Minkowski (1881–1930), oil on canvas, 1910. Based on the Talmudic narrative above, this work reflects the struggle of European Jews in the 18th and 19th centuries between tradition and modernity, with contemporary representations of the rabbis mentioned in the Talmud. (The Jewish Museum, New York)

III. DISCOVERING SPIRITUALITY

For the sake of *experiencing* our soul's spiritual awareness, we must access the soul's spiritual *perspective*. This is accomplished through contemplation of spiritual ideas. Naturally, these concepts are abstract, and they require cognitive meditation to properly appreciate them and assimilate them into our conscious thinking.

binah—understanding

FIGURE 2.1

	HITBODEDUT	HITBONENUT
HEBREW ROOT WORD	*Badad*	*Binah*
TRANSLATION	**Alone/Secluded**	**Contemplation**
ACTION	Detaching from material engagement	Developing spiritual awareness

TALMUD TORAH
Ephraim Moshe Lilien, Israel,
etching on paper, 1915

TEXT 9

Hitbonenut Meditation

Rabbi Yosef Yitzchak Schneersohn, *Igrot Kodesh* 3, p. 525

וְהִנֵּה עִקָּר גָּדוֹל בְּלִמּוּד זֶה, הוּא לְהִתְעַמֵּק בְּמַחֲשָׁבָה זְמַן
נָכוֹן כַּמָּה פְּעָמִים בְּהָעִנְיָן שֶׁלָּמַד, וְהוּא עִנְיַן הַהִתְבּוֹנְנוּת,
דְּפֵרוּשׁוֹ הִסְתַּכְּלוּת חֲזָקָה בְּעִיּוּן וּבְהַעֲמָקָה גְדוֹלָה.

A central foundation of this study [of mysticism] is to repeatedly spend considerable time in deep contemplation on the subject matter being studied. This is the practice that is referred to as *hitbonenut*, which means to firmly visualize the concept and to analyze it deeply.

RABBI YOSEF YITZCHAK SCHNEERSOHN (RAYATZ, FRIERDIKER REBBE, PREVIOUS REBBE) 1880–1950

 Chasidic rebbe, prolific writer, and Jewish activist. Rabbi Yosef Yitzchak, the sixth leader of the Chabad movement, actively promoted Jewish religious practice in Soviet Russia and was arrested for these activities. After his release from prison and exile, he settled in Warsaw, Poland, from where he fled Nazi occupation and arrived in New York in 1940. Settling in Brooklyn, Rabbi Schneersohn worked to revitalize American Jewish life. His son-in-law Rabbi Menachem Mendel Schneerson succeeded him as the leader of the Chabad movement.

A letter written by the Previous Rebbe, Rabbi Yosef Yitzchak Schneersohn, describing a reception held in St. Louis, one of the cities that he traveled to during his historic visit to America in 1930.

Study & think!

Take It to Heart

Rabbi Bachya ben Asher, Deuteronomy 4:39

TEXT 10

RABBI
BACHYA BEN ASHER
(RABBEINU BECHAYE)
C. 1255–1340

Biblical commentator.
Rabbeinu Bechaye lived
in Spain and was a
disciple of Rabbi Shlomo
ben Aderet, known as
Rashba. He is best known
for his multifaceted
commentary on the
Torah, which interprets
the text on literal,
Midrashic, philosophical,
and kabbalistic levels.
Rabbeinu Bechaye also
wrote *Kad Hakemach*, a
work on philosophy
and ethics.

"וַהֲשֵׁבֹתָ אֶל לְבָבֶךָ" (דְּבָרִים ד, לט): זֶה מִצְוַת עֲשֵׂה מִן הַתּוֹרָה
בִּידִיעַת הַשֵּׁם יִתְבָּרַךְ, שֶׁנִּצְטַוִּינוּ לָדַעַת אוֹתוֹ וְלַחֲקֹר עַל אַחְדוּתוֹ
וְשֶׁלֹּא נִסְמֹךְ עַל הַקַּבָּלָה בִּלְבַד . . . וּמִפְּנֵי שֶׁאֵין עִנְיָן הָאֱלֹקוּת שֶׁיַּשִּׂיגֶנּוּ
הָאָדָם בְּשִׂכְלוֹ בִּתְחִלַּת מַחֲשַׁבְתּוֹ, לְכָךְ הִזְכִּיר בּוֹ לָשׁוֹן "וַהֲשֵׁבֹתָ
אֶל לְבָבֶךָ" כְּאָדָם שֶׁמִּתְבּוֹנֵן בַּדָּבָר וְיַצְטָרֵךְ לַחֲזֹר וּלְהִתְבּוֹנֵן . . .
וְעִנְיַן הֲשָׁבַת הַלֵּב הוּא הַדָּבָר שֶׁצָּרִיךְ עִיּוּן גָּדוֹל וְדֵעָה יְתֵרָה.

"You shall take it to heart" (DEUTERONOMY 4:39): This is a positive commandment to know G-d. We are enjoined to investigate and develop an appreciation of G-d's unity, and not rely solely on received tradition. . . . However, since the spiritual understanding of the Divine is abstract and not easily understood, the verse emphasizes that we must "take it to heart" [the Hebrew term for "take it" in this verse more literally means "return it"], indicating that we must *repeatedly* contemplate the concept until it settles in our mind. . . . The term "take to heart" always refers to a matter that requires profound concentration and extra-focused thinking.

TEXT 11A

Inner Dialogue

Rabbi Yosef Yitzchak Schneersohn, *Sefer Hamaamarim* 5701, p. 99

אָמְנָם עִנְיַן הַהִתְבּוֹנְנוּת הוּא שַׁקְלָא וְטַרְיָא שִׂכְלִית. וְהַיְנוּ דְּכָל דָּבָר
שֵׂכֶל הַבָּא בְּמֻשָּׂג, עִם הֱיוֹתוֹ כְּבָר מְפֹרָט לְרִבּוּי פְּרָטִים, עִנְיָנִים וַחֲלָקִים
וּמְבֹאָרִים וּמְסֻבָּרִים בְּבֵאוּר וְהֶסְבֵּר, הִנֵּה כֹּחַ הַהִתְבּוֹנְנוּת הוּא הַשַּׁקְלָא
וְטַרְיָא בְּהַהַשָּׂגָה הַהִיא. אִם כֵּן, הוּא בֶּאֱמֶת כְּפִי אֲשֶׁר פְּרָט כָּל הַפְּרָטִים
וְהָעִנְיָנִים וְהַחֲלָקִים הָהֵם . . . וְעַל יְדֵי שְׁקִידַת הַהִתְבּוֹנְנוּת הֲרֵי הוּא בָּא
לִידֵי הִסְתַּכְּלוּת הַחֲזָקָה בְּנִשְׁמַת הַהַשָּׂגָה, שֶׁהוּא צִיּוּר הַמֻּשָׂג הַהוּא.

Hitbonenut is an internal dialogue with an idea.
Once we have studied something well in all its fine
details, explanations, and commentaries—until
we have developed a thorough understanding of
it—the practice of *hitbonenut* meditation is to
then mentally analyze the idea to verify whether
our understanding is true and accurate in all of its
details. . . . Through diligent meditation we develop
a strong visualization of the soul of the concept,
which is the animating core of the idea itself.

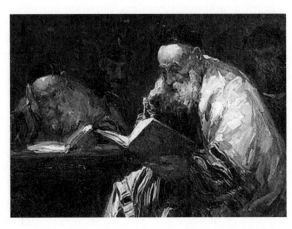

TALMUDYŚCI—
THE TALMUDISTS
Adolf Behrman (1876–1943), oil
on canvas. A Polish painter who
portrayed scenes of Polish Jewish
life, Behrman spent most of his life
in Lodz, escaping to Bialystok after
the Nazi invasion of Poland. He was
killed during the liquidation of the
Bialystok ghetto, and many of his
works were destroyed in World War II.
(Jewish Historical Institute, Warsaw)

We have to learn about G-d to think about G-d

TEXT 11B

Expanding Awareness

Frumma Rosenberg-Gottlieb,
"On Mindfulness and Jewish Meditation (a Brief History),"
chabad.org

FRUMMA ROSENBERG-GOTTLIEB

Author and speaker.
Frumma Rosenberg-Gottlieb is an educator and life coach. She lives in Miami and is the author of *Awesome Aging: Happier, Healthier, Smarter, and Younger than Yesterday.*

The chassidic practice of *hitbonenut* meditation involves actively contemplating a spiritual concept until it expands our creative intelligence, deepens our awareness, and becomes an indelible part of our consciousness.

TEXT 12

For the Love of G-d

Rabbi Shalom DovBer Schneersohn, *Kuntres Haavodah*, p. 50

RABBI SHALOM DOVBER SCHNEERSOHN (RASHAB)
1860–1920

Chasidic rebbe. Rabbi Shalom DovBer became the 5th leader of the Chabad movement upon the passing of his father, Rabbi Shmuel Schneersohn. He established the Lubavitch network of *yeshivot* called Tomchei Temimim. He authored many volumes of Chasidic discourses and is renowned for his lucid and thorough explanations of kabbalistic concepts.

שֶׁעַל יְדֵי הַתְבּוֹנְנוּת אֲמִתִּי וּבְהַעֲמָקַת הַדַּעַת, יִהְיֶה קָרוֹב
וּדְבֵקוּת נַפְשׁוֹ לֶאֱלוֹקוּת בֶּאֱמֶת (רְצוֹנוֹ לוֹמַר: בֶּאֱמֶת
שֶׁלוֹ לְפִי מַדְרֵגָתוֹ), וּמְקַיֵּם בָּזֶה מִצְוַת אַהֲבַת ה'.

Through honest contemplation with deep focus, a person's soul develops an authentic closeness and attachment with G-d, commensurate to their spiritual standing. Through this, one fulfills the mitzvah to love G-d.

IV. *HITBONENUT* MEDITATION EXERCISE

The following is a *hitbonenut* exercise. It begins by analyzing a spiritual teaching to reach an awareness of the spiritual energy that breathes within everything. That energy is the force responsible for each entity's continued existence and is its innermost identity. This meditation develops our spiritual awareness and reframes our perspective of the world.

TEXT 13

The Soul Existence

Rabbi Shalom DovBer Schneersohn,
Sefer Hamaamarim 5659, p. 28

כִּי בְּכָל דָּבָר בָּעוֹלָם הַזֶּה יֵשׁ גַּשְׁמִיּוּת וְרוּחָנִיּוּת, וְהָרוּחָנִיּוּת הוּא בְּחִינַת הַחַיּוּת הָאֱלֹקִי הַמְחַיֶּה וּמְהַוֶּה אֶת גֶּשֶׁם הַנִּבְרָא. וּכְמוֹ בְּחַי וּמְדַבֵּר, הִנֵּה הַנֶּפֶשׁ שֶׁבּוֹ הוּא הַמְחַיֶּה אֶת גּוּף הַבַּעַל חַי אוֹ הַמְדַבֵּר, לִהְיוֹת בִּבְחִינַת חַי אוֹ מְדַבֵּר. וּבְהִסְתַּלֵּק הַנֶּפֶשׁ מִן הַגּוּף, יָצָא הַגּוּף מִגֶּדֶר חַי וְיִתְבַּטֵּל חַיּוּתוֹ, וְגַם גּוּפוֹ נִרְקָב וְנַעֲשֶׂה לְעָפָר. וְהַיְנוּ מִשּׁוּם דְּקִיּוּם הַגּוּף הוּא גַּם כֵּן מִצַּד הַחַיּוּת הַמְחַיָּה אוֹתוֹ. וְכֵן בַּצּוֹמֵחַ, יֵשׁ בּוֹ נֶפֶשׁ הַצּוֹמַחַת הַמְחַיָּה אוֹתוֹ. וְכֵן בַּדּוֹמֵם, יֵשׁ בּוֹ חַיּוּת הַמְחַיֶּה וּמְקַיֵּם אוֹתוֹ שֶׁלֹּא יִתְבַּטֵּל יֵשׁוּתוֹ, וְלֹא יַחֲזֹר לִהְיוֹת אַיִן וְאֶפֶס כְּמוֹ קֹדֶם הַבְּרִיאָה.

וְלָכֵן הָרוּחָנִיּוּת וְהַחַיּוּת הָאֱלֹקִי נִקְרָא חַיִּים וְטוֹב, לִהְיוֹת שֶׁהוּא בְּחִינַת הַחַי אֲשֶׁר נִשְׁאָר חַי וְקַיָּם לְעוֹלָם. וְהַגַּשְׁמִי נִקְרָא מָוֶת וָרַע, לְפִי שֶׁהוּא כָּלֶה וְנִפְסָד בְּהִסְתַּלֵּק הַנֶּפֶשׁ מִמֶּנּוּ, וְאֵין לוֹ קִיּוּם מִצַּד עַצְמוֹ כְּלָל.

וּמִבְּשָׂרִי אֶחֱזֶה אֱלוֹקַהּ (אִיּוֹב יט, כו): כְּשֵׁם שֶׁהָאָדָם מַרְגִּישׁ בְּנַפְשׁוֹ שֶׁיֵּשׁ בּוֹ חַיּוּת הַמְחַיֶּה אוֹתוֹ, וְהָעִקָּר הוּא הַחַיּוּת, וּבְהִסְתַּלֵּק הַנֶּפֶשׁ מִן הַגּוּף נִשְׁאָר כְּאֶבֶן דּוֹמֵם, וְגַם הַגּוּף כָּלֶה וְנִפְסָד כַּנַּ"ל, כְּמוֹ כֵן יָבִין בִּכְלָלוּת הָעוֹלָמוֹת, שֶׁיֵּשׁ בָּהֶם חַיּוּת אֱלֹקִי הַמְחַיֶּה אוֹתָם, וּמִזֶּה כָּל

חַיּוֹת וְקַיָּים הָעוֹלָמוֹת, רַק מִצַּד הָאוֹר וְהַחַיּוּת הָאֱלֹקִי שֶׁבָּהֶם. וְאִם הָיָה מִסְתַּלֵּק הַחַיּוּת חַס וְשָׁלוֹם, הָיָה נַעֲשֶׂה מֵהֶם לְאַיִן וְאֶפֶס מַמָּשׁ . . .

וְהִנֵּה כְּשֶׁיִּתְבּוֹנֵן הָאָדָם בְּכָל זֶה, אֵיךְ שֶׁבְּכָל דָּבָר יֵשׁ אוֹר וְחַיּוּת הָאֱלֹקִי, וְהָעִקָּר הוּא הָאוֹר הָאֱלֹקִי שֶׁבּוֹ, וְהַנִּבְרָאִים בֶּאֱמֶת בְּטֵלִים לְהָאוֹר הָאֱלֹקִי שֶׁבָּהֶם וּלְשָׁרְשָׁם וְלִמְקוֹרָם הַמְחַיֶּם כוּ', עַל יְדֵי זֶה יִתְעוֹרֵר בִּרְצוֹן וּתְשׁוּקָה וְאַהֲבָה גְדוֹלָה לֶאֱלֹקוּת, שֶׁזֶּה יִהְיֶה כָּל חֶפְצוֹ וּמְגַמָּתוֹ רַק בֶּאֱלֹקוּת לְבַד, וְלֹא יִרְצֶה בְּחִיצוֹנִית וְגַשְׁמִיּוּת הָעוֹלָם, שֶׁהֵם מָוֶת מִצַּד עַצְמָם, הַוֶֹים וְנִפְסָדִים כוּ', רַק יִרְצֶה בְּהַחַיּוּת הָאֱלֹקִי שֶׁהוּא הָעִקָּר.

Everything that exists is comprised of a physical form and a spiritual, Divine energy that creates and animates the entity's physical existence. This is clearly demonstrable in animals and humans: They have an animating spirit. If the spirit were to leave their body, the body would no longer be classified as alive, and the body would begin to decompose and turn to dust. That is because the very existence of the body hinges upon the spiritual energy that animates it. The same is true of vegetation: it also possesses an animating spirit. Even inanimate objects possess some sort of energizing spirit that keeps them in existence and prevents their disappearance.

Based on this awareness, spirituality is referred to as "good" and "life"—because it is a living force that remains alive and in existence forever—whereas physical matter is referred to as "negative" and "death," because it decomposes and ceases to exist without the spirit within it, and it has no means of existing independently.

"From my flesh, I can perceive G-d" (JOB 19:26)
[meaning that human experience informs our
understanding of G-d]: We intuitively sense that
we have a life force that provides us with our life;
and that it is our primary identity; and that were
our soul to leave our body, the body would be left
like an inanimate rock and eventually decompose
and disappear. The same is true with all that exists.
The entire cosmos and all its contents exist due to
a Divine spirit that gives existence to everything.
That Divine light and force is the entire life and
sustaining power of all that exists. If it departs, all
existence will revert to absolute nothingness. . . .

If we meditate on this idea . . . we will realize that
the material existence of each entity is entirely
dependent on the spiritual force within it, and that
physicality is nullified before the presence of the
Divine light that is its source of existence. This
realization will inspire a powerful desire, love, and
yearning for the Divine. We will no longer desire
that which exists only superficially, and which is
in fact death—decomposing and disappearing.
All we will desire is to attach to the Divinity
that is true life and the mainstay of existence.

Is G-d real? Watch an
animated conversation
between a mother
and baby lamp:
myjli.com/meditation

Record three key ideas that Text 13 reveals:

1

2

3

Identify the "body" and "soul" of the following scenarios:

Dinner with a spouse or close friend

Body

Soul

Disciplining a child

Body

Soul

Exercising at the gym

Body

Soul

Shaking hands on a deal

Body

Soul

TEXT 14

Choose Life

Deuteronomy 30:9

הַעִידֹתִי בָכֶם הַיּוֹם אֶת הַשָּׁמַיִם וְאֶת הָאָרֶץ: הַחַיִּים וְהַמָּוֶת נָתַתִּי לְפָנֶיךָ, הַבְּרָכָה וְהַקְּלָלָה; וּבָחַרְתָּ בַּחַיִּים, לְמַעַן תִּחְיֶה אַתָּה וְזַרְעֶךָ.

This day, I call upon Heaven and earth as witnesses [that I have warned] you: I have set before you life and death, the blessing and the curse. You shall choose life, so that you and your offspring will live.

*Soul
spirituality
don't choose
just the material
world, is by itself
lifeless*

QUESTION

The choice between life and death seems obvious. Why would G-d need to encourage us to choose life?

Opening pages of the book of Deuteronomy in a parchment manuscript of the Pentateuch and *haftarot* from the last quarter of the 15th century. (Braginsky Collection, Zurich)

Loving Life

Rabbi Shalom DovBer Schneersohn,
Sefer Hamaamarim 5659, p. 30

וְזֶהוּ "לְאַהֲבָה אֶת ה' אֱלֹקֶיךָ . . . כִּי הוּא חַיֶּיךָ" (דְּבָרִים ל, כ), דִּכְמוֹ שֶׁהָאָדָם אוֹהֵב חַיֵּי נַפְשׁוֹ, מִפְּנֵי שֶׁמַּרְגִּישׁ בְּעַצְמוֹ שֶׁהָעִקָּר הוּא הַחַיּוּת הַנֶּפֶשׁ, וּלְזֹאת הוּא אוֹהֵב אֶת הַנֶּפֶשׁ . . . וּכְמוֹ כֵן "לְאַהֲבָה אֶת ה' אֱלֹקֶיךָ כִּי הוּא חַיֶּיךָ", כְּשֶׁמִּתְבּוֹנֵן אֵיךְ שֶׁהָאֱלֹקוּת הוּא חַיֵּי הַחַיִּים, דְּכָל חַיּוּת הָעוֹלָם וְהַנִּבְרָאִים הוּא מֵאֱלֹקוּת וְהוּא הָעִקָּר, הֲרֵי יִרְצֶה וְיֹאהַב אֶת ה', דְּהַיְנוּ דְּבְכָל עֲשִׂיּוֹתָיו בְּחִיצוֹנִיּוּת הָעוֹלָם, כְּמוֹ בַּאֲכִילָה וּשְׁתִיָּה וּבְעֵסֶק מַשָּׂא וּמַתָּן וְכַדּוֹמֶה, לֹא יִרְצֶה אֶת הַדָּבָר הַגַּשְׁמִי, כִּי אִם הָאֱלֹקוּת שֶׁבּוֹ.

The Torah instructs us: "Love the L-rd your G-d
. . . because He is your life" (DEUTERONOMY
30:20). When we love ourselves, it is the state of
life that our soul provides that we love, because we
sense that it is our core self. . . . By the same token,
we should love G-d, for He is the source of life for
all existence. When we meditate on the reality
that Divinity is the life of all life, we will desire and
love G-d. Consequently, in all our interactions
with the externality of the universe, such as eating
or drinking, conducting business, and so on, our
focus will shift from the material and corporeal
elements to embrace the Divinity within them.

V. TAKEAWAY

The above teachings and meditations have provided a renewed understanding of spirituality, which is not a specific thing or experience, but rather, the *soul* of each thing and experience. However, for this awareness to truly take shape, we will need to practice *hitbonenut* consistently.

EXERCISE 2.5

How would you define spirituality?

How might spirituality be experienced?

FOREST GLORY
Yehoshua Wiseman,
Israel, oil on canvas

FIGURE 2.2   The Benefits of Spirituality

> "Spiritual people are relatively happier than non-spiritual people, have superior mental health, cope better with stressors, have more satisfying marriages, use drugs and alcohol less often, are physically healthier, and live longer lives."
>
> — *Sonja Lyubomirsky,* The How of Happiness *(New York: Penguin Press, 2007)*

There are many tangible benefits to spirituality. In the past, researchers of psychology typically hesitated to study spirituality and religion, but a growing body of research suggests a direct link between spirituality/religion and overall health and happiness.

Some suggest that such benefits should be attributed to the communal and social support systems built into religious or spiritual communities, and not necessarily to the substance of an individual's convictions and beliefs. However, further analysis demonstrates that this is not the case, and instead draws a direct line from commonly held religio-spiritual beliefs to the enhanced health benefits typically enjoyed by members of faith communities.

Spirituality Increases Happiness and Well-Being

 MEANING AND SECURITY

To be happy, humans need a sense of meaning in life, a purpose to existence, and to feel that their actions are imbued with significance. They need a reason to focus on something beyond themselves. Lastly, they must feel secure and safe in their position in life. Religion and spirituality are obvious ways to provide that meaning, transcendence, and security.[1]

 POSITIVE EMOTIONS AND EXPERIENCES

Practicing religion and nurturing a sense of spirituality, such as regularly praying—in private or with others—can engender a wide range of positive emotions, experiences, and traits. Some examples are hope, gratitude, love, awe, compassion, joy, and even ecstasy.[2]

 PHYSICAL AND MENTAL HEALTH

Studies demonstrate the positive impact of spirituality on physical and mental health and other positive health outcomes, such as subjective well-being, health-related quality of life, recovery from mental illness, and reduction in addictive or suicidal behaviors.[3]

DISPOSITION TO FORGIVE

A slew of studies demonstrates that highly religious and spiritual individuals value forgiveness to a greater extent and consider themselves as more forgiving than their less spiritual or religious peers.[4]

COMMITTED RELATIONSHIPS

Research published by the American Psychological Association reveals that romantic partners who pray for their significant others experience stronger commitment in their relationship.[5] These studies exemplify an emerging subfield called relational spirituality, which focuses on the ways that diverse couples can rely on specific spiritual beliefs and behaviors, for better or worse, to motivate them to create, maintain, and transform their intimate relationships.[6]

Spirituality Protects

COPING WITH GRIEF

In one study, parents who had lost a baby to sudden infant death syndrome (SIDS) were interviewed three weeks and eighteen months later. Those who attended religious services frequently and who reported religion as being important to them were better able to cope eighteen months after the loss, showing relatively less depression at this time and greater well-being than nonreligious parents.[7]

FINDING MEANING IN TRAGEDY

Spirituality and religion provide a sense of meaning, remove the randomness from life, and arm those suffering from tragedy with answers or insights. Spiritual or religious individuals generally believe that "there is a reason for everything G-d does." This belief provides a coping mechanism that reduces stress and a form of emotion regulation.[8]

ABILITY TO ADJUST

In a study of patients undergoing chemotherapy, those who believed that G-d had a measurable control over their cancers had higher self-esteem, and were rated as better-adjusted by their nurses (happier, more serene, more active, and able to relate better to others). Belief in G-d as "a controlling force" helped them cope better than belief in their own control. When these patients spoke of "control," they actively expressed that through prayer and faith.

1. Benson, P. L., et al., "Spiritual Development in Childhood and Adolescence: Toward a Field of Inquiry," *Applied Developmental Science*, 2003:7, pp. 205–213.

2. Pargament, K. I., Mahoney, A., "Spirituality: Discovering and Conserving the Sacred," in C. R. Snyder and S. J. Lopez (eds.), *Handbook of Positive Psychology* (New York: Oxford University Press, 2002), pp. 646–659.

3. Mueller, P. S., et al., "Religious Involvement, Spirituality, and Medicine: Implications for Clinical Practice," *Mayo Clinic Proceedings*, Dec. 1976 (12), pp. 1225–35.

4. McCullough, M. E., Worthington, E. L., "Religion and the Forgiving Personality," *Journal of Personality*, 74 (2001), pp. 1257–1292.

5. https://www.apa.org/news/press/releases/2014/12/religion-relationships

6. https://www.apa.org/pubs/journals/releases/fam-0000030.pdf

7. McIntosh, D. N., et al., "Religion's Role in Adjustment to a Negative Life Event: Coping with the Loss of a Child," *Journal of Psychiatry and Social Psychology*, 65 (1993), pp. 812–821.

8. Ellison, C. G., "Religion, the Life Stress Paradigm, and the Study of Depression," in Levin, J. S. (ed.), *Religion in Aging and Health: Theoretical Foundations and Methodological Frontiers* (Thousand Oaks, Calif., Sage Publishing, 1994), pp. 78–121.

KEY POINTS

1   We are comprised of a body and soul, each of
which has a unique character and drive.

2   The body is driven by material gain and the soul by
spirituality. We all possess an innate spiritual drive
within us that we can come to feel and experience.

3   One way to perceive the spiritual drive of the soul is by
distancing ourselves from the immediate distractions of
materialism. This is the root of *hitbodedut* meditation.

4   The most effective way to develop our spiritual calling
is by learning about it and contemplating the spiritual
ideas. This meditation practice is known as *hitbonenut*.

5   Just as we have a soul that gives us life and is
our true identity, the world has a soul that
sustains it and is its most authentic identity.

6   We "choose life" by focusing on the spiritual
content of every experience and valuing
the Divine potential within it.

APPENDIX A

TEXT 16

Aloneness with G-d

Rabbi Nachman of Breslov, *Likutei Moharan* II, 25:1

הַהִתְבּוֹדְדוּת הוּא מַעֲלָה עֶלְיוֹנָה וּגְדוֹלָה מִן הַכֹּל, דְּהַיְנוּ לִקְבֹּעַ לוֹ, עַל כָּל פָּנִים, שָׁעָה אוֹ יוֹתֵר לְהִתְבּוֹדֵד לְבַדּוֹ בְּאֵיזֶה חֶדֶר אוֹ בַּשָּׂדֶה, וּלְפָרֵשׁ שִׂיחָתוֹ בֵּינוֹ לְבֵין קוֹנוֹ בְּטַעֲנוֹת וַאֲמַתְלָאוֹת, בְּדִבְרֵי חֵן וְרָצוּי וּפִיּוּס, לְבַקֵּשׁ וּלְהִתְחַנֵּן מִלְּפָנָיו יִתְבָּרַךְ שֶׁיְּקָרְבוֹ אֵלָיו לַעֲבוֹדָתוֹ בֶּאֱמֶת.

וּתְפִלָּה וְשִׂיחָה זוֹ יִהְיֶה בַּלָּשׁוֹן שֶׁמְּדַבְּרִים בּוֹ, דְּהַיְנוּ בִּלְשׁוֹן אַשְׁכְּנַז (בִּמְדִינָתֵנוּ), כִּי בִּלְשׁוֹן הַקֹּדֶשׁ קָשֶׁה לוֹ לְפָרֵשׁ כָּל שִׂיחָתוֹ . . . וּבִלְשׁוֹן אַשְׁכְּנַז יָכוֹל לְפָרֵשׁ כָּל שִׂיחָתוֹ. וְאֶת כָּל אֲשֶׁר עִם לְבָבוֹ יָשִׂיחַ וִיסַפֵּר לְפָנָיו יִתְבָּרַךְ, הֵן חֲרָטָה וּתְשׁוּבָה עַל הֶעָבָר, וְהֵן בַּקָּשַׁת הַתַּחֲנוּנִים לִזְכּוֹת לְהִתְקָרֵב אֵלָיו יִתְבָּרַךְ מֵהַיּוֹם וְהָלְאָה בֶּאֱמֶת, וְכַיּוֹצֵא בָּזֶה כָּל חַד לְפוּם דַּרְגֵּהּ . . .

וְהַנְהָגָה זוֹ הִיא גְּדוֹלָה בְּמַעֲלָה מְאֹד מְאֹד, וְהוּא דֶרֶךְ וְעֵצָה טוֹבָה מְאֹד לְהִתְקָרֵב אֵלָיו יִתְבָּרַךְ, כִּי זֹאת הִיא עֵצָה כְּלָלִיּת, שֶׁכּוֹלֵל הַכֹּל . . .

וְדַע, שֶׁכַּמָּה וְכַמָּה צַדִּיקִים גְּדוֹלִים מְפֻרְסָמִים סִפְּרוּ, שֶׁלֹּא בָּאוּ לְמַדְרֵגָתָם, רַק עַל יְדֵי הַנְהָגָה זוֹ. וְהַמַּשְׂכִּיל יָבִין מֵעַצְמוֹ גֹּדֶל מַעֲלַת הַנְהָגָה זוֹ, הָעוֹלָה לְמַעְלָה לְמַעְלָה, וְהוּא דָבָר הַשָּׁוֶה לְכָל נֶפֶשׁ מִקָּטֹן וְעַד גָּדוֹל, כִּי כֻלָּם יְכוֹלִים לִנְהֹג הַנְהָגָה זוֹ, וְעַל יְדֵי זֶה יָבוֹאוּ לְמַעֲלָה גְדוֹלָה. אַשְׁרֵי שֶׁיֹּאחֵז בָּזֶה.

Hitbodedut (seclusion) is the highest asset, greater than everything. It requires setting aside at least an hour for secluding yourself in a room or field and finding ways to enter into a dialogue with your Creator. Use words that evoke favor, placate, and conciliate in order to

RABBI NACHMAN
OF BRESLOV
1772-1810

Chasidic rebbe and thinker. Rabbi Nachman was a great-grandson of the Baal Shem Tov, the founder of the Chasidic movement. His magnum opus, *Likutei Moharan*, was published and disseminated by his disciple, Rabbi Noson Steinhartz. Reb Nachman died of tuberculosis at the age of 38, without appointing a successor. He is buried in Uman, Ukraine, where his followers continue to make pilgrimages, especially for Jewish holidays.

entreat and plead with G-d that He bring you closer to Him—to genuine Divine worship.

Conduct this prayer and conversation in the language you normally use, your native tongue, because it is difficult to express all that you desire to say in the Holy Tongue [if it is not your native language]. . . . In your native tongue, you can express yourself fully. Share with G-d everything that is in your heart: express your remorse and repentance for the past, your pleas to genuinely merit drawing closer to G-d from this day forward, and similar conversations, each individual according to their spiritual standing. . . .

This practice is extraordinarily beneficial. It is an extremely good path and guideline for drawing closer to G-d, because it is a universal guide that encompasses everything. . . .

You should know that many renowned *tzadikim* related that they attained their high degree of spirituality only through this practice. A perceptive individual will readily appreciate the great benefit of this practice, which raises a person higher and higher. Furthermore, it is a practice that is accessible to all people. Anyone can make use of this practice and thereby climb to spiritual heights. Fortunate are those who seize the opportunities this practice provides.

TEXT 17

Hitbodedut Meditation

Rabbi Nachman of Breslov, *Likutei Moharan* I, 52:3

אַךְ לִזְכּוֹת לָזֶה לְהִכָּלֵל בְּשָׁרְשׁוֹ, דְּהַיְנוּ לַחֲזֹר וּלְהִכָּלֵל בְּאַחְדוּת הַשֵּׁם יִתְבָּרַךְ, שֶׁהוּא מְחֻיַּב הַמְּצִיאוּת, זֶה אִי אֶפְשָׁר לִזְכּוֹת, כִּי אִם עַל יְדֵי בִּטּוּל, שֶׁיְּבַטֵּל עַצְמוֹ לְגַמְרֵי, עַד שֶׁיִּהְיֶה נִכְלָל בְּאַחְדוּתוֹ יִתְבָּרַךְ. וְאִי אֶפְשָׁר לָבוֹא לִידֵי בִּטּוּל, כִּי אִם עַל יְדֵי הִתְבּוֹדְדוּת, כִּי עַל יְדֵי שֶׁמִּתְבּוֹדֵד וּמְפָרֵשׁ שִׂיחָתוֹ בֵּינוֹ לְבֵין קוֹנוֹ, עַל יְדֵי זֶה הוּא זוֹכֶה לְבַטֵּל כָּל הַתַּאֲווֹת וְהַמִּדּוֹת רָעוֹת, עַד שֶׁזּוֹכֶה לְבַטֵּל כָּל גַּשְׁמִיּוּתוֹ, וּלְהִכָּלֵל בְּשָׁרְשׁוֹ . . .

וְגַם צְרִיכִין שֶׁיִּהְיֶה הַהִתְבּוֹדְדוּת בְּמָקוֹם מְיֻחָד, דְּהַיְנוּ חוּץ מֵהָעִיר בְּדֶרֶךְ יְחִידִי, בְּמָקוֹם שֶׁאֵין הוֹלְכִים שָׁם בְּנֵי אָדָם, כִּי בְּמָקוֹם שֶׁהוֹלְכִים שָׁם בְּנֵי אָדָם בַּיּוֹם, הָרוֹדְפִים אַחַר הָעוֹלָם הַזֶּה, אַף עַל פִּי שֶׁכָּעֵת אֵינָם הוֹלְכִים שָׁם, הוּא מְבַלְבֵּל גַּם כֵּן הַהִתְבּוֹדְדוּת, וְאֵינוֹ יָכוֹל לְהִתְבַּטֵּל וּלְהִכָּלֵל בּוֹ יִתְבָּרַךְ. עַל כֵּן צָרִיךְ שֶׁיֵּלֵךְ לְבַדּוֹ בַּלַּיְלָה בְּדֶרֶךְ יְחִידִי, בְּמָקוֹם שֶׁאֵין שָׁם אָדָם, וְשָׁם יֵלֵךְ וְיִתְבּוֹדֵד, וִיפַנֶּה לִבּוֹ וְדַעְתּוֹ מִכָּל עִסְקֵי עוֹלָם הַזֶּה, וִיבַטֵּל הַכֹּל, עַד שֶׁיִּזְכֶּה לִבְחִינַת בִּטּוּל בֶּאֱמֶת . . .

וְאָזַי, כְּשֶׁזּוֹכֶה לְבִטּוּל בֶּאֱמֶת, וַאֲזַי נִכְלָל נַפְשׁוֹ בְּשָׁרְשׁוֹ, דְּהַיְנוּ בּוֹ יִתְבָּרַךְ, שֶׁהוּא מְחֻיַּב הַמְּצִיאוּת. אֲזַי נִכְלָל כָּל הָעוֹלָם עִם נַפְשׁוֹ בְּשָׁרְשׁוֹ, שֶׁהוּא מְחֻיַּב הַמְּצִיאוּת, כִּי הַכֹּל תָּלוּי בּוֹ כַּנַּ"ל, וַאֲזַי נַעֲשֶׂה כָּל הָעוֹלָם עַל יָדוֹ בִּבְחִינַת מְחֻיַּב הַמְּצִיאוּת, כַּנַּ"ל.

To merit this—to return and be encompassed in G-d's oneness—is possible only through *bitul* (self-surrender). We must surrender ourselves until we are encompassed in G-d's oneness. The only way to attain *bitul* is through *hitbodedut*, through secluding ourselves and conversing at length with our Master. We thereby merit to negate all our physical desires and bad character traits, to the point that we merit negating all our corporeality and are encompassed in our Divine source. . . .

In addition, the *hitbodedut* should take place in a special place—away from the city, on a secluded road, in a place not frequented by people. For a place frequented during the day by people who chase after this world, even if at present they are not there, nonetheless disturbs the *hitbodedut* and we are unable to attain *bitul* and be encompassed in G-d. Therefore, we must go alone at night on a secluded road, in a location where no one else goes, and there engage in *hitbodedut*—emptying our heart and mind of all worldly matters, negating everything until we merit true *bitul*. . . .

When we merit true *bitul,* our soul is encompassed in its source—G-d, the True Existence. In this way, together with our own soul, the entire world is encompassed in its source, the True Existence upon which all existence is utterly dependent. Through this experience, we allow the entire universe to become the true reality.

TEXT 18

Silencing the Mind

Rabbi Klonymus Kalman of Piaseczno, *Derech Hamelech*
(Jerusalem: Vaad Chassidei Piaseczno, 1998), p. 450

**RABBI KLONYMUS
KALMAN SHAPIRA
OF PIASECZNO
1889–1943**

Chasidic rebbe
and educator.
Born into a long line of
Chasidic rebbes, Rabbi
Klonymus Kalman
Shapira served as a
Rebbe in Piaseczno,
near Warsaw. He was
the head of Yeshiva
Daat Moshe and was
renowned for his original
educational approach.
Rabbi Shapira is best
known for *Aish Kodesh*
(*Holy Fire*), a collection
of the weekly sermons
he gave in the Warsaw
ghetto, inspiring his
listeners with a message
of faith, self-sacrifice,
compassion, and hope.

אֲדוֹנֵנוּ מוֹרֵנוּ וְרַבֵּנוּ זצללה"ה הִתְחִיל אָז בְּהַמַּאֲמָר חֲזַ"ל (בְּרָכוֹת
נז, ב) "חֲלוֹם, אֶחָד מִשִּׁשִּׁים בַּנְּבוּאָה". כַּנּוֹדָע דַּרְכּוֹ שֶׁל הָאַדְמוֹ"ר
בִּסְפָרָיו, כִּי הַיֵּשׁוּת שֶׁל הָאָדָם הוּא הַמִּתְנַגֵּד לְהַשְׁרָאָה מִמָּרוֹם,
וְאִם דַּעְתּוֹ וּמַחְשְׁבוֹתָיו עֵרִים אָז קָשֶׁה שֶׁתִּשְׁרֶה עָלָיו הַשְׁרָאָה
מִמָּרוֹם, וּבְעֵת שֶׁהָאָדָם יָשֵׁן וְדַעְתּוֹ וּמַחְשְׁבוֹתָיו שׁוֹקְטִים, אָז
דַּוְקָא, כֵּיוָן שֶׁאֵין לוֹ דַעַת לְעַצְמוֹ, אֶפְשָׁר שֶׁתִּשְׁרֶה עָלָיו הַשְׁרָאָה
מִמָּרוֹם, וְזֶה הָעִנְיָן "חֲלוֹם אֶחָד וְכוּ'" . . . אֲבָל בְּעֵת שֶׁהָאִישׁ
יָשֵׁן, אָז אִי אֶפְשָׁר לוֹ לִרְצוֹת דְּבַר מָה, כִּי הֲלֹא יָשֵׁן הוּא.

וּבְכֵן הָעִקָּר לָבוֹא בְּהָקִיץ בְּעֵת שֶׁאֶפְשָׁר לוֹ לִרְצוֹת
לְמַצָּב שֶׁל שֵׁנָה, הַיְנוּ בְּהַשְׁקָטַת מַחְשְׁבוֹתָיו וּרְצוֹנוֹתָיו
הַשּׁוֹטְפִים בָּאָדָם בְּלִי קֵץ, כִּי כָּךְ דַּרְכָּהּ שֶׁל הַמַּחֲשָׁבָה,
שֶׁמִּסְתַּבֶּכֶת זוֹ בָזוֹ, וְקָשֶׁה לוֹ לְהָאָדָם לִפְרֹשׁ מֵהֶן . . .

וְנָתַן בָּזֶה עֵצוֹת מַעֲשִׂיּוֹת אֵיךְ לְהַשְׁקִיט מַחְשְׁבוֹתָיו.

וְדִבֶּר אָז שֶׁיַּתְחִיל הָאִישׁ לְהַבִּיט עַל מַחְשְׁבוֹתָיו שָׁעָה קַלָּה לְעֵרֶךְ אֵיזֶה
רְגָעִים, הַיְנוּ, מָה אֲנִי חוֹשֵׁב. אָז יַרְגִּישׁ לְאַט לְאַט שֶׁרֹאשׁוֹ מִתְרוֹקֵן
וּמַחְשְׁבוֹתָיו עָמְדוּ מִשִּׁטְפָן הָרָגִיל. וְאָז יַתְחִיל לֵאמֹר פָּסוּק אֶחָד, כְּגוֹן
"ה' אֱלֹקִים אֱמֶת", כְּדֵי לְקַשֵּׁר עַכְשָׁו רֹאשׁוֹ הֶחָלָל מִשְּׁאָר מַחֲשָׁבוֹת
לְמַחְשָׁבָה אַחַת שֶׁל קְדֻשָׁה, וְאַחַר כָּךְ כְּבָר יָכוֹל הוּא לְבַקֵּשׁ צְרָכָיו
בְּאֵיזֶה מִדָּה שֶׁהוּא צָרִיךְ לְהִתְתַּקֵּן בְּחִזּוּק אֱמוּנָה אוֹ אַהֲבָה וְיִרְאָה.
וְזָכִיתִי לִשְׁמֹעַ אָז מִמֶּנּוּ אֹפֶן הַשְׁקָטָה בְּחִזּוּק אֱמוּנָה. וְאָמַר בִּלְשׁוֹנוֹ
הַקָּדוֹשׁ, "אֲנִי מַאֲמִין בֶּאֱמוּנָה שְׁלֵמָה, שֶׁהַבּוֹרֵא הוּא הַנִּמְצָא הַיְחִידִי
בָּעוֹלָם, וְאֵין שׁוּם מְצִיאוּת זוּלָתוֹ, וְכָל הָעוֹלָם וְכָל אֲשֶׁר בּוֹ הֵם רַק
הֶאָרַת אוֹר ה'", וְכָךְ שָׁנֵן אֵיזֶה פְּעָמִים. אֲבָל לֹא שֶׁיֹּאמַר זֹאת בְּחָזְקָה,
כִּי כָּל הָעִנְיָן הוּא רַק לְהַשְׁקִיט מַחְשְׁבוֹתָיו, וּבַאֲמִירָה בְּתֹקֶף יָכוֹל
הוּא רַק לְעוֹרֵר אֶת הָאֲנֹכִיּוּת שֶׁלוֹ, רַק אַדְּרַבָּה, בְּאֹפֶן קַל מְאֹד.

גַּם זָכִיתִי לִשְׁמֹעַ בְּעִנְיַן אַהֲבָה, וְזֶה הָיָה לְשׁוֹנוֹ:
"רָצִיתִי מְאֹד לִהְיוֹת קָרוֹב לְהַשֵּׁם יִתְבָּרַךְ, הָיִיתִי מְאֹד
רוֹצֶה לְהַרְגִּישׁ הִתְקָרְבוּת לְהַבּוֹרֵא הַגָּדוֹל".

The Talmud states that a dream is a sixtieth of prophecy (BERACHOT 57B). The explanation of this is that our self-awareness prevents us from experiencing the Divine. As long as we are awake and conscious of ourselves, the spiritual presence of the Divine cannot rest on us. Conversely, when we are asleep, our awareness and consciousness are quieted—our sense of self is no longer present, and the Divine spirit can rest on us. . . . For that reason, our dreams contain a fraction of prophecy— because while we sleep, our sense of self is not present to disturb the Divinity.

Our goal, however, is to attain this sleep-consciousness while *awake*. This is achieved through silencing our thoughts and desires that control us incessantly. . . .

Here is practical direction to achieve this:

First, we simply pay attention to our flow of thoughts for a set time. We will eventually notice that our mind is emptying, and our thoughts are slowing from their habitual hurried flow. We should then repeat a single verse or phrase, such as "G-d is truly G-d," in order to insert a thought of holiness into our now open mind. After these steps, we can articulate a need for help in any of the many areas of character development with which we require assistance to improve, be it our faith or our love or awe for G-d.

Here is a suggestion for work on strengthening faith: "I believe with complete faith that G-d is the only existence in the universe. There is no reality other than G-d. All the world and all that exists is but a ray of His light." This should be repeated several times, but not forcefully. The whole point is to *quiet* the self. Speaking with forcefulness is likely to *arouse* the ego. Rather, we utter the phrase with extreme gentleness.

Or if you wish to arouse love for G-d, say: "I wish so much to be close to His blessed Essence. My deepest desire is to feel that I am forever growing nearer to the mighty Creator."

TEXT 19

Meditative Prophets

Maimonides, *Mishneh Torah*,
Laws of the Foundations of the Torah 7:1–4

אָדָם שֶׁהוּא מְמֻלָּא בְּכָל הַמִּדּוֹת הָאֵלּוּ שָׁלֵם בְּגוּפוֹ, כְּשֶׁיִּכָּנֵס לַפַּרְדֵּס
וְיִמָּשֵׁךְ בְּאוֹתָן הָעִנְיָנִים הַגְּדוֹלִים הָרְחוֹקִים, וְתִהְיֶה לוֹ דֵּעָה נְכוֹנָה
לְהָבִין וּלְהַשִּׂיג, וְהוּא מִתְקַדֵּשׁ וְהוֹלֵךְ וּפוֹרֵשׁ מִדַּרְכֵי כְּלַל הָעָם הַהוֹלְכִים
בְּמַחֲשַׁכֵּי הַזְּמָן, וְהוֹלֵךְ וּמְזָרֵז עַצְמוֹ וּמְלַמֵּד נַפְשׁוֹ שֶׁלֹּא תִּהְיֶה לוֹ
מַחֲשָׁבָה כְּלָל בְּאֶחָד מִדְּבָרִים בְּטֵלִים וְלֹא מֵהַבְלֵי הַזְּמָן וְתַחְבּוּלוֹתָיו.

אֶלָּא דַעְתּוֹ פְּנוּיָה תָּמִיד לְמַעְלָה, קְשׁוּרָה תַּחַת הַכִּסֵּא, לְהָבִין בְּאוֹתָן הַצּוּרוֹת הַקְּדוֹשׁוֹת הַטְּהוֹרוֹת, וּמִסְתַּכֵּל בְּחָכְמָתוֹ שֶׁל הַקָּדוֹשׁ בָּרוּךְ הוּא כֻּלָּהּ, מִצּוּרָה רִאשׁוֹנָה עַד טַבּוּר הָאָרֶץ וְיוֹדֵעַ מֵהֶן גָּדְלוֹ, מִיָּד רוּחַ הַקֹּדֶשׁ שׁוֹרָה עָלָיו . . . כָּל הַנְּבִיאִים אֵין מִתְנַבְּאִין בְּכָל עֵת שֶׁיִּרְצוּ, אֶלָּא מְכַוְּנִים דַּעְתָּם וְיוֹשְׁבִים שְׂמֵחִים וְטוֹבֵי לֵב וּמִתְבּוֹדְדִים.

In order to achieve prophecy, an aspiring prophet who is advanced in all the required character traits enters the orchard [*pardes*; the Torah's mystical wisdom] and is drawn into these great and sublime concepts. If they possess an adequate mental capacity to comprehend and grasp them, they will become holy. They must train themselves to avoid thinking about meaningless things and contemporary vanities.

Instead, their mind should constantly be directed upward, bound beneath G-d's throne of glory, striving to comprehend the holy and pure forms and gazing at the wisdom of the Holy One, blessed be He, in its entirety, in its manifold manifestations from the most elevated spiritual form until the navel of the earth, appreciating His greatness from them. After these preparations, the Divine spirit will immediately rest upon him. . . .

All the prophets do not prophesy whenever they desire. Rather, they must concentrate their attention on spiritual concepts in a joyful frame of mind and enter a state of seclusion [*hitbodedut*].

RABBI MOSHE BEN MAIMON (MAIMONIDES, RAMBAM) 1135–1204

Halachist, philosopher, author, and physician. Maimonides was born in Córdoba, Spain. After the conquest of Córdoba by the Almohads, he fled Spain and eventually settled in Cairo, Egypt. There, he became the leader of the Jewish community and served as court physician to the vizier of Egypt. He is most noted for authoring the *Mishneh Torah*, an encyclopedic arrangement of Jewish law; and for his philosophical work, *Guide for the Perplexed*. His rulings on Jewish law are integral to the formation of halachic consensus.

APPENDIX B

TEXT 20

Mystical Visions

Talmud, Chagigah 14b

תָּנוּ רַבָּנָן: מַעֲשֶׂה בְּרַבָּן יוֹחָנָן בֶּן זַכַּאי שֶׁהָיָה רוֹכֵב עַל הַחֲמוֹר
וְהָיָה מְהַלֵּךְ בַּדֶּרֶךְ, וְרַבִּי אֶלְעָזָר בֶּן עֲרָךְ מְחַמֵּר אַחֲרָיו.
אָמַר לוֹ: רַבִּי, שְׁנֵה לִי פֶּרֶק אֶחָד בְּמַעֲשֵׂה מֶרְכָּבָה!

אָמַר לוֹ: לֹא כָּךְ שָׁנִיתִי לָכֶם, "וְלֹא בַּמֶּרְכָּבָה בְּיָחִיד,
אֶלָּא אִם כֵּן הָיָה חָכָם מֵבִין מִדַּעְתּוֹ"?

אָמַר לוֹ: רַבִּי, תַּרְשֵׁנִי לוֹמַר לְפָנֶיךָ דָּבָר אֶחָד שֶׁלְּמַדְתָּנִי.

אָמַר לוֹ: אֱמֹר.

מִיָּד יָרַד רַבָּן יוֹחָנָן בֶּן זַכַּאי מֵעַל הַחֲמוֹר
וְנִתְעַטֵּף, וְיָשַׁב עַל הָאֶבֶן תַּחַת הַזַּיִת.

אָמַר לוֹ: רַבִּי, מִפְּנֵי מָה יָרַדְתָּ מֵעַל הַחֲמוֹר?

אָמַר: אֶפְשָׁר אַתָּה דּוֹרֵשׁ בְּמַעֲשֵׂה מֶרְכָּבָה, וּשְׁכִינָה עִמָּנוּ,
וּמַלְאֲכֵי הַשָּׁרֵת מְלַוִּין אוֹתָנוּ, וַאֲנִי אֶרְכַּב עַל הַחֲמוֹר?

מִיָּד פָּתַח רַבִּי אֶלְעָזָר בֶּן עֲרָךְ בְּמַעֲשֵׂה הַמֶּרְכָּבָה וְדָרַשׁ, וְיָרְדָה אֵשׁ מִן
הַשָּׁמַיִם וְסִבְּבָה כָּל הָאִילָנוֹת שֶׁבַּשָּׂדֶה, פָּתְחוּ כֻּלָּן וְאָמְרוּ שִׁירָה . . .

נַעֲנָה מַלְאָךְ מִן הָאֵשׁ וְאָמַר: הֵן הֵן מַעֲשֵׂה הַמֶּרְכָּבָה.

וּכְשֶׁנֶּאֶמְרוּ הַדְּבָרִים לִפְנֵי רַבִּי יְהוֹשֻׁעַ, הָיָה הוּא וְרַבִּי יוֹסֵי הַכֹּהֵן
מְהַלְּכִים בַּדֶּרֶךְ, אָמְרוּ: אַף אָנוּ נִדְרֹשׁ בְּמַעֲשֵׂה מֶרְכָּבָה.

פָּתַח רַבִּי יְהוֹשֻׁעַ וְדָרַשׁ, וְאוֹתוֹ הַיּוֹם תְּקוּפַת תַּמּוּז הָיָה, נִתְקַשְּׁרוּ שָׁמַיִם
בֶּעָבִים וְנִרְאָה כְּמִין קֶשֶׁת בֶּעָנָן, וְהָיוּ מַלְאֲכֵי הַשָּׁרֵת מִתְקַבְּצִין וּבָאִין
לִשְׁמֹעַ, כִּבְנֵי אָדָם שֶׁמִּתְקַבְּצִין וּבָאִין לִרְאוֹת בְּמַזְמוּטֵי חָתָן וְכַלָּה.

A story occurred involving Rabbi Yochanan ben Zakai, who was traveling along the way, riding on a donkey, accompanied by his student, Rabbi Elazar ben Arach. Rabbi Elazar entreated, "My teacher! Please teach me one chapter in the Design of the Divine Chariot."

Rabbi Yochanan replied, "Have I not taught you that one may not teach the Design of the Divine Chariot to an individual unless he is a sage who is capable of understanding it on his own?"

Rabbi Elazar responded, "My teacher! Please allow me to repeat one thing that you taught me."

Rabbi Yochanan said to him, "Speak."

Rabbi Yochanan immediately alighted from the donkey, wrapped his head in his cloak in a manner of reverence, and sat on a stone under an olive tree.

Rabbi Elazar inquired, "My teacher, why did you alight from the donkey?"

Rabbi Yochanan replied, "How can I possibly ride a donkey while you are expounding on the Design of the Divine Chariot? The Divine Presence is with us! The ministering angels are accompanying us!"

Immediately, Rabbi Elazar began to discuss the Design of the Divine Chariot. As he spoke, fire descended from Heaven and encircled all the trees in the field, and the trees began singing. . . . An angel responded from the fire, saying, "This is the very Design of the Divine Chariot, just as you have described it!" . . .

Rabbi Yehoshua was informed of this incident involving his colleague Rabbi Elazar. At the time, he was also on the road, accompanied by Rabbi Yosei the Priest. They said to each other, "Let us similarly discuss the Design of the Divine Chariot, like Rabbi Yochanan and Rabbi Elazar did."

Rabbi Yehoshua began expounding and, although it was a clear summer day without a cloud in the sky, the heavens became filled with clouds, and there the form of a rainbow appeared in a cloud. Ministering angels gathered and came to listen, like humans gathering to witness the rejoicing of a bride and groom.

Soul Elevation

TEXT 21

Rabbi Yisrael Baal Shem Tov, *Keter Shem Tov* 1

בְּרֹאשׁ הַשָּׁנָה שְׁנַת תק"ז עָשִׂיתִי הַשְׁבָּעַת עֲלִיַת הַנְּשָׁמָה כַּיָדוּעַ לְךָ, וְרָאִיתִי דְּבָרִים נִפְלָאִים בְּמַרְאֶה, מַה שֶׁלֹּא רָאִיתִי עַד הֵנָּה מִיּוֹם עָמְדִי עַל דַּעְתִּי. וַאֲשֶׁר רָאִיתִי וְלָמַדְתִּי בַּעֲלוֹתִי שָׁם בִּלְתִּי אֶפְשָׁרִי לְסַפֵּר וּלְדַבֵּר, אֲפִלּוּ פֶּה אֶל פֶּה.

On Rosh Hashanah of the year 5507 [1746], I performed—by means of a mystical oath which you are familiar with—an elevation of soul to the higher spiritual realms. I saw wondrous things that I had never seen before. That which I saw and learned there is impossible to convey in words, even face-to-face.

RABBI YISRAEL BAAL SHEM TOV (BESHT) 1698–1760

Founder of the Chasidic movement. Born in Slutsk, Belarus, the Baal Shem Tov was orphaned as a child. He served as a teacher's assistant and clay digger before founding the Chasidic movement and revolutionizing the Jewish world with his emphasis on prayer, joy, and love for every Jew, regardless of his or her level of Torah knowledge.

The Soul as a Flame

In Proverbs (20:27), King Solomon depicts the Divine soul that breathes within each living human to the flame of a lit lamp. His depiction was subsequently reflected in every branch of Jewish literature. The simple, poignant image of a flickering flame seemingly pining to fly higher evokes the yearning of a Divine spirit to soar Heavenward. This correlation inspired Jewish thinkers, teachers, and artists throughout the ages. Beyond the basic metaphor, the depiction has been broken down into a surprising tally of specific elements, feeding an army of ramifications in terms of philosophical, kabbalistic, and Chasidic insights— and even delivering practical ramifications.

I. The Metaphor Unpacked

FLAME

Hold a lit candle sideways or upside down; nothing will convince its flame to end its perpetual struggle to defy gravity and soar upward. It will ignore you even if you whisper, "Little flame, stop striving, because if you succeed in soaring upward, you will expire and go up in smoke!" But the flame is deliberately engaged in a desperate act of self-destruction. That is its basic nature, and it cannot back down.

Our soul is similarly trapped in a corporeal body and desperately seeks to return home—to fly up to its Maker, to fuse with G-d's glory. Although the independent identity it acquired while housed in a body will expire, it craves nothing else.

More specifically, the soul's yearning for G-d is analogous to a "fiery," passionate love. Investigate every culture and you will find love predominantly associated with warmth. The greater the love, the greater the warmth. Our soul is a flame seeking to reunite with the Source of all Divine fire.

— *Rabbi Shneur Zalman of Liadi*, Tanya, Likutei Amarim, *ch. 19*

OIL/CANDLE

Combustible material with lesser resistance will produce cleaner fire. For that reason, virgin olive oil burns steadily and charmingly, whereas a moist twig will resist and obstruct the act of combustion, creating a harsh, crackling flame.

Similarly, the manner of our relationship with G-d determines the quality of our soul's flame. The appropriate manner to bond with G-d is through removing resistance, offering a pure and complete surrender to G-d.

The metaphor goes even further: oil must be regularly added to prolong the life of a flame, failing which it will sputter and die. So, too, we must we regularly replenish our dedication to G-d's service and reinforce our sense of surrender, to ensure an undying relationship with G-d.

— *Rabbi Shneur Zalman of Liadi*, Likutei Torah, Acharei 26b; *Rabbi Chaim Tirer*, Be'er Mayim Chayim, Shemot 27:20

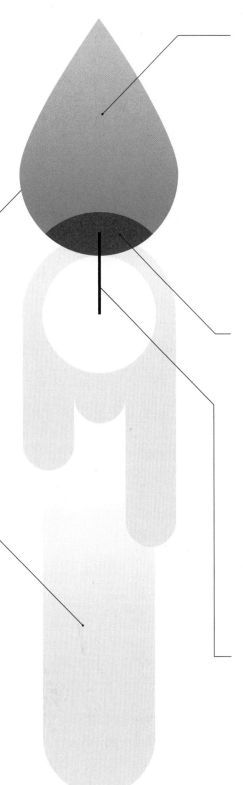

CLEAN FIRE

Beyond the blueish-blackish hue of a flame's immediate grasp on a wick's head, a flame's upper tiers are bright and clean. Rising above the combat of combustion, its experience is more pure.

Our soul can similarly experience a higher and purer yearning for and love of G-d. This is the stage at which we rise above the wonderful rational reasons for our attachment to G-d, and soar into the flickering, delightful bonding that is a love too deep and real, too genuine and true, to be explained. Intellect can only sully such intimacy. It is not a matter of knowing G-d or appreciating G-d. It is experiencing G-d. When that occurs, we become bright and translucent with love.

— *Rabbi Yosef Yitzchak Schneersohn*, Sefer Hamaamarim *5708, pp. 164–5; Rabbi Shneur Zalman of Liadi*, Likutei Torah, *Shelach 45a*

DARK FIRE

Peer into a flame: bright, light, translucent. Now gaze toward its base, closest to the wick, where a material is being gobbled into a brilliant energy. Here, the tension of material breakdown occurs. Here, the flame is darker and appears less clean and translucent.

Our soul's flame—its yearning and passion for G-d—also harbors a less translucent base. There, its love is of lower, more primitive form. It is the stage at which we begin our spiritual journey, when our love remains somewhat rational. It is a love we feel intuitively within our souls, but one that we can also explain rationally: We love G-d because G-d is omnipresent, forgiving, loving, and brilliant. Because G-d created a mind-blowing universe. There is a lot to be excited about, and it all leads to love.

— *Rabbi Yosef Yitzchak Schneersohn*, Sefer Hamaamarim *5708, pp. 164–5; Rabbi Shneur Zalman of Liadi*, Siddur Im Dach *82b; Rabbi DovBer of Lubavitch*, Shaarei Orah *41a*

WICK

A wick tethers a flame, keeping it securely tied to a pool of combusting fuel. Remove the wick, and the flame will be free to escape into the ethers of its smoky destination.

Similarly, our corporeal body hosts our soul and prevents it from leaping upward out of this world and returning to G-d's heavenly embrace from where it originated.

— *Rabbi Shneur Zalman of Liadi*, Tanya, Likutei Amarim, *ch. 19*

The Soul as a Flame *continued*

II. What Does It Mean?

SOURCE

The source of this metaphor is a verse in Proverbs (20:27):

נֵר ה׳ נִשְׁמַת אָדָם חֹפֵשׂ כָּל חַדְרֵי בָטֶן.

The human soul is the candle of G-d, which searches out all the innermost parts.

What, exactly, is the metaphor?

In what way is the soul comparable to "the candle of G-d?"

There are several interpretations:

FULL TRANSPARENCY

G-d uses your soul to search your innermost parts. In other words, just as you might light a lamp to search for an item in the dark, so does G-d use your soul to discover your innermost thoughts and beliefs. After all, your soul is always with you, it is witness to your internal machinations, and it is willing to report back to G-d whatever it sees.

—*Rashi, Ibn Ezra, Rabbeinu Yonah, and* Metzudat David *on Proverbs 20:27*

SHINING AN INTELLECTUAL LIGHT

The soul spoken of in this verse is a reference to the pinnacle of human capacity—our intellect, cognition. A wise person (to whom reference was made in the preceding verse) employs their intellect to shine a light on everything they perceive, constantly seeking to explore and discover with the light of that intellectual beam.

—*Ralbag on Proverbs 20:27*

G-D'S WATCHING YOU

G-d does not limit His providence and unique attention to your external actions. Rather, G-d pays attention—shines a light—to your internal dynamics, including the contents of your soul.

—*Radak to Proverbs 20:27*

III. Other Ramifications of the Metaphor

SWAYING DURING PRAYER AND STUDY

Jews famously sway during prayer and Torah study. One reason for this phenomenon is that, as implied in this verse, our soul is "on fire." Just as a flame leaps and surges from its wick, so do Jews move and surge forward as they pray or study.

– Zohar 3, 218b

YAHRTZEIT CANDLE

It is customary to light a candle for one who has passed. This is done during the *shivah* (initial seven days of mourning), on the *yahrtzeit* (anniversary of death), and some light it during the entire first year after passing. It is done to honor the soul of the deceased.

–See sources collected in Rabbi Ovadia Yosef, Yabia Omer, vol. 4, Yoreh De'ah, section 34; Rabbi Yosef Chaim of Baghdad, Responsa Torah Lishmah, section 520: see also Rabbeinu Bechaye on Shemot 25:31

LIGHTING CANDLES IN THE *SHUL*

It is appropriate to light many candles in the synagogue, because the flames are reminiscent of our soul and its G-dly light.

–Rabbi Eliyahu de Vidas, Reishit Chochmah, Shaar Hayirah 15:77

ABSTAINING FROM RUBBING OILS ON YOM KIPPUR

Five activities related to our bodies are proscribed on Yom Kippur— eating and drinking; bathing; rubbing oil onto skin; intimate relations; and wearing leather footgear. One reason for this rule is that on Yom Kippur we seek to imitate the angels. As such, we divest to the degree possible from our bodies, to better relate to our souls and thereby become more angelic.

As explained in kabbalah, there are five dimensions to the soul, each with a unique name. The five prohibited bodily functions correspond to these five dimensions. Through abstaining from each of these, we free another element of our soul from its bodily captor.

Our verse refers to the soul with the title *neshamah*, which corresponds to the prohibition of rubbing oils onto our skin. As the verse indicates, this *neshamah* is luminescent. Were we to pamper our body with rubbing oils on this sacred day of Yom Kippur, the light of our *neshamah* would be unable to shine through.

–Rabbi Yehudah Loew of Prague, Derashot Maharal, Derush for Shabbat Shuvah, section 43

3

MASTERMIND

The Benefits of Divine Closeness

*G-d is often perceived as some distant force, and
spirituality as something static. This lesson rips off the veil,
demonstrating that G-d's presence is dynamically animating
all of existence in the present, and that G-d is purposefully
guiding all of reality in all of its diverse details. It promotes
the application of this awareness as a guide to developing
a Divine consciousness, and shows how this can be effective
in increasing our joy, resilience, and sense of purpose.*

I. REFRAMING REALITY

In the previous lesson, we explored cognitive meditation as a tool to develop a sense of the universe's spiritual dimension. We will now focus on the ultimate goal of this meditation, which is not to transcend the material world or experience a peak spiritual moment, but to develop a deeper perspective of reality and change the way we experience life.

TEXT 1

Cognitive Construction

Rabbi Shlomo Wolbe, *Alei Shur, 2,* p. 271

שְׁנֵי שָׁרָשִׁים מַרְכִּיבִים אֶת הַמִּלָּה הִתְבּוֹנְנוּת: "בִּנְיָן" וּ"בִינָה". הַמִּתְבּוֹנֵן, בּוֹנֶה אֶת עַצְמוֹ עַל יְדֵי בִּינָתוֹ בְּכָל הַסּוֹבֵב אוֹתוֹ.

The Hebrew word *hitbonenut* [contemplative meditation] stems etymologically from two root words: *binyan* [building] and *binah* [contemplation]. When we practice cognitive meditation, we "build" ourselves as a result of gaining a more profound understanding of our environment.

**RABBI SHLOMO WOLBE
1914-2005**

Educator and ethicist. Rabbi Shlomo Wolbe was born in Berlin to a secular Jewish family and studied at the University of Berlin. He went on to attend *yeshivot,* including the yeshiva in Mir, Lithuania, where he studied under the tutelage of Rabbi Yerucham Levovitz. After participating in rescue work during the Holocaust, Rabbi Wolbe moved to Israel, where he became the *mashgiach* (spiritual guide) at the yeshiva in Beer Yaakov. He is known for *Alei Shur,* a guide for spiritual growth and character development for yeshiva students.

FIGURE 3.1

Hitbonenut Etymology

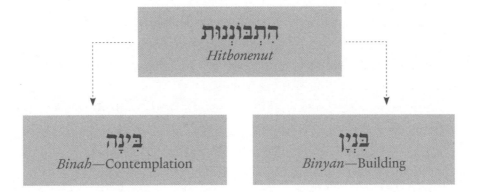

הִתְבּוֹנְנוּת
Hitbonenut

בִּינָה
Binah—Contemplation

בִּנְיָן
Binyan—Building

THE PRAYING JEW
Marc Chagall, France,
1923, oil on canvas

II. DIVINE CONSCIOUSNESS

The spiritual force that animates creation is a manifestation of G-d's presence. Every detail within creation is an expression of G-d. Therefore, G-d is consciously present within our lives and within the world.

Meditating on G-d's presence opens an awareness to a deeper dimension of reality, which leads in turn to a sense of wonder and joy. It also provides the comforting sense that results from being aware of G-d's closeness to us.

TEXT 2

The Soul of the Universe

Midrash Tehilim 103:3

"בָּרְכִי נַפְשִׁי אֶת ה'" (תְּהִלִּים קג, א). לָמָה מְקַלֵּס דָּוִד לְהַקָּדוֹשׁ בָּרוּךְ הוּא בַּנֶּפֶשׁ? אָמַר: מָה הַנֶּפֶשׁ מְמַלְּאָה אֶת הַגּוּף, כָּךְ הַקָּדוֹשׁ בָּרוּךְ הוּא מְמַלֵּא אֶת עוֹלָמוֹ . . . אָמַר דָּוִד: תָּבוֹא הַנֶּפֶשׁ שֶׁיֵּשׁ בָּהּ כָּל הַמִּדּוֹת הַלָּלוּ, וּתְהַלֵּל לְהַקָּדוֹשׁ בָּרוּךְ הוּא שֶׁיֵּשׁ בּוֹ כָּל הַמִּדּוֹת הַלָּלוּ.

King David exclaimed, "My soul blesses G-d!" (PSALMS 103:1). Why did he feel the need to emphasize that it was his soul that praised G-d? He told himself: Just as the soul fills the body, so does G-d fill the universe. . . . So, King David concluded, let the soul, which possesses the same qualities as G-d, praise Him.

MIDRASH TEHILIM

A rabbinic commentary on the Book of Psalms. Midrash is the designation of a particular genre of rabbinic literature usually forming a running commentary on specific books of the Bible. This particular Midrash provides textual exegeses and develops and illustrates the principles of the Book of Psalms.

TEXT 3

Exposing the Divine

Rabbi Yosef Yitzchak Schneersohn,
Sefer Hamaamarim 5697, p. 254

RABBI YOSEF YITZCHAK SCHNEERSOHN (RAYATZ, FRIERDIKER REBBE, PREVIOUS REBBE)
1880–1950

 Chasidic rebbe, prolific writer, and Jewish activist. Rabbi Yosef Yitzchak, the sixth leader of the Chabad movement, actively promoted Jewish religious practice in Soviet Russia and was arrested for these activities. After his release from prison and exile, he settled in Warsaw, Poland, from where he fled Nazi occupation and arrived in New York in 1940. Settling in Brooklyn, Rabbi Schneersohn worked to revitalize American Jewish life. His son-in-law Rabbi Menachem Mendel Schneerson succeeded him as the leader of the Chabad movement.

וְהִנֵּה, מֵהַיְדִיעָה פְּרָטִית הַלָּזוֹ שֶׁאָדָם יוֹדֵעַ בִּפְרָטֵי פְּרָטִיּוּת
אֹפֶן גִּלּוּי חַיּוּת נַפְשׁוֹ בְּגוּפוֹ, הֲרֵי יוֹדֵעַ וּמֵבִין וּמַשִּׂיג בְּכָל בְּרוּאֵי
הָעוֹלָם אֵיךְ דְּהַכֹּל הוּא חַי בַּחַיּוּת הָאֱלֹקִי, ד"מָה הַנְּשָׁמָה
מְמַלְּאָה אֶת הַגּוּף, כָּךְ הַקָּדוֹשׁ בָּרוּךְ הוּא מְמַלֵּא אֶת הָעוֹלָם",
וּ"מִבְּשָׂרִי אֶחֱזֶה אֱלֹקַהּ" (אִיּוֹב יט, כו), דְּכָל עִנְיְנֵי מִקְרֵי הַגּוּף,
גַּם הַקְּטַנִּים וְהַקַּלִּים בְּיוֹתֵר, בָּאִים עַל פִּי הַנֶּפֶשׁ. אֲשֶׁר כְּמוֹ כֵן
הוּא גַם בְּחַיּוּת הָעוֹלָם, בְּכָל פְּרָטֵי פְּרָטִיּוּת עִנְיְנֵי הַנִּבְרָאִים.

וְלֹא זוֹ בִּלְבַד שֶׁרוֹאֶה עִנְיְנֵי הַשְׁגָּחָה פְּרָטִית בְּמוּחָשׁ,
אֶלָּא שֶׁבְּכָל פִּנָּה שֶׁהוּא פּוֹנֶה הוּא רוֹאֶה אֱלֹקוּת בְּמוּחָשׁ
מַמָּשׁ, עֶר זֶעהט גֶעטְלִיכְקַייט כְּמוֹ אָהֶן אַ לְבוּשׁ.

A highly detailed self-awareness of the manner in which our own soul operates within our body will allow us to appreciate that the Divine is manifest within every detail of the universe—and that each detail exists and is sustained through Divine energy. This parallel is expressed in the teaching, "Just as the soul fills the body, so does G-d fill the world" (MIDRASH TEHILIM 103:3), and is expressed in the verse, "*From my flesh* I can perceive the Divine" (JOB 19:26). Every sensation and experience of the body, even the most insignificant, is an active expression of the soul. Similarly, even the smallest detail or phenomenon within the universe is actively directed by G-d.

Watch a short animated video on the nature of existence:
myjli.com/meditation

When we develop this awareness, we sense
not only the Divine *providence* in everything,
but we see *Divinity* clearly wherever we turn.
We can literally see the Divine exposed.

Animating Every Detail

Rabbi Yosef Yitzchak Schneersohn,
Sefer Hamaamarim 5696, pp. 119–120

אַךְ הָעִנְיָן הוּא, דְּהִנֵּה כָּל הַנִּבְרָאִים שֶׁלְּמַטָּה כֻּלָּם נֶחֱלָקִים
בְּד' מַדְרֵגוֹת כּוֹלְלִים, וְהֵם: דּוֹמֵם, צוֹמֵחַ, חַי, מְדַבֵּר. אֲשֶׁר
כָּל אֶחָד מֵד' אֵלּוּ כּוֹלְלִים מִינִים רַבִּים בְּרִבּוּי מָפְלָג.

וְיוּבַן זֶה בְּצוֹמֵחַ, דְּהִנֵּה בְּצוֹמֵחַ הֲרֵי יֵשׁ מִינִים רַבִּים: אִילָנוֹת,
תְּבוּאוֹת, יְרָקוֹת, עֲשָׂבִים וּדְשָׁאִים. וּבְכָל מִין יֵשׁ רִבּוּי מֻפְלָג, כְּמוֹ
בְּאִילָנוֹת - רִבּוּי עָצוּם הַחֲלוּקִים זֶה מִזֶּה בְּעֶצֶם מַהוּתָם וּבְפִרְיָם,
וְכֵן בַּעֲשָׂבִים אוֹ דְשָׁאִים - שֶׁיֵּשׁ בָּהֶם רִבּוּי מִינִים הַחֲלוּקִים
בִּסְגֻלּוֹתֵיהֶם, מִסַּמֵּי רְפוּאָה וְסַמֵּי מָוֶת, וּבְמַרְאֵיהֶם וְטִבְעָם.
וּבְכָל אֶחָד מֵהַמִּינִים יֵשׁ בָּהֶם רִבּוּי מֻפְלָג עַד אֵין שִׁעוּר.

וְכָל הָרִבּוּי מֻפְלָג הַלָּזֶה, הִנֵּה כָּל אֶחָד וְאֶחָד מֵהֶם יֵשׁ לוֹ חַיּוּת מְיֻחָד
וּמֻגְבָּל לוֹ לְבַדּוֹ, אֲשֶׁר הַחַיּוּת הַהִיא הִיא נַפְשׁוֹ הַמְחַיָּה אוֹתוֹ, מַצְמִיחוֹ,
מְגַדְּלוֹ וּמַנְהִיגוֹ לְכָל פְּרָטֵי עִנְיָנָיו בְּכָל תְּנוּעוֹתָיו, מֵעֵת צֵאתוֹ מִבֶּטֶן
הָאֲדָמָה עַד רֶגַע הָאַחֲרוֹן שֶׁבָּא קִצּוֹ עַל פִּי גְּזֵרַת הַהַשְׁגָּחָה, אִם לְהִקָּצֵר
בְּחֶרְמֵשׁ וּמַגַּל יָד לְהָבִיא תּוֹעֶלֶת הַנִּרְאֶה בְּמִרְעֶה הַבַּעֲלֵי חַיִּים, אוֹ
לִהְיוֹת לְמִרְמָס רֶגֶל בְּלִי תּוֹעֶלֶת נִרְאֶה, אוֹ לִהְיוֹת כָּלֶה וְנִפְסָד בְּעֵת
בּוֹא זְמַנּוֹ, דְּכָל זֶה הוּא עַל פִּי דִין וּמִשְׁפָּט הַהַשְׁגָּחָה הָעֶלְיוֹנָה.

דְּכָל אֶחָד יֵשׁ לוֹ נַפְשׁוֹ הַפְּרָטִי, שֶׁזֶּהוּ חַיּוּתוֹ וּמַנְהִיגוֹ. וְלָכֵן, הִנֵּה כָּל
דֶּשֶׁא פְּרָטִי יֵשׁ לוֹ צִיּוּר מְיֻחָד, דְּעִם הֱיוֹתָם כֻּלָּם בְּתַבְנִית וּמַרְאֶה

וּסְגֻלָּה כְּלָלִית, וּמִכָּל מָקוֹם - הִנֵּה בְּעֶצֶם גּוּפָם יֵשׁ בָּהֶם אֵיזֶה דָבָר
פְּרָטִי מָה שֶׁאֵין הָאֶחָד דּוֹמֶה מַמָּשׁ לַחֲבֵרוֹ, וְהוּא לְפִי דְכָל אֶחָד
הֲרֵי יֵשׁ לוֹ חַיּוּת מְיֻחָד וּמֻגְבָּל לוֹ לְבַדּוֹ, לְהַחֲיוֹתוֹ וּלְהַנְהִיגוֹ.

The entirety of creation divides into four kingdoms: mineral, vegetable, animal, and human. Each of these is subdivided into myriads of specific species.

If we examine the world of plants, for example, we encounter a broad spectrum of vegetation—such as trees, crops, vegetables, grass, and herbs—each category of which is further divided into multiple species. There is an astonishing variety of trees, and each kind is unique and distinguished from all other trees. There is a tremendous diversity of plants and herbs—and again, each kind offers a unique nutritional value, some are beneficial while others are poisonous, and they each carry a unique design and set of properties. Furthermore, within each of these subspecies there are countless individual units, each of which is similarly unique.

Now, each individual unit possesses a unique life-force—Divine energy—that is tailored for it. That life-force is what we call its "soul"—the spiritual entity that animates it, causes it to grow, and guides everything that happens to it from the moment it sprouts from the earth until its last moment when it is plucked. Even the plant's final fate is within the jurisdiction of a specific Divine providence that determines whether the plant will be harvested for an overt purpose such as animal fodder, trampled underfoot in an apparently aimless manner, or wither in due course and disintegrate entirely. Such a matter is the result of a specific decision and calculation of Divine providence.

Everything in this world has a unique Divine energy that is its life and guide. Each blade of grass is unique. It may appear identical to another blade, but closer examination reveals specific features that set a specific blade apart from every other blade of grass in the universe. This distinction is the result of the *specific* Divine energy that G-d invests into *this* blade; it is an entirely individualized Divine manifestation.

TEXT 5

Spiritual Growth

Midrash, *Bereshit Rabah* 10:6

אָמַר רַבִּי סִימוֹן: אֵין לְךָ כָּל עֵשֶׂב וְעֵשֶׂב שֶׁאֵין לוֹ מַזָּל בָּרָקִיעַ שֶׁמַּכֶּה אוֹתוֹ וְאוֹמֵר לוֹ: גְּדַל!

Rabbi Simon said: Each blade of grass has a spiritual force that strikes it and tells it to grow.

BERESHIT RABAH

An early rabbinic commentary on the Book of Genesis. This Midrash bears the name of Rabbi Oshiya Rabah (Rabbi Oshiya "the Great"), whose teaching opens this work. This Midrash provides textual exegeses and stories, expounds upon the biblical narrative, and develops and illustrates moral principles. Produced by the sages of the Talmud in the Land of Israel, its use of Aramaic closely resembles that of the Jerusalem Talmud. It was first printed in Constantinople in 1512 together with 4 other Midrashic works on the other 4 books of the Pentateuch.

TEXT 6

The Cosmic Symphony

Rabbi Moshe Chaim Efraim of Sudilkov,
Degel Machaneh Efraim, Yitro

**RABBI MOSHE CHAIM
EFRAIM OF SUDILKOV
1748-1800**

Chasidic teacher and
author. Rabbi Moshe
Chaim Efraim was a
grandson of the Baal
Shem Tov, who took a
personal interest in his
education. After the Baal
Shem Tov's passing, he
studied under the Magid
of Mezeritch and Rabbi
Yaakov Yosef of Polonye.
He later settled in
Sudilkov, where he
served as rabbi. His
Chasidic work, *Degel
Machaneh Efraim,* is a
commentary on the
weekly Torah portions; it
was printed
posthumously by his
grandson Rabbi Yaakov
Yechiel of Kuritz.

שֶׁשָּׁמַעְתִּי מָשָׁל מִן אֲדוֹנִי
אָבִי זְקֵנִי זִכְרוֹנוֹ לִבְרָכָה לְחַיֵּי הָעוֹלָם הַבָּא:

שֶׁהָיָה אֶחָד מְנַגֵּן בִּכְלִי זֶמֶר יָפֶה מְאוֹד בִּמְתִיקוּת וַעֲרֵבוּת גָּדוֹל.
וְאוֹתָם שֶׁהֵם שׁוֹמְעִים זֶה, לֹא יָכְלוּ לְהִתְאַפֵּק מִגֹּדֶל הַמְּתִיקוּת
וְהַתַּעֲנוּג, עַד שֶׁהָיוּ רוֹקְדִים כִּמְעַט עַד לַתִּקְרָה מֵחֲמַת גֹּדֶל הַתַּעֲנוּג
וְהַנְעִימוּת וְהַמְתִיקוּת. וְכָל מִי שֶׁהָיָה קָרוֹב יוֹתֵר וְהָיָה מְקָרֵב עַצְמוֹ
לִשְׁמֹעַ הַכְּלִי זֶמֶר, הָיָה לוֹ בְּיוֹתֵר תַּעֲנוּג, וְהָיָה רוֹקֵד עַד מְאוֹד.

וּבְתוֹךְ כָּךְ, בָּא אֶחָד חֵרֵשׁ שֶׁאֵינוֹ שׁוֹמֵעַ כְּלַל הַקּוֹל שֶׁל כְּלִי
זֶמֶר הָעָרֵב, רַק רָאָה שֶׁאֲנָשִׁים רוֹקְדִים עַד מְאוֹד, וְהֵם בְּעֵינָיו
כִּמְשֻׁגָּעִים. וְאוֹמֵר בְּלִבּוֹ, כִּי לְשִׂמְחָה מָה זֶה עוֹשָׂה? וּבֶאֱמֶת, אִלּוּ
הָיָה הוּא חָכָם, וְיָדַע וְהֵבִין שֶׁהוּא מֵחֲמַת גֹּדֶל הַתַּעֲנוּג וְהַנְעִימוּת
קוֹל שֶׁל כְּלִי זֶמֶר, הָיָה הוּא גַּם כֵּן רוֹקֵד שָׁם. וְהַנִּמְשָׁל מוּבָן.

The following parable I heard from
my master, my grandfather [the Baal
Shem Tov], of blessed memory:

There was once a talented musician that played
beautiful, sweet music. All who heard it were
mesmerized by the sweet, pleasurable, blissful
sounds. They could not hold themselves back
from dancing to the rafters in sheer ecstasy.
The closer the people drew to the source
of music, the more entranced they became
and the more ecstatic their dancing.

Watch a video of
people's reaction
to seeing in color
for the first time:
myjli.com/meditation

Just then, a deaf individual came across the scene. Not noticing the musician, he simply observed people dancing wildly and regarded them as crazy. "What on earth could make people so ridiculously joyful all of a sudden?" he muttered to himself. Now, if he were intelligent, wise, and knowledgeable, he would deduce that they must be dancing to a delightful melody. In fact, contemplating the depth of pleasure they must be experiencing—judging by their response—he would be moved to join them in delightful dance.

The analogy is obvious.

SIMCHAT TORAH
Zalman Kleinman (1933–1995)
On the holiday of Simchat Torah, the Torah is completed and started again amidst much joy and dancing.

TEXT 7

Meditating on G-d's Presence

Rabbi Yisrael Baal Shem Tov, *Tzava'at Harivash* 15

RABBI YISRAEL BAAL SHEM TOV (BESHT) 1698–1760

Founder of the Chasidic movement. Born in Slutsk, Belarus, the Baal Shem Tov was orphaned as a child. He served as a teacher's assistant and clay digger before founding the Chasidic movement and revolutionizing the Jewish world with his emphasis on prayer, joy, and love for every Jew, regardless of his or her level of Torah knowledge.

יַחֲשֹׁב שֶׁהַבּוֹרֵא מְלֹא כָל הָאָרֶץ כְּבוֹדוֹ, וּשְׁכִינָתוֹ תָּמִיד
אֶצְלוֹ . . . וְיִהְיֶה תָּמִיד בְּשִׂמְחָה, וְיַחֲשֹׁב וְיַאֲמִין בֶּאֱמוּנָה
שְׁלֵמָה שֶׁהַשְּׁכִינָה אֶצְלוֹ וְשׁוֹמֶרֶת אוֹתוֹ.

וְהוּא מִסְתַּכֵּל עַל הַבּוֹרֵא יִתְבָּרַךְ, וְהַבּוֹרֵא יִתְבָּרַךְ מִסְתַּכֵּל בּוֹ. וְהַבּוֹרֵא
יִתְבָּרַךְ יָכוֹל לַעֲשׂוֹת כָּל מָה שֶׁהוּא רוֹצֶה . . . וּבוֹ יִתְבָּרַךְ מָשְׁרָשִׁים
כָּל הַטּוֹבוֹת וְהַדִּינִים שֶׁיֵּשׁ בָּעוֹלָם, שֶׁבְּכָל דָּבָר יֵשׁ שִׁפְעוֹ וְחַיּוּתוֹ.

Meditate on the fact that the Divine presence fills the entire universe, and that G-d's intimate presence is with you constantly. . . . This will allow you to be constantly joyful, realizing and believing with perfect faith that the Divine presence is with you, protecting you.

Realize that you are gazing at the Divine! And that G-d is gazing at you! G-d can do as He pleases . . . and is the source of all of the goodness and suffering in the world, for His Divinity and sustaining force is within each item of existence.

A common combination of prayers during the eighteenth century was Birkat Hamazon (Grace after meals), Birkat Hanehenin (Blessings over Enjoyments), Shalosh Mitzvot Nashim (the Three Mitzvot for Women), and Kriat Shema al Hamitah (Shema prayer before retiring at night). This illustrated manuscript was likely given to a woman as a wedding present. Although it is not signed, the manuscript is attributed to the well-known scribe Aaron Wolf Herlingen, done on parchment in the eastern Austrian town of Deutschkreutz in 1751. Detail shown here is the blessing recited upon hearing thunder: "Blessed are You . . . Whose power and might fill the world" is captioned above the scene of a thunderstorm. (Braginsky Collection, Zurich)

TEXT 8

Developing Divine Consciousness

Rabbi Yisrael Baal Shem Tov, *Keter Shem Tov* 196

מַעֲלָה גְדוֹלָה כְּשֶׁאָדָם מְחַשֵּׁב וּמְהַרְהֵר תָּמִיד בְּלִבּוֹ שֶׁהוּא
אֵצֶל הַבּוֹרֵא יִתְבָּרֵךְ, וְהוּא מַקִּיף אוֹתוֹ מִכָּל צְדָדָיו . . .

וְיִהְיֶה דָבוּק כָּל כָּךְ שֶׁלֹּא יְהֵא צָרִיךְ לְיַשֵּׁב אֶת עַצְמוֹ בְּכָל פַּעַם
שֶׁהוּא אֶצְלוֹ יִתְבָּרֵךְ, רַק שֶׁיִּרְאֶה הַבּוֹרֵא יִתְבָּרֵךְ בְּעֵין הַשֵּׂכֶל, וְשֶׁהוּא
יִתְבָּרֵךְ "מְקוֹמוֹ שֶׁל עוֹלָם" (בְּרֵאשִׁית רַבָּה סח, ט) [וְהַכַּוָּנָה, שֶׁהֲרֵי
הוּא הָיָה קֹדֶם שֶׁבָּרָא הָעוֹלָם, וְהָעוֹלָם הוּא עוֹמֵד בַּבּוֹרֵא יִתְבָּרֵךְ],
וְכֵן הָאָדָם שֶׁנִּקְרָא עוֹלָם קָטָן. וִיקַיֵּם "שִׁוִּיתִי ה' לְנֶגְדִּי תָמִיד"
(תְּהִלִּים טז, ח) כְּמוֹ שֶׁכָּתוּב בְּשֻׁלְחָן עָרוּךְ אֹרַח חַיִּים, סִימָן א.

It is a tremendous achievement to constantly
meditate on the fact that we are close to
G-d and that we are literally and entirely
encompassed by His presence. . . .

We should try to remain connected to this reality
to the extent that reflection becomes unnecessary
because we mentally envision G-d everywhere,
constantly. At that point, we see that "G-d is the
place of the world" (*BERESHIT RABAH* 68:9)—
He preexists all of existence, and all of existence
exists within G-d. This includes, of course, each of us
as well. With this meditation, we fulfill the directive
recorded in the Code of Jewish Law (*ORACH
CHAYIM* 1:1), to set G-d before us at all times.

III. EVERYTHING IS ON PURPOSE

Judaism teaches that G-d is everywhere and that His presence fills the universe. But G-d's presence is not merely passive. Rather, it constantly and deliberately guides and orchestrates each detail of existence. Nothing occurs by chance; all is guided by G-d's hand in accord with His grand master plan for the universe He created. This leads us to the understanding that everything is exactly as it is supposed to be, and that G-d has arranged our lives the way He did for a reason. This meditation can be a valuable tool for overcoming negative feelings and adversity.

TEXT 9

Divine Director

Psalms 147:8–9

הַמְכַסֶּה שָׁמַיִם בְּעָבִים,
הַמֵּכִין לָאָרֶץ מָטָר,
הַמַּצְמִיחַ הָרִים חָצִיר.
נוֹתֵן לִבְהֵמָה לַחְמָהּ,
לִבְנֵי עֹרֵב אֲשֶׁר יִקְרָאוּ.

He covers the heavens with clouds,
prepares rain for the earth,
and causes mountains to sprout grass.
He gives an animal its food,
[and, as well] to the [hungry]
young ravens that call out.

PSALMS

Biblical book. The book of Psalms contains 150 psalms expressing praise for G-d, faith in G-d, and laments over tragedies. The primary author of the psalms was King David, who lived in the 9th century BCE. Psalms also contains material from earlier figures. The feelings and circumstances expressed in the psalms resonate throughout the generations and they have become an important part of communal and personal prayer.

QUESTION

Identify an occasion in which matters beyond your control unexpectedly and inexplicably shifted your plans or altered the outcome you had intended for yourself. With hindsight, are you able to recognize value in that change?

TEHILIM—PSALMS 147
Yehoshua Wiseman, Israel.

TEXT 10

Careful Watchfulness

The Rebbe, Rabbi Menachem Mendel Schneerson, English correspondence, 25 Elul 1975

With reference to your writing about doubts and difficulty and about a feeling of insecurity in general, I trust it is unnecessary to elaborate to you at length that such feelings arise when a person thinks that he is alone; and can only rely upon himself and his own judgment and therefore feels doubtful and insecure about each move he has to make. And while he also trusts in G-d, this trust is somehow superficial, without permeating him and his way of life in every detail; and only on certain days, such as the High Holy Days, he feels more close to G-d.

But when a person's faith in G-d is deep, and when he reflects that G-d's benevolent Providence extends to each and every person and to each and every detail and each and every minute, surely he must develop a profound sense of security and confidence. The concept of Divine Providence is better understood in the original term of *Hashgocho Protis,* for *Hashgocho Protis* means careful watchfulness, for which reason the term *hashgocho* is used also in connection with the law of *kashrus,* where every detail has to be carefully watched. Nor is another translation which is sometimes used in connection with *Hashgocho Protis,* namely "supervision," entirely satisfactory in

RABBI MENACHEM MENDEL SCHNEERSON 1902–1994

The towering Jewish leader of the 20th century, known as "the Lubavitcher Rebbe," or simply as "the Rebbe." Born in southern Ukraine, the Rebbe escaped Nazi-occupied Europe, arriving in the U.S. in June 1941. The Rebbe inspired and guided the revival of traditional Judaism after the European devastation, impacting virtually every Jewish community the world over. The Rebbe often emphasized that the performance of just one additional good deed could usher in the era of Mashiach. The Rebbe's scholarly talks and writings have been printed in more than 200 volumes.

this case, because supervision implies "overseeing," that is to say, seeing from above, whereas *hashgocho* in the sense of G-d's watchfulness means knowing matters through and through.

The belief in such *Hashgocho Protis* is basic to our religion and way of life, so much so that before every new year and during the beginning of the new year, we say twice daily Psalm 27, "G-d is my light and my salvation, whom shall I fear? G-d is the strength of my life, of whom shall I be afraid?" From this it follows that even if things happen not as desired according to human calculations and even if it seems that even according to the *Torah* it should have been different, a Jew still puts his trust in G-d.

Psalm 27 is written in the lower margins of The Northern French Miscellany beneath the text of Ecclesiastes. The initial word of each psalm is decorated. (British Museum [MS 11639], London)

EXERCISE 3.1

Identify a recent experience that triggered a negative emotion, and make note of it below:

Pause for a moment. Reflect on what happened, and consider that it was specifically designed by G-d. You may not know why, but it was supposed to be.

Record how you feel now about the same matter, post-reflection:

Detail from the Bird's Head Hagaddah, depicting G-d's hand providing manna to the Jewish people. Named for the griffin-like faces of the Jewish people in its drawings of scenes from the Exodus and preparations for the Passover *seder*, the Bird's Head Haggadah is the oldest known illustrated Ashkenazi Haggadah. It was produced in the Upper Rhine region of Southern Germany in the early fourteenth century and reveals the cultural practices in dress and ritual of the Jewish people living there at the time. (Israel Museum [B46.04.0912], Jerusalem)

IV. COSMIC SIGNIFICANCE

Everything that happens is relevant to the overall purpose of existence. The smallest nod of a solitary blade of grass carries cosmic significance and is necessary for the fulfillment of the purpose of creation. Surely, this is even truer of each human. Each of us matters greatly to G-d. We each play indispensable roles in the cosmic drama of history and destiny. This profound awareness injects purpose and significance to each moment of our lives.

TEXT 11

Designed for a Purpose

Rabbi Yosef Yitzchak Schneersohn,
Sefer Hamaamarim 5696, p. 120

וְכַיָּדוּעַ בְּעִנְיַן הַהַשְׁגָּחָה פְּרָטִית שֶׁמְּבָאֵר מוֹרֵנוּ הַבַּעַל שֵׁם טוֹב נִשְׁמָתוֹ עֵדֶן, דְּלֹא זוּ בִּלְבַד דְּכָל פְּרָטֵי תְּנוּעוֹת הַנִּבְרָאִים לְמִינֵיהֶם הִיא בְּהַשְׁגָּחָה פְּרָטִית מֵהַבּוֹרֵא יִתְבָּרֵךְ, וְהַשְׁגָּחָה פְּרָטִית הַלָּזוֹ הִיא חַיּוּת הַנִּבְרָא וְקִיּוּמוֹ - אֶלָּא דְּעוֹד זֹאת, דִּתְנוּעָה פְּרָטִית דְּנִבְרָא פְּרָטִי, הֲרֵי יֵשׁ לוֹ יַחַס כְּלָלִי לִכְלָלוּת כַּוָּנַת הַבְּרִיאָה.

וְעַל דֶּרֶךְ דְּגְמָא: הִנֵּה תְּנוּעַת אֶחָד הַדְּשָׁאִים הַצּוֹמֵחַ בְּעָמְקֵי יַעַר, אוֹ בְּאֶחָד הֶהָרִים הַגְּבוֹהִים, אוֹ בָּעֲמָקִים הַיּוֹתֵר עֲמֻקִּים אֲשֶׁר לֹא עָבַר שָׁם אִישׁ - הִנֵּה לֹא זוּ בִּלְבַד דִּתְנוּעַת הַדֶּשֶׁא הַהוּא לִימִינוֹ וְלִשְׂמֹאלוֹ לְפָנִים וּלְאָחוֹר בְּכָל מֶשֶׁךְ יְמֵי חַיָּיו הוּא עַל פִּי הַהַשְׁגָּחָה פְּרָטִית, אֲשֶׁר הוּא יִתְבָּרֵךְ גָּזַר אֹמֶר אֲשֶׁר דֶּשֶׁא פְּרָטִי זֶה חָיָה יִחְיֶה חֳדָשִׁים יָמִים וְשָׁעוֹת קְצוּבוֹת, וּבְמֶשֶׁךְ זֶה יָסֹב וְיִכֹּף לִימִינוֹ וּשְׂמֹאלוֹ לְפָנָיו וְלַאֲחוֹרָיו בְּמִסְפָּר כָּזֶה וְכָזֶה.

אֶלָּא עוֹד זֹאת, דִּתְנוּעַת הַדֶּשֶׁא הַפְּרָטִי הַלָּזֶה יֵשׁ לוֹ יַחַס כְּלָלִי לִכְלָלוּת כַּוָּנַת הַבְּרִיאָה, דְּבִצֵרוּף וְאִחוּד כָּל הַפְּעֻלּוֹת הַפְּרָטִיִּים שֶׁל הָרִבּוּי רְבָבוֹת פְּרָטִים אֵין מִסְפָּר שֶׁיֶּשְׁנָם בְּכָל

"How to See the Consciousness in Everything"—
Dr. Shmuel Klatzkin shares his personal journey:
myjli.com/meditation

הָאֲלָפִים וְרִבּוֹת מִינִים שֶׁיֶּשְׁנָם בְּהַד' חֲלוּקוֹת דְּדוֹמֵם צוֹמֵחַ חַי מְדַבֵּר - הִנֵּה נִשְׁלְמָה כַּוָּנָה הָעֶלְיוֹנָה בְּסוֹד הַבְּרִיאָה כֻּלָּהּ.

וְאִם כֵּן, הִנֵּה לֹא זוֹ בִּלְבַד דִּתְנוּעָה אַחַת שֶׁל דֶּשֶׁא פְּרָטִי הִיא בָּאָה בְּהַשְׁגָּחָה פְּרָטִית, אֶלָּא עוֹד זֹאת, דְּגַם תְּנוּעָה אַחַת שֶׁל דֶּשֶׁא פְּרָטִי מַשְׁלִים הַכַּוָּנָה הָעֶלְיוֹנָה בְּעִנְיַן הַבְּרִיאָה.

The Baal Shem Tov taught that Divine providence does not only mean that G-d orchestrates the individual movement of each of the manifold created entities— and that the same providence is actually determining the existence and life of that entity. It also means that the particular movement of a *single* entity bears a direct impact on the *overall* purpose of creation.

Take, for example, the slightest quiver of a solitary sliver of a plant flourishing in the belly of the forest, or upon some tremendous mountain, or in one of our planet's deepest valleys that has never been traversed by a human. The plant's movements to the right, to the left, forward, or backward throughout the duration of its lifespan are actively determined by ongoing Divine providence. G-d has issued a specific decree: this particular plant will live for a specific amount of months, days, and hours—and that during this time, it will turn and bend in these directions a certain amount of times.

Beyond all that, however, each of these particular movements is significant for the overall purpose of creation! Through the combination and synthesis of all the myriad particular occurrences, involving countless millions of species and subdivisions that exist within all of the four kingdoms, the sublime Divine intent that underpins all of creation is consummated.

Not only is every feature of every entity Divinely orchestrated, it plays an indispensable role in the Divine purpose of creation.

FIGURE 3.2

Pixelated Purpose

Every moment and occurrence is like a single pixel. It may seem plain and meaningless in isolation, but it plays an integral part in the complete picture.

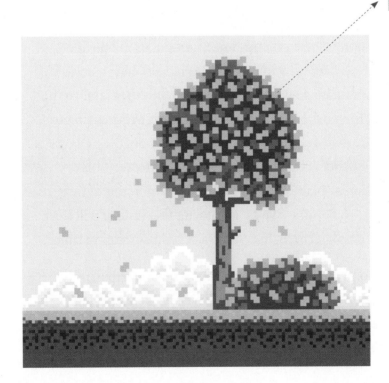

TEXT 12

You Matter

Rabbi Tzadok Hakohen Rabinowitz, *Tzidkat Hatzadik* 154

כְּשֵׁם שֶׁצָּרִיךְ אָדָם לְהַאֲמִין בְּהַשֵׁם יִתְבָּרַךְ, כָּךְ צָרִיךְ אַחַר כָּךְ לְהַאֲמִין בְּעַצְמוֹ. רְצוֹנִי לוֹמַר, שֶׁיֵּשׁ לְהַשֵׁם יִתְבָּרַךְ עֵסֶק עִמּוֹ וְשֶׁאֵינֶנּוּ פּוֹעֵל בָּטֵל... רַק צָרִיךְ לְהַאֲמִין כִּי נַפְשׁוֹ מִמְּקוֹר הַחַיִּים יִתְבָּרַךְ שְׁמוֹ, וְהַשֵׁם יִתְבָּרַךְ מִתְעַנֵּג וּמִשְׁתַּעֲשֵׁעַ בָּהּ כְּשֶׁעוֹשָׂה רְצוֹנוֹ.

Just as we are enjoined to believe in G-d, so must we subsequently believe in ourselves. In other words, we must believe that G-d has provided us with a mission in life, and our lives are not meaningless. . . . But rather, our souls come from G-d, the Source of life, and G-d is delighted and satisfied when we execute His will.

RABBI TZADOK HAKOHEN RABINOWITZ OF LUBLIN 1823–1900

Chasidic rebbe and author. Born into a Lithuanian rabbinic family, Rabbi Tzadok joined the Chasidic movement and became a student of Rabbi Mordechai Yosef Leiner of Izbica and Rabbi Leibel Eiger. He succeeded Rabbi Eiger after his passing and became a rebbe in Lublin, Poland. A distinctly original thinker, Rabbi Tzadok authored many works on Jewish law, Chasidism, and ethics, as well as scholarly essays on astronomy, geometry, and algebra.

ASHREINU—HOW FORTUNATE ARE WE
Michoel Muchnik, mixed media

TEXT 13

Guided Footsteps

Rabbi Levi Yitzchak of Berditchev, cited in *Pitgamin Kadishin*, p. 16

**RABBI LEVI YITZCHAK
OF BERDITCHEV
1740–1809**

Chasidic rebbe. Rabbi
Levi Yitzchak was one of
the foremost disciples of
the Magid of Mezeritch
and later went on to serve
as rabbi in Berditchev,
Ukraine. His Chasidic
commentary on the
Torah, *Kedushat Levi*, is a
classic that is popular to
this day. He is known in
Jewish history and
folklore for his all-
encompassing love,
compassion, and
advocacy on behalf of the
Jewish people.

יֵדַע הָאָדָם בִּידִיעָה בְּרוּרָה וּצְלוּלָה, שֶׁכָּל נְסִיעוֹת וַהֲלִיכוֹת
הָאָדָם לְאֵיזֶה מְקוֹמוֹת, הַכֹּל לֹא בְּמִקְרֶה הוּא חָלִילָה, רַק
מֵאֵת ה' הָיְתָה זֹאת וּבְהַשְׁגָּחָה פְּרָטִית. וְכַוָּנַת הַבּוֹרֵא בָּרוּךְ
הוּא בָּזֶה, שֶׁיֵּשׁ לוֹ לָאָדָם הַלָּזֶה שׁוּם חֵלֶק מָה לְתַקֵּן שָׁמָה
בַּמָּקוֹם הַלָּזֶה, הֵן בְּכֹחַ תּוֹרָה וּתְפִלָּה, וְהֵן בְּכֹחַ אֲכִילָה וּשְׁתִיָּה
וְשֵׁנָה לְשֵׁם שָׁמַיִם, וְהֵן בִּשְׁאָר עֲבוֹדוֹת לְשֵׁם שָׁמַיִם . . .

וּכְמוֹ שֶׁאָמַר הַבַּעַל שֵׁם טוֹב זְכוּתוֹ יָגֵן עָלֵינוּ:
"מֵה' מִצְעֲדֵי גֶבֶר כּוֹנָנוּ" (תְּהִלִּים לז, כג),
דְּהַיְנוּ שֶׁהַשֵּׁם יִתְבָּרֵךְ עוֹשֶׂה לְהָאָדָם חֵשֶׁק לֵילֵךְ וְלִנְסֹעַ
לְאֵיזֶה מָקוֹם, וְכַוָּנָתוֹ יִתְבָּרֵךְ הוּא . . . שֶׁיַּעֲשֶׂה שָׁם
הָאָדָם הַלָּזֶה אֵיזֶה עוּבְדָּא מֵעֲבוֹדָתוֹ יִתְבָּרֵךְ, כְּדֵי שֶׁיְּתַקֵּן
שָׁם הָאָדָם אֵיזֶה תִּקּוּן הַצָּרִיךְ לוֹ, כַּנִּזְכָּר לְעֵיל.

וְעַל כֵּן חַיָּב הָאָדָם לִרְאוֹת אֶת עַצְמוֹ בִּהְיוֹתוֹ בָּא אֶל
אֵיזֶה מָקוֹם, לָתֵן אֶל לִבּוֹ מַה זֶּה וְעַל מַה זֶּה הֵבִיא
אוֹתוֹ הַשֵּׁם יִתְבָּרֵךְ לְכָאן, וַדַּאי לֹא לְחִנָּם הוּא.

We should recognize and fully appreciate that
our travels to various locations are not random;
each journey is specifically directed by G-d. The
Divine intention in orchestrating these journeys
is that each individual has been allotted a specific
portion of the material world to spiritually rectify.
Our portions are in specific locations, to which
we must journey. We accomplish these acts of
rectification in a variety of ways, such as through
studying Torah or praying in that location; or
through eating, drinking, and sleeping there for the

sake of properly serving G-d; or through another means of performing G-d's will in that place. . . .

The Baal Shem Tov associated this concept with the verse, "G-d establishes the steps of man" (PSALMS 37:23), meaning that a person's desire to relocate to a specific place is actually inspired by G-d for the purpose of that individual to engage in a particular aspect of Divine service . . . thereby rectifying whatever this person has been appointed to rectify.

Therefore, when we arrive at any given location, we must reflect on this deeper reality and challenge ourselves: "Why am I here? It is certainly not random! For what achievement did G-d lead me to this spot?"

Perhaps one of the most accomplished painters among his contemporaries, Moshe Yehudah Leib ben Wolf Brada of Trebitsch created several illustrated manuscripts including this book of Tehillim (psalms) copied and decorated on parchment in 1723. The emblem of the De Pinto family of Amsterdam is found on both the front and back covers. Notable decorations are the architectural title page with Moses and Aharon standing in arches, and the depiction after the initial word of Psalm 1 of King David playing the harp while looking at an open book. Shown here is a portion of Psalm 37. (Braginsky Collection, Zurich)

V. TAKEAWAY

Each of the three meditations presented above has its own application, but together they form a comprehensive Divine consciousness: a deep awareness of G-d's presence in our lives and the world around us. However, for the meditation to truly liberate our thinking, consistent practice is necessary.

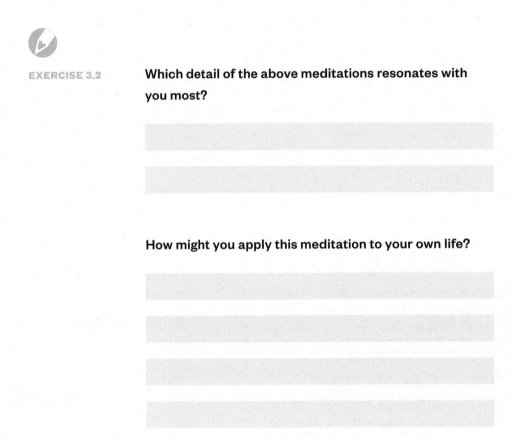

EXERCISE 3.2

Which detail of the above meditations resonates with you most?

How might you apply this meditation to your own life?

FIGURE 3.3   Providence and Psychological Well-Being

Throughout this course, we have highlighted many aspects of religion and spirituality and their effects on an individual's psychology and well-being. In this lesson, we explored the belief in Divine providence, that an omniscient and omnipotent G-d directs the world. Studies show that people who believe in G-d and that events— significant and small—are not random but controlled by G-d, for a purpose, enjoy psychological benefits in a range of areas.

SECURITY AND SELF-ESTEEM

We shouldn't ignore the one "ultimate" supportive relationship for many religious individuals, one that doesn't require any formal participation in religious services or programs, and that is their relationship with G-d. This relationship is not only a source of comfort in troubled times but a source of self-esteem, feeling unconditionally valued, loved, and cared for. Those of you who feel this way have a sense of security that others only wish for. Your belief that G-d will intervene when needed gives you a sense of peace and calm.

Sonja Lyubomirsky, PhD, *The How of Happiness* (New York: Penguin Press, 2008), p. 230

GRATITUDE

A slew of studies demonstrates that highly religious and spiritual individuals value forgiveness to a greater extent and consider themselves as more forgiving than their less spiritual or religious peers.

Christopher Kaczor, PhD, "Does Belief in G-d Enhance Gratitude?" *The Washington Post* (August 21, 2015)

HAPPINESS

Psychologists who have studied whether religious people are happy or unhappy have often reached a general conclusion—religious people are on the whole happier than the non-religious. In the vast majority of studies, religious people report higher well-being than their nonbelieving counterparts. Even when researchers define religiosity in various ways—such as attending church or having self-professed spiritual beliefs—studies show that religious people are, on average, mildly happier.

In one study, conducted by one of the authors (Ed) and the Gallup Organization, about a thousand people living in St. Louis were contacted through random-digit telephone dialing and asked to answer a survey related to spiritual beliefs and satisfaction. It was found that respondents who believed in G-d and in an afterlife were more likely to be satisfied with their lives. . . .

Some scholars have accused us of pushing religion, and of not being objective scientists. Our response is that whether people are religious or secular, they can learn something about how to practice happiness from the findings on religion and happiness.

Ed Diener, PhD, and Robert Biswas-Diener, PhD, *Happiness: Unlocking the Mysteries of Psychological Wealth* (Malden, Mass.: Blackwell Pub., 2008), pp. 114–125

COPING

In their empirical studies, researchers have shown that individuals who interpret negative life events within a more benevolent religious framework generally experience better adjustment to those crises (see Pargament, 1997, for a review). For example, Jenkins and Pargament (1988) asked patients with cancer about the degree to which they felt that G-d was in control of their illness. Attributions of control over the illness to G-d were tied to self-reports of greater self-esteem and nurses' reports of better patient adjustment. . . .

In contrast, those who are unable to sustain their belief in a loving G-d following stressful events may be more vulnerable to problems. In a study of primary hospice caregivers for terminally ill patients, Mickley, Pargament, Brant, and Hipp (1998) found that benevolent religious reframing of the experience (e.g., viewing the situation in a spiritual light, attributions to G-d's will) was associated with perceptions of greater coping efficacy, more positive spiritual outcomes, and greater purpose in life.

Kenneth Pargament, PhD, and Annette Mahoney, PhD, "Spirituality: Discovering and Conserving the Sacred," in C. R. Snyder and S. J. Lopez (eds.), *Handbook of Positive Psychology* (New York: Oxford University Press, 2002), pp. 646–659

MEANING

Divine interaction may affect well-being by deepening the sense of the coherence, comprehensibility, and meaningfulness of reality (Antonovsky 1979). Belief in a divine other can contribute to perceptions of the orderliness and predictability of events and can provide a basis for explaining problematic occurrences (Greeley 1982; Spilka, et al., 1985). In a related vein, interaction with a Divinity may affect well-being by investing otherwise alienating events with meaning: individuals may feel that trivial, painful, or odious activities have significance before an omniscient Divinity. Thus as a source of new cognitions in problematic situations, as a source of empowerment and enhancement of the self, and as a contributor to a sense of meaningfulness, interaction with a divine other may be expected to have a significant effect on well-being.

Melvin Pollner, "Divine Relations, Social Relations, and Well-Being," *Journal of Health and Social Behavior,* 30(1), March 1989, pp. 92–104

KEY POINTS

1   G-d is the soul of the world, and His presence animates all of existence.

2   Every detail of creation is deliberately designed by G-d and is formed by a unique expression of His presence in that being.

3   G-d is with us always, and we can feel His presence.

4   Nothing is by chance. Everything that happens is directed by G-d and is supposed to happen.

5   Everything that happens is an integral part of the master plan of creation.

6   Each one of us, and every circumstance of our lives, is relevant and important to the overall purpose of existence.

Stories of Divine Providence

A collection of stories from the sages of the Talmud and the Chassidic masters on the theme of Divine providence.

Talmud, Berachot 60b–61a

Rav Huna said in the name of Rav, who said in the name of Rabbi Meir, and so it was also taught in a Beraita in the name of Rabbi Akiva: A person should always be accustomed to saying, "Everything that G-d does, He does for the best."

Rabbi Akiva was once traveling along the road. When he reached a certain city he inquired about lodgings, but no one provided him any. Rabbi Akiva said, "Everything that G-d does, He does for the best," and went to sleep in the field.

In Rabbi Akiva's possession were a rooster, a donkey and a candle. A gust of wind came and extinguished the candle; a cat came and ate the rooster; and a lion came and ate the donkey. Rabbi Akiva said, "Everything that G-d does, He does for the best."

That very night, an army came and captured the city. Rabbi Akiva said, "Did I not tell you? Everything that G-d does, He does for the best."

Talmud, Taanit 21a

Nachum Ish Gam Zu was called Gam Zu because regarding everything that happened to him he would say, "This too is for the good [gam zu letova].*"*

Once, the Jews wished to send a gift to the court of the emperor. They said, "Who should go and present this gift? Let Nachum Ish Gam Zu go, as he is accustomed to having miracles performed on his behalf." They sent with him a chest filled with precious stones and pearls. On his way, he spent the night at a particular inn. During the night, the residents of the inn arose and took all of the precious jewels and pearls from the chest, and filled it with dirt. The next day, when he saw what had happened, Nachum Ish Gam Zu said, "This too is for the good."

When Nachum Ish Gam Zu arrived at the palace, they opened the chest and saw that it was filled with dirt. The emperor, enraged, wanted to kill them all, declaring, "The Jews are mocking me." Nachum Ish Gam Zu said, "This too is for the good."

Elijah the Prophet came and appeared before the ruler as one of his officials. He said to the ruler, "Perhaps this dirt is from the earth of their father Abraham. When Abraham threw earth, it turned into swords, and when he threw straw, it turned into arrows, as the verse says, "He made his sword like dirt, his bow like wind-blown straw" (Isaiah 41:2).

There was one city that the Romans had been unable to conquer. They took some of this dirt and tested it by throwing it at their enemies, and they successfully conquered that city. After their victory, the emperor's officers entered the royal treasury and filled Nachum Ish Gam Zu's chest with precious stones and pearls, and sent him off with great honor.

Rabbi Yisrael Baal Shem Tov, 1698-1760, as related in *Shomer Emunim, Maamar Hashgachah Peratit*, ch. 17

The Baal Shem Tov was once walking with his students in the field. A strong wind suddenly blew, and a few leaves fell from the tree to the ground. The Baal Shem Tov said to his students: "My children, you should know that the wind that just blew was all for the sake of one worm that was exposed to the sunlight and was suffering from the heat. The worm cried out to G-d, and he sent this wind that blew the leaves down in order to provide shade for this worm."

The Baal Shem Tov concluded, "See how carefully G-d watches over all of His creations, and how great is His mercy for them."

Based on: Rabbi Yosef Yitzchak Schneersohn, 1880-1950, *Sefer Hasichot* 5702, pp. 84–85

Rabbi Shalom Huminer was a star student of Rabbi Hillel of Paritch, a master teacher of *Chasidut* in Russia in the nineteenth century. One of the innovations of Chasidism is the many hours certain individuals spend in contemplative prayer. These sessions comprise an extensive preparatory period, which includes the study of Chasidic texts and then prayer itself, which entails meditating about G-d and His relationship with the world, probing deeper meanings to the words of prayer, thinking about self-improvement, and so forth.

When Reb Hillel used to travel, he would take along his student, Reb Shalom Huminer. One evening, they came to an inn in the Ukraine. Reb Shalom began the evening prayer and spent such a long time meditating and praying that morning came. So how can one lie down to sleep? So Reb Shalom set to prepare himself for the morning prayers, taking an hour or so. He then recited the morning prayers, and this took the entire day. By the time he came to the Shema, it was already time for the afternoon prayer.

The innkeeper, a simple villager, came to recite the afternoon prayer and saw that Reb Shalom was still in middle of his morning prayers. He cried out, "What is it with this Jew? Last night, he spent the whole night praying, and now he has prayed the whole day! I'm different. I can just say, 'Shema Yisrael,' unlike this man who takes so long. There is only one way to understand this: obviously, this man is a simpleton!"

Reb Shalom had already completed his prayers and heard what the villager had said. In accordance with the teaching of *Chassidus* that everything that a person sees or hears is by Divine providence, and contains a lesson for us to learn from it, Reb Shalom took the simple innkeeper's words to heart.

Reb Hillel said afterward, "Three years of studying the teachings of Chasidism with Reb Shalom did not have as much of an effect on him, in terms of self-improvement, as these words of the simple villager."

Stories of Divine Providence *continued*

Rabbi Yosef Yitzchak Schneerson,
Likutei Diburim, 1880-1950, vol. 1,
pp. 168–170

Translated by Yanki Tauber, *Chabad.org*

It was the summer of 1896, and Father and I were strolling in the fields of Balivka, a hamlet near Lubavitch. The grain was near to ripening, and the wheat and grass swayed gently in the breeze.

Said Father to me: "See G-dliness! Every movement of each stalk and grass was included in G-d's primordial thought of creation, in G-d's all-embracing vision of history, and is guided by divine providence toward a G-dly purpose."

Walking, we entered the forest. Engrossed in what I had heard, excited by the gentleness and seriousness of Father's words, I absentmindedly tore a leaf off a passing tree. Holding it a while in my hands, I continued my thoughtful pacing, occasionally tearing small pieces of leaf and casting them to the winds.

"The Holy Ari," said Father to me, "says that not only is every leaf on a tree a creation invested with divine life, created for a specific purpose within G-d's intent in creation, but also that within each and every leaf there is a spark of a soul that has descended to earth to find its correction and fulfillment.

"The Talmud," Father continued, "rules that 'a man is always responsible for his actions, whether awake or asleep.' The difference between wakefulness and sleep is in the inner faculties of man, his intellect and emotions. The external faculties function equally well in sleep; only the inner faculties are confused. So, dreams present us with contradictory truths. A waking man sees the real world; a sleeping man does not. This is the deeper significance of wakefulness and sleep: when one is awake one sees Divinity; when asleep, one does not.

"Nevertheless, our sages maintain that man is always responsible for his actions, whether awake or asleep. Only this moment we have spoken of divine providence, and unthinkingly you tore off a leaf, played with it in your hands, twisting and squashing and tearing it to pieces, throwing it in all directions.

"How can one be so callous towards a creation of G-d? This leaf was created by the Almighty towards a specific purpose, and is imbued with a divine life-force. It has a body, and it has its life. In what way is the 'I' of this leaf inferior to yours?"

Based on: The Rebbe, Rabbi Menachem Mendel Schneerson, 1902-1994, *Likutei Sichot* 23, p. 468 (February 19, 1979)

In February 1979, Chabad's women's organization's midwinter convention was held in suburban Detroit, Michigan. By the time the convention ended, a blizzard on the East Coast grounded all New-York-bound flights. The women wrote to the Rebbe, highlighting their stressful situation of being delayed, away from their families, etc. The Rebbe wrote a brief note that was read to the women over the phone. It said:

The Baal Shem Tov's teaching—that every occurrence contains a directive in serving G-d—is a topic that has been spoken of and discussed at length many, many times; I am sure that you, too, have given speeches on this topic. Yet, now, when an incident has happened to you (i.e., your being delayed in Detroit by the New York snowstorm) whose occurrence has a clear meaning and purpose, you seek to attach to the incident most distorted interpretations (e.g., "Perhaps the delay is designed to distress us," G-d forbid, or "How are we going to return home?" etc.)—anything but the simple and obvious interpretation.

The simple and obvious reason for the delay is: It is possible to disseminate Torah and *mitzvot* to a far greater degree than was accomplished during the Convention. You are therefore being granted the merit—through the snow which descends from Heaven—of completing the above task with an extraordinary abundance and storm intensity of Judaism, similar to the extraordinary abundance of the snowstorm.

Your efforts in completing the Convention's task of disseminating Torah and *mitzvot* should be extended to the city, the airport, publicity in the newspapers, etc.

Of course, the women did just that. They spent the day connecting with fellow Jews, inspiring many of them to added mitzvah performance. They returned home the next day.

That evening, after reporting to the Rebbe on the activities of the day, they received an additional reply:

It is a particularly great merit when the A-mighty from On High "points with a finger" and clearly shows one what to do. May all your activities (undertaken as a result of this Divine indication) be highly successful. It is obvious that each and every woman will soon travel and reach home—for she will have completed her mission.

Aspects and Implications of Divine Providence

The following texts explore various aspects of Divine providence and its practical meaning for us.

Divine Providence and Free Choice

Rabbi Shmuel de Uceda, 1545-1604, Midrash Shmuel, *Avot 3:15*

G-d sees in the present what the future will be. He foreknows everything that will befall us until the day we die. From the beginning of time, He observes our inevitable demise and all of our choices during our lifetime. For He is not subject to the limitations of time. The lines between past and future are not drawn.

Accordingly, our choices were not decreed by Him, G-d forbid. Rather, He looks and sees what we will choose until our last day....

Rabbi Moshe Almosnino suggested the following parable:

If I see Reuben running, although my knowledge of this fact is flawless, one cannot say that Reuben is forced to run due to my seeing and knowing that he is running. Despite my knowledge, he is running by choice.

Similarly, G-d's knowledge does not compel our choices. G-d's knowledge is knowledge of the present. There is no future for Him, because He transcends the confines of time. Our future is G-d's present. And just like our knowledge of the present does not affect people's choices, so too, His knowledge—always about the present—does not affect our choices.

The confusion that we have in this regard is rooted in the fact that we cannot fathom the notion of G-d knowing the future in the present, which, in turn, is due to our thinking of G-d's knowledge through the prism of our own limited knowledge.

Is Our World Beneath G-d?

The Rebbe, Rabbi Menachem Mendel Schneerson, 1902-1994 , Sefer Hamaamarim Melukat, *vol. 1, p. 322*

The nations acknowledge G-d's existence but they describe Him as "the G-d of gods." This is implied in the verse, "G-d is high above every nation, upon the heavens is His glory" (Psalms 113:4). Meaning, they insist that G-d is high and supremely exalted, and they therefore conclude that "upon the heavens is His glory," that only the heavens contain His revelation, whereas active involvement in this world and its lower forms of life are beneath G-d's exalted dignity. They therefore claim that G-d abandoned this world to the administration of the stars and heavenly forces [the "gods"].

At the root of their misconception is the belief that the world was created according to the principle of a cause being relative to the effect it produces, so that a creative power bears some relationship and at least a remote comparability to the created entity. Accordingly, they argue that only the supernal entities—the "heavens"—are exalted enough for G-d to have a relationship with, leading them to conclude that G-d therefore tasked these entities with running this world. By contrast, they believe that G-d considers the dismal end-products of the creative process—the material world and its contents—as irrelevant and insignificant to Him.

This is false. The same psalm continues to describe G-d as He "Who dwells on high, Who lowers Himself to look in the heavens and the earth" (Ibid. verses 5–6). G-d is indeed high and exalted, but He is higher than, and infinitely separated from, *all* of existence. He must lower Himself to be watchful over "the heavens and the earth"—equally. Not only the physical universe, but also the spiritual heavens along with the supernal Divine forces [that the nations refer to as "gods"] are all equally insignificant to G-d. He is both infinitely above them all, and yet, at the same time, He intensely watches over them all equally.

Creation and Providence

Rabbi Yosef Yitzchak Schneersohn, **1880-1950, Igrot Kodesh,** *vol. 4, pp. 548–549*

"Who in His goodness renews every day, continuously, the work of Creation" (Siddur, Morning Prayers) . . .

On the practical level, this passage teaches us about the phenomenon of Divine providence—the core of which, if we distill profundity into

a single sentence, is that G-d's individual Divine guidance of each entity within Creation is the actual life-force, existence, and truest identity of that entity.

If we direct our minds and hearts to contemplate ourselves and that which we understand of the surrounding world, we will observe clearly that G-d is personally watching and guiding each entity that exists in all its fine details. We can observe this truth in our personal experiences when, for example, something good happens to us—something that is extremely important to us—without any initiative on our part, without our prior knowledge, and completely unplanned. Or, when we are protected or rescued from a harmful scenario without having done anything to produce that outcome, and without any prior knowledge of the harm. This is all G-d's active and detailed individual guidance. Such occurrences are demonstrative of the Divine providence that fills all of Creation—in the words of the Shabbat prayers, "He conducts His world with kindness and His creations with mercy."

This, then, is the service required from us, as per the teachings of *Chasidut*: to train ourselves to see Divine providence, to observe that G-d in His goodness renews at every moment all of creation and every created entity, with constant individual attention, and that this attention, and only this attention, is each entity's very life and existence.

Once we train ourselves to observe and recognize Divine providence, we gradually allow our soul's internal purity to emerge, which enables us to gradually climb the many-stepped ladder of our intellectual perception of G-dliness.

Aspects and Implications
of Divine Providence *continued*

Appreciating Providence

Rabbi Yosef Yitzchak Schneersohn, **1880-1950,**
Sefer Hamaamarim Kuntresim, vol. 1, p. 374

"For I, G-d, have not changed; and you, the descendants of Jacob, have not expired" (Malachi 3:6). We can read this verse as the prophet expressing his astonishment at the Jewish people. He tells them:

Do you not observe that G-d does not renege on His promise to you? [He promised to preserve you as a people,] as it is stated, "For G-d will not forsake His people, nor will He abandon His inheritance" (Psalms 94:14). Indeed, each of you plainly observes individual Divine providence! And our sages taught that the Jewish people is like a single sheep surrounded by seventy wolves—and yet, they are divinely protected and continue to survive! If so, why is it that "you, the descendants of Jacob, have not expired"? How are you not drawn to cleave to G-d through studying His Torah and observing His commandments with the blazing passion of a soul that expires from sheer love?

When Stones Will Talk

Rabbi Yosef Yitzchak Schneersohn,
1880-1950, *Igrot Kodesh, vol. 4, pp. 145–151*

The Almighty L-rd, G-d of Hosts, desired to contract Himself, so to speak, and to conceal Himself through countless veils and concealments, and to thereby create a physical, corporeal world that appears pleasing to the human eye, replete with food and drink that is pleasant to a corporeal being, and with all sorts of things that the spirits of material creatures find attractive. Within this setting, He chose us and gave us the Torah, the commandments, and paths of Divine worship. With these, and through these, it is possible to empower the soul to overcome corporeality. When an individual does so, that person's body and associated portion of the material world becomes spiritually refined.

Now, in order to fulfill G-d's purpose in terms of refining and purifying the corporeality and physicality of material existence, G-d engages in intricate orchestration of events. "For the L-rd is a G-d of thoughts, and to Him are deeds counted" (I Samuel 2:3). *Alilot,* "deeds," can also means "schemes." The supernal thoughts of G-d orchestrate, through a brilliant scheme of causations, that a particular person who is empowered to introduce spiritual refinement and to elevate a particular material matter will encounter the specific material that requires their attention.

However, G-d also provides freedom of choice. Each of us can choose, upon arriving at the location containing the materiality requiring our specific attention, the kind of influence we will have. We might choose to act according to our personal wishes—to indulge in corporeal pleasures, and to commit wrong deeds there, thereby increasing the spiritual coarseness and egotistical nature of materiality in that location. Or we can choose to engage in words of Torah, pure speech, and stories that inspire people to pursue Torah, *mitzvot,* service of the heart, fear of

Heaven, faith in our sages, positive character traits, love for a fellow Jew, and spiritually elevated ideas. With these, we purify the material coarseness of our location and all that it contains, reducing its general egocentricity [that acts as a barrier to Divinity].

At a previous gathering, we had opportunity to explain the passage, "A stone will cry from the wall, and a chip will answer it from a beam" (Habakkuk 2:11). This prophecy describes the world in the future era [of Redemption]. . . . At present, the mineral, vegetable, and animal kingdoms are mute and do not speak at all. In the future era, however, "A stone will cry from the wall, and a chip will answer it from a beam."

Right now, inanimate matter is silent. We trample over it and it keeps quiet. But there will yet arrive an era, amid the Divine revelations of the future, in which inanimate entities will begin to speak. Physical objects will begin to recount and share their experiences. They will then demand to know why we trampled over them. If we failed to contemplate or speak words of Torah, then by what right did we trample them! You see, whenever we think about or discuss Torah matters, then even the physical materials in our surroundings sense it—although they presently maintain their silence. In the future, they will not keep silent but will recount all of their past experiences.

The Master of all worlds—the Primary Cause responsible for all possible causes, and the ultimate Orchestrator of all—guides complex chains of events. . . . "From G-d are a person's steps established" (Psalms 37:23), for the sake of executing the supernal goal: to illuminate Earth's darkness with the light of Torah, *mitzvot*, prayer, refining and repairing character traits, and loving our fellow Jews.

Purposeful Direction

Rabbi Yosef Yitzchak Schneersohn, 1880-1950, Igrot Kodesh, vol. 3, pp. 112–113

King David declared, "From G-d are a person's steps established" (Psalms 37:23). Each individual, by virtue of being human, must be fully aware that they are an ambassador of the supernal providence, sent to this world to introduce illumination specifically through the light of Torah and personal Divine service. The target of this illumination is the specific location and social scene in which we find ourselves, into which we were placed by deliberate decree of G-d's individualized guidance. We have been granted the free will to choose goodness, and when we do, G-d is pleased with the way we conduct our lives.

King Solomon declared, "A person's steps are from G-d" (Proverbs 20:24). Each and every step we take, wherever we are, is from G-d. It is G-d who provides us the ability and strength to take each step in life, so that we can fulfill the supernal purpose for the Creation. If we harbor complaints about our location or other elements of our personal situations, we should note that King Solomon concluded the above insight with, "What do humans understand about their own ways?" We cannot fathom G-d's plans, but we must remain secure in the knowledge that G-d has given us the ability to achieve goodness.

4

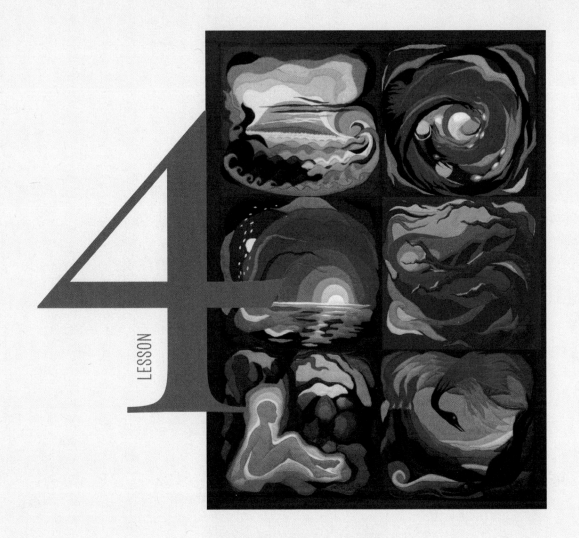

MIND YOUR TIME

The Purpose and Power of the Present

*Perhaps now more than ever, we can all relate to the
struggle of feeling mentally or emotionally scattered and
distracted. This lesson presents a path of meditation
that focuses on the perpetual nature of creation,
through which it highlights a revolutionary depth to
living in the present moment. The lesson promotes
a mindful awareness that allows us to recognize the
value of each moment as an end, in and of itself.*

THE CREATION
Bracha Lavee, print of felt on canvas tapestry

I. INTRODUCTION

The goal of Jewish spiritual meditation is to reframe the way we live our day-to-day lives. Our lives are fast paced and busy, and we often feel scattered between so many different responsibilities. This study provides a framework, based upon spiritual meditation, for removing the rush from the race and becoming fully invested in the present moment.

when we cram things in, we are doing less, living less

EXERCISE 4.1

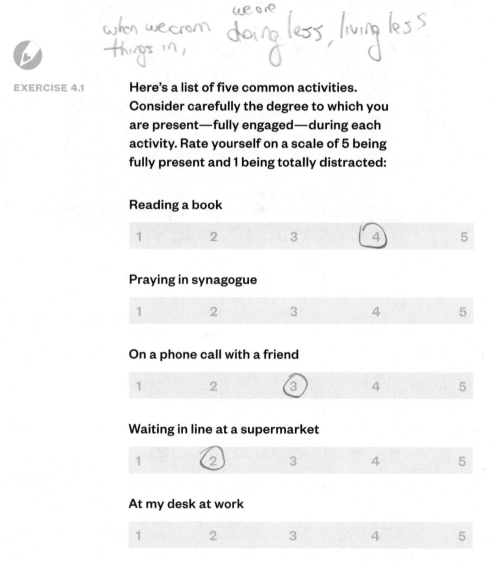

Here's a list of five common activities. Consider carefully the degree to which you are present—fully engaged—during each activity. Rate yourself on a scale of 5 being fully present and 1 being totally distracted:

Reading a book

| 1 | 2 | 3 | 4 | 5 |

Praying in synagogue

| 1 | 2 | 3 | 4 | 5 |

On a phone call with a friend

| 1 | 2 | 3 | 4 | 5 |

Waiting in line at a supermarket

| 1 | 2 | 3 | 4 | 5 |

At my desk at work

| 1 | 2 | 3 | 4 | 5 |

TEXT 1

Scattered Soul

Rabbi Ovadiah Bartenura, Mishnah, Avot 2:7

וְחָסִיד אֶחָד הָיָה מִתְפַּלֵּל, "הַמָּקוֹם יַצִילֵנִי מִפְּזוּר הַנֶּפֶשׁ".

וְשָׁאֲלוּ מִמֶּנּוּ, מַהוּ פִּזוּר הַנֶּפֶשׁ?

אָמַר לָהֶם "שֶׁיִּהְיוּ לוֹ נְכָסִים מְרֻבִּים מְפֻזָרִים בִּמְקוֹמוֹת הַרְבֵּה וְצָרִיךְ לְפַזֵּר נַפְשׁוֹ לַחֲשֹׁב לְכָאן וּלְכָאן".

One pious fellow would often pray, "May G-d protect me from enduring a scattered soul."

People in earshot would ask,
"What is a scattered soul?"

He would respond, "Those who own many assets that are located in several divergent locations are forced to divide their attention to stay on top of all of them at once, causing the soul to scatter [its energies]."

RABBI OVADIAH OF BARTENURA C. 1445–1524

Scholar and author. Born in Italy, Rabbi Ovadiah is commonly known as "the Bartenura," after the city in which he held the rabbinate. Arriving in Jerusalem in 1488, he quickly became an effective leader of the oppressed Jewish community, especially focusing his energies on the influx of Sephardic Jews to Jerusalem following the Spanish expulsion. His highly-acclaimed commentary on the Mishnah appears in almost every printed edition.

A richly illuminated page of the opening text of Tractate Avot. Part of a 15th-century prayer book manuscript on parchment that was owned by Rabbi Yisrael Friedman of Ruzhin (1796–1850) and his descendants. (The Israel Museum [B51.12.3026], Jerusalem)

TEXT 2

Slow Down

Rabbi Yisrael Baal Shem Tov, *Baal Shem Tov al HaTorah,* Ekev 62

"וַאֲבַדְתֶּם מְהֵרָה" (דְּבָרִים יא, יז). הַבַּעַל שֵׁם טוֹב אָמַר
שֶׁהָאָדָם צָרִיךְ לִהְיוֹת תָּמִיד בְּדֵעָה מְיֻשֶּׁבֶת, וְלֹא בִּמְהִירוּת,
וְזֶהוּ "וַאֲבַדְתֶּם מְהֵרָה" - צָרִיךְ לְאַבֵּד אֶת הַמְּהִירוּת.

The Baal Shem Tov explained that we must always maintain a settled mind, and not be in a rush. He would refer to the verse: "You will be swiftly eradicated" (DEUTERONOMY 11:17). The Hebrew phrase, *avadetem meherah,* allows for an alternative reading in the form of a directive: "You must eradicate the swiftness."

We must eradicate swiftness.

RABBI YISRAEL BAAL SHEM TOV (BESHT) 1698–1760

Founder of the Chasidic movement. Born in Slutsk, Belarus, the Baal Shem Tov was orphaned as a child. He served as a teacher's assistant and clay digger before founding the Chasidic movement and revolutionizing the Jewish world with his emphasis on prayer, joy, and love for every Jew, regardless of his or her level of Torah knowledge.

An Israeli 0.25 lira stamp commemorating two hundred years from the passing of the Baal Shem Tov. Depicted is his synagogue with the caption "The synagogue of the Besht in Mezhibuzh." It was designed by A. Vardimon and issued on August 21, 1961.

II. LIVE IN THE MOMENT

The classic tool for slowing down and focusing is mindfulness—the art of becoming fully present and aware of the present moment. However, mindfulness has its drawbacks, and can turn into a hollow practice used to escape from, rather than to embrace, life's responsibilities.

QUESTION

What tool do you use to slow down and focus?

"Don't Just Do Something. . . . Sit There"— a one-minute meditation that can save your life: **myjli.com/meditation**

THE LAST PRAYER
Samuel Hirszenberg, 1897, oil on canvas. (Museum of Art, Ein Harod, Israel)

TEXT 3

Don't Worry about Tomorrow

Talmud, Sanhedrin 100b

BABYLONIAN TALMUD

A literary work of monumental proportions that draws upon the legal, spiritual, intellectual, ethical, and historical traditions of Judaism. The 37 tractates of the Babylonian Talmud contain the teachings of the Jewish sages from the period after the destruction of the 2nd Temple through the 5th century CE. It has served as the primary vehicle for the transmission of the Oral Law and the education of Jews over the centuries; it is the entry point for all subsequent legal, ethical, and theological Jewish scholarship.

אָמַר רַב יוֹסֵף: מִילֵי מְעַלְיָיתָא דְּאִית בֵּיהּ, דָּרְשִׁינַן לְהוּ . . .
אַל תָּצֵר צָרַת מָחָר כִּי לֹא תֵדַע מַה יֵּלֶד יוֹם, שֶׁמָּא לְמָחָר
אֵינֶנּוּ וְנִמְצָא מִצְטַעֵר עַל עוֹלָם שֶׁאֵינוֹ שֶׁלּוֹ.

Rabbi Yosef stated, "The valuable passages within the Book of Ben Sira may be taught. . . . 'Grieve not over tomorrow's woes for you know not what a day may bring; you may not be [alive] tomorrow and you are worrying about a world to which you will not belong.'"

TEXT 4

Don't Worry

Rabbi Yosef Yuspa Nordlinger, *Yosef Ometz*, p. 168

הֶעָבָר אַיִן
הֶעָתִיד עֲדַיִן
וְהַהֹוֶה כְּהֶרֶף עַיִן
אִם כֵּן, דְּאָגָה מְנַיִן?

The past is no longer here.
The future has yet to appear.
In a blink the present will disappear.
So, what case is there for fear?

**RABBI YOSEF YUSPA NORDLINGER
C. 1570–1637**

Rabbi Yosef Yuspa Nordlinger served as a judge on the rabbinic court of his native Frankfurt. He is known for *Yosef Ometz*, a work of Halachah and ethics and an important source regarding the customs of the German Jewish communities.

III. A WHOLE NEW WORLD

Meditation on the nature of Creation can add new depth and substance to the mindfulness practice. Creation was not a one-time event; G-d constantly recreates all of existence from nonexistence. Created existence is a product of Divine creative energy, and consequently, that energy must perpetually flow into existence in order for it to exist. At every moment, the universe is recreated with a fresh burst of Divine energy.

Perpetual Creation

TEXT 5

Rabbi Yeshayahu Halevi Horowitz, *Shenei Luchot Haberit, Asarah Maamarot, Maamar* 1, 40b–41a

הִנֵּה סְבָרַת הָעוֹלָם הִיא . . . כָּךְ: הַבּוֹרֵא בָּרוּךְ הוּא חִידֵּשׁ הַכֹּל יֵשׁ מֵאַיִן הַמּוּחְלָט . . . בְּרֵאשִׁית נָתַן הַקָּדוֹשׁ בָּרוּךְ הוּא לִצְבָא הַשָּׁמַיִם כֹּחַ וִיכוֹלֶת לְהַנְהִיג הָעוֹלָם . . . הָעוֹלָם כְּמִנְהָגוֹ נוֹהֵג, וְכִבְיָכוֹל זֶזֶה יָדוֹ מֵהֶם, רַק אִם לְעֵת מֵהָעִתִּים רוֹצֶה לְשַׁדֵּד אוֹתָם. וְכָל זְמַן שֶׁאֵינוֹ מְשַׁדֵּד, אָז מַנְהִיגִים בְּכֹחַ שֶׁהוּשַׂג לָהֶם בְּעֵת הַבְּרִיאָה.

אָמְנָם אֲמִתַּת הָאֱמוּנָה . . . הִיא: הַשֵּׁם יִתְבָּרֵךְ מְחַדֵּשׁ בְּטוּבוֹ בְּכָל יוֹם תָּמִיד מַעֲשֵׂה בְרֵאשִׁית, בְּכַוָּנָה מְכֻוֶּנֶת שׁוֹפֵעַ שִׁפְעוֹ. וְאִילוּ הָיָה מוֹנֵעַ רֶגַע אֶחָד, הָיָה הַכֹּל כְּלֹא הָיָה, בָּטֵל הַמְצִיאוּת.

A common perception . . . is that G-d created everything out of absolute nothingness . . . and that in the beginning of Creation, G-d imparted to the hosts of Heaven [i.e., the forces of nature] the power and ability to run the world. . . . The world thus operates according to its manner, as if G-d has let go of His creation; it is only that occasionally

RABBI YESHAYAHU HALEVI HOROWITZ (*SHALAH*)
1565–1630

Kabbalist and author. Rabbi Horowitz was born in Prague and served as rabbi in several prominent Jewish communities, including Frankfurt am Main and his native Prague. After the passing of his wife in 1620, he moved to Israel. In Tiberias, he completed his *Shenei Luchot Haberit*, an encyclopedic compilation of kabbalistic ideas. He is buried in Tiberias, next to Maimonides.

G-d may desire to override [the natural order]. As long as G-d does not override it, the world runs on the power it obtained at the time of its creation.

But the proper belief . . . is that G-d "in His goodness renews each day, constantly, the first act of Creation," actively directing His flow of vitality. Should G-d cease to do so for even an instant, all would be as naught; its existence would be utterly nullified.

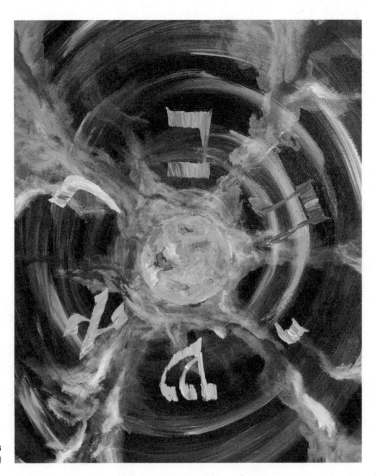

BERESHIT: GENESIS
Yehoshua Wiseman, Israel

TEXT 6

From Scratch

Rabbi Shneur Zalman of Liadi, *Tanya*,
Shaar Hayichud Veha'emunah, ch. 2

**RABBI SHNEUR
ZALMAN OF LIADI
(ALTER REBBE)
1745–1812**

Chasidic
rebbe, halachic
authority, and founder of
the Chabad movement.
The Alter Rebbe was
born in Liozna, Belarus,
and was among the
principal students of the
Magid of Mezeritch. His
numerous works include
the *Tanya*, an early
classic containing the
fundamentals of Chabad
Chasidism; and *Shulchan
Aruch Harav*, an
expanded and reworked
code of Jewish law.

הִנֵּה, מִכָּאן תְּשׁוּבַת הַמִּינִים וְגִלּוּי שׁוֹרֶשׁ טָעוּתָם, הַכּוֹפְרִים בְּהַשְׁגָּחָה
פְּרָטִית וּבְאוֹתוֹת וּמוֹפְתֵי הַתּוֹרָה, שֶׁטוֹעִים בְּדִמְיוֹנָם הַכּוֹזֵב שֶׁמְּדַמִּין
מַעֲשֵׂה ה' "עוֹשֶׂה שָׁמַיִם וָאָרֶץ" לְמַעֲשֵׂה אֱנוֹשׁ וְתַחְבּוּלוֹתָיו, כִּי
כַּאֲשֶׁר יָצָא לַצּוֹרֵף כְּלִי - שׁוּב אֵין הַכְּלִי צָרִיךְ לִידֵי הַצּוֹרֵף, כִּי אַף שֶׁיָּדָיו
מְסוּלָּקוֹת הֵימֶנּוּ וְהוֹלֵךְ לוֹ בַּשּׁוּק - הַכְּלִי קַיָּם בְּתַבְנִיתוֹ וְצַלְמוֹ מַמָּשׁ
כַּאֲשֶׁר יָצָא מִידֵי הַצּוֹרֵף, כָּךְ מְדַמִּין הַסְּכָלִים הָאֵלּוּ מַעֲשֵׂה שָׁמַיִם וָאָרֶץ.

אַךְ "טַח מֵרְאוֹת עֵינֵיהֶם" הַהֶבְדֵּל הַגָּדוֹל שֶׁבֵּין מַעֲשֵׂה אֱנוֹשׁ
וְתַחְבּוּלוֹתָיו, שֶׁהוּא יֵשׁ מִיֵּשׁ, רַק שֶׁמְּשַׁנֶּה הַצּוּרָה וְהַתְּמוּנָה מִתְּמוּנַת
חֲתִיכַת כֶּסֶף לִתְמוּנַת כְּלִי, לְמַעֲשֵׂה שָׁמַיִם וָאָרֶץ, שֶׁהוּא יֵשׁ מֵאַיִן . . .

בִּבְרִיאַת יֵשׁ מֵאַיִן . . . שֶׁבְּהִסְתַּלְּקוּת כֹּחַ הַבּוֹרֵא מִן הַנִּבְרָא
חַס וְשָׁלוֹם - יָשׁוּב הַנִּבְרָא לְאַיִן וָאֶפֶס מַמָּשׁ. אֶלָּא צָרִיךְ
לִהְיוֹת כֹּחַ הַפּוֹעֵל בַּנִּפְעָל תָּמִיד, לְהַחֲיוֹתוֹ וּלְקַיְּימוֹ.

Herein lies the answer to those who deny individual
Divine providence and the miracles recorded in
the Torah, and the root of their error. They err in
comparing the work of G-d, the Creator of Heaven
and earth, to the work of man and his schemes.
When a silversmith has completed crafting a vessel,
that vessel is no longer dependent upon the hands
of the craftsman, and even when his hands are
removed from it and he goes on his way, the vessel
remains in exactly the same image and form as when
it left the hands of the smith. These fools conceive
the creation of Heaven and earth in the same way.

However, their eyes are blinded from seeing the great difference between the work of man and the making of Heaven and earth. The work of man consists of fashioning one existent thing out of another already existent thing, merely changing the form and appearance, e.g., processing silver into a vessel. Creation of Heaven and earth, however, is creating something from nothing. . . .

When something is created out of nothing . . . if the power of the Creator is withdrawn from the thing created, G-d forbid, the created being would revert to naught and utter nonexistence. The activating force of the Creator must continuously be present in the thing created to give it life and ongoing existence.

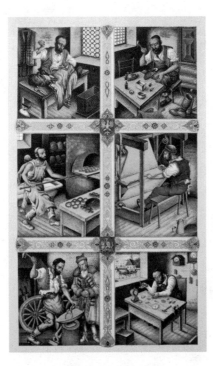

JEWISH CRAFTSMEN AND TRADESMEN
Arthur Szyk (1894–1951), Paris, 1927. Pubished in 1932, his work was a visual interpretation of the Statue of Kalisz—issued by Boleslaw the Pious in 1264—granting unprecedented legal rights to the Jews of Poland including religious freedom and the right to trade and travel. The watercolor and gouache miniatures were made in the style of a medieval illuminated manuscriptand sought to remind Poles and Jews of the 20th century of this historic precedent.

TEXT 7

Constant Renewal

Siddur, Blessings before the Shema Prayer

הַמְחַדֵּשׁ בְּטוּבוֹ בְּכָל יוֹם תָּמִיד מַעֲשֵׂה בְרֵאשִׁית.

In His goodness, He renews the work of Creation each day, continuously.

SIDDUR

The siddur is the Jewish prayer book. It was originally developed by the sages of the Great Assembly in the 4th century BCE, and later reconstructed by Rabban Gamliel after the destruction of the Second Temple. Various authorities continued to add prayers, from then until contemporary times. It includes praise of G-d, requests for personal and national needs, selections from the Bible, and much else. Various Jewish communities have slightly different versions of the siddur.

Part of the blessings before the Shema, in a prayer book written on parchment in the 15th century. (British Museum [MS 26971], London)

Rabbi YY Jacobson explores the Jewish value of living in the present moment: **myjli.com/meditation**

IV. INVESTING IN THE PRESENT

This meditation reveals the incredible inherent value of each moment. A moment in time is a unique and deliberate creation of G-d with an entire purpose of its own. Living with this perspective leads a person to be fully invested in each moment. This approach to mindfulness does not negate the past or future; rather, it incorporates them only inasmuch as they are relevant within the present moment in time.

TEXT 8

Unique Moment in Time

The Rebbe, Rabbi Menachem Mendel Schneerson,
Torat Menachem 5744:3, pp. 1674–1675

RABBI MENACHEM MENDEL SCHNEERSON 1902-1994

The towering Jewish leader of the 20th century, known as "the Lubavitcher Rebbe," or simply as "the Rebbe." Born in southern Ukraine, the Rebbe escaped Nazi-occupied Europe, arriving in the U.S. in June 1941. The Rebbe inspired and guided the revival of traditional Judaism after the European devastation, impacting virtually every Jewish community the world over. The Rebbe often emphasized that the performance of just one additional good deed could usher in the era of Mashiach. The Rebbe's scholarly talks and writings have been printed in more than 200 volumes.

אֲפִלּוּ בֶּן אָדָם שֶׁאֵינוֹ בְּתַכְלִית הַשְּׁלֵמוּת לֹא יַעֲשֶׂה דָבָר לְלֹא כָּל תּוֹעֶלֶת, לְהֶבֶל וְלָרִיק (אֶלָּא אִם כֵּן הוּא לְגַמְרֵי לֹא בְסֵדֶר . . .) וְעַל אַחַת כַּמָּה וְכַמָּה בּוֹרֵא הָעוֹלָם וּמַנְהִיגוֹ וּבוֹרֵא אָדָם וּמַנְהִיגוֹ, שֶׁבְּוַדַּאי "לֹא בָּרָא דָבָר אֶחָד לְבַטָּלָה" . . .

וּמִכֵּיוָן שֶׁכָּל יוֹם וָיוֹם (וְכָל רֶגַע וָרֶגַע) דְּכָל סֵדֶר הִשְׁתַּלְשְׁלוּת הַזְּמַן הוּא בְּרִיאָה בִּפְנֵי עַצְמָהּ - מוּבָן, שֶׁעִנְיָנוֹ הַמְיֻחָד שֶׁל יוֹם זֶה שׁוֹנֶה מִכָּל שְׁאָר הַיָּמִים דְּכָל סֵדֶר הִשְׁתַּלְשְׁלוּת הַזְּמַן.

כְּלוֹמַר, יִחוּדוֹ שֶׁל יוֹם זֶה בְּ"עֲבִידְתֵּיהּ" הַשַּׁיֶּכֶת אֵלָיו, אֵינוֹ רַק בְּיַחַס לִשְׁאָר יְמֵי שָׁבוּעַ זֶה, חֹדֶשׁ זֶה אוֹ שָׁנָה זוֹ, כִּי אִם בְּיַחַס לְכָל הַיָּמִים דְּכָל סֵדֶר הִשְׁתַּלְשְׁלוּת הַזְּמַן.

וְהַהוֹכָחָה לְכָךְ בְּפַשְׁטוּת: מִכֵּיוָן שֶׁיּוֹם זֶה נִבְרָא עַל יְדֵי הַקָּדוֹשׁ בָּרוּךְ הוּא בְּתוֹר בְּרִיאָה בִּפְנֵי עַצְמָהּ, הֲרֵי בְּוַדַּאי שֶׁיֵּשׁ בּוֹ עִנְיָן מְיֻחָד שֶׁאֵינוֹ בְּכָל שְׁאָר הַיָּמִים שֶׁבְּכָל סֵדֶר הִשְׁתַּלְשְׁלוּת הַזְּמַן, כִּי לוּלֵי זֹאת לֹא הָיָה צֹרֶךְ בִּבְרִיאַת יוֹם זֶה.

וְזֶהוּ תַּפְקִידוֹ שֶׁל יְהוּדִי - "אֲנִי נִבְרֵאתִי לְשַׁמֵּשׁ אֶת קוֹנִי" לְנַצֵּל כָּל יוֹם וָיוֹם בְּהֶתְאֵם לִרְצוֹנוֹ שֶׁל הַקָּדוֹשׁ בָּרוּךְ הוּא, עַל יְדֵי זֶה שֶׁמְּמַלֵּא אֶת הָעֲבוֹדָה הַמְיֻחֶדֶת שֶׁרָצָה הַקָּדוֹשׁ בָּרוּךְ הוּא שֶׁתֵּעָשֶׂה בְּיוֹם זֶה.

Humans, even if they are not in a perfect state of balanced mind (with the exception of truly extreme cases) will not do anything without a reason and motivation. Certainly, the [absolutely perfect] Creator and Director of the universe, Who is also the Creator and Director of each human, does not create an entity that lacks a definite purpose. . . .

Each individual day, and each and every moment of the cosmic dimension of time, is an individually created entity. It therefore follows that the theme and purpose of a specific day is distinguishable from that of every other day in the entire realm of time.

In other words, the *purpose* of any single day in terms of that which G-d expects us to accomplish is unique. It is unique not only within the week to which it belongs, or that month, or even that year. Rather, our mission in regard to this day is unique among *all* of the days that are supported by the *entire* dimension of time.

The proof is straightforward: G-d created this day as an individual unit of time. He surely has a unique purpose for this unit of time—this unique creation of His—that cannot be accomplished with any other unit of time. Were that not the case, G-d would have no need for it, and He would not have created it.

The task of a Jew, who was created for the overt goal of serving G-d, is to utilize each day consonant with G-d's will—through accomplishing the purpose unique to that particular day.

TEXT 9

Investing in Now

The Rebbe, Rabbi Menachem Mendel Schneerson,
Torat Menachem 5751:4, pp. 56–57

וְכַיָּדוּעַ פִּתְגָם כְּבוֹד קְדֻשַּׁת אַדְמוֹ"ר (מְהוֹרַשַׁ"ב) נִשְׁמָתוֹ עֵדֶן . . .
שֶׁפְּנִימִי, כָּל דָּבָר שֶׁהוּא עוֹשֶׂה, הֲרֵי הוּא שָׁקוּעַ בָּזֶה לְגַמְרֵי.

פַּעַם אַחַת בְּהִתְוַעֲדוּת הִרְגִּישׁ כְּבוֹד קְדֻשַּׁת אַדְמוֹ"ר נִשְׁמָתוֹ עֵדֶן
שֶׁהַבַּחוּרִים מְנַגְּנִים נִגּוּן בְּחִפָּזוֹן, כְּהַקְדָּמָה לְמָה שֶׁיָּבוֹא לְאַחֲרֵי הַנִּגּוּן
(אֲמִירַת חֲסִידוּת וְכַיּוֹצֵא בָּזֶה). וְהִקְדִּישׁ שִׂיחָה שְׁלֵמָה שֶׁתָּכְנָהּ הוּא
שֶׁבַּעֲבוֹדָתוֹ שֶׁל יְהוּדִי צָרִיךְ הוּא לַעֲשׂוֹת כָּל דָּבָר בִּשְׁלֵמוּת. אֲפִלּוּ
כַּאֲשֶׁר מְדֻבָּר אוֹדוֹת עִנְיָן שֶׁהוּא הַקְדָּמָה לְעִנְיָן אַחֵר - הֲרֵי כַּאֲשֶׁר
נִמְצָאִים עֲדַיִן בְּמַצָּב זֶה, צְרִיכִים לִהְיוֹת שְׁקוּעִים בָּזֶה לְגַמְרֵי. "בִּכְלַל
הֲרֵי זֶה עִקָּר גָּדוֹל, שֶׁבַּמָּקוֹם שֶׁנִּמְצָאִים - צְרִיכִים לִהְיוֹת בֶּאֱמֶת".

There is a famous saying of [the fifth Chabad Rebbe,] Rabbi Shalom DovBer . . . that a *penimi* [person of profound internal integrity] is fully invested in each and every undertaking.

At one of his public gatherings, Rabbi Shalom DovBer sensed that his younger students were leading the customary singing [of a Chasidic melody] at a furious pace because they were

eager to hear the profound spiritual teachings
that were to be delivered following the singing. In
response, he devoted an entire address to explaining
that a Jew must accomplish *each* individual
undertaking of Divine service *wholesomely*.
We may be engaged in an activity that serves
merely as a preparatory bridge to a main task.
Nevertheless, as long as we are engaged with
this particular activity, we must be *fully* invested
in the activity. "This is a fundamental principle
for all situations," he declared, "that wherever
you find yourself, you must be fully present."

TEXT 10

Forward Looking

Talmud, Tamid 32a

אָמַר לָהֶם: אֵידִין מִתְקָרֵי חַכִּים?

אָמְרוּ לֵיה: אֵיזֶהוּ חָכָם, הָרוֹאֶה אֶת הַנּוֹלָד.
birth

Alexander of Macedon said to the elders,
"Who do you consider wise?"

They replied, "Who is wise? Those who see
[anticipate] the consequences [of their behavior]."

The Present Future

Rabbi Shimon ben Tzemach Duran, *Magen Avot* 2:9

TEXT 11

RABBI SHIMON BEN
TZEMACH DURAN
(RASHBATZ)
C. 1361–1444

וְצִוּוּי זֶה אֵינוֹ סוֹתֵר מַה שֶּׁכָּתוּב בְּסֵפֶר בֶּן סִירָא, וְנִזְכַּר בְּפֶרֶק חֵלֶק (סַנְהֶדְרִין ק, ב) וּבְפֶרֶק "הַבָּא עַל יְבִמְתּוֹ" (יְבָמוֹת סג, ב), וְהוּא אָמְרוּ "אַל תָּצֵר עַל צָרַת מָחָר כִּי לֹא תֵדַע מַה יֵּלֶד יוֹם". וְכֵן מַה שֶּׁאָמְרוּ בָּאַחֲרוֹן מִסּוֹטָה (מח, ב): "כָּל מִי שֶׁיֵּשׁ לוֹ פַּת בְּסַלּוֹ וְאוֹמֵר 'מָה אֹכַל מָחָר', הֲרֵי זֶה מִקְטַנֵּי אֲמָנָה".

כִּי יֵשׁ לוֹ לָאָדָם לַחֲשֹׁב עַל הֶעָתִיד וְיִקַּח תַּחְבּוּלָה לְהַצִּיל לוֹ מֵרָעָתוֹ, וּמַה שֶּׁאֵינוֹ בְּיָדוֹ - יִבְטַח בָּאֵ-ל, וְאַל יִדְאַג עָלָיו.

This directive [to anticipate consequences] does not contradict the statement of Ben Sira, quoted in the Talmud (SANHEDRIN 100B), "Grieve not over tomorrow's woes for you know not what a day may bring." It is stated similarly in the Talmud, "Those with bread in their basket for today's meals who say, 'What will I eat tomorrow?' exhibit diminished faith" (SOTAH 48B).

This is no contradiction, because we are supposed to consider the future and set plans in motion that will rescue us from future harm—but concerning that which is *not* within our control, we should have full confidence in G-d and not worry about it.

Physician, poet, rabbi, and philosopher. Duran was a student of philosophy, astronomy, mathematics, and especially of medicine, which he practiced for a number of years in Palma, Spain. He left Spain in the aftermath of the 1391 massacres and moved to Algiers, where, in addition to practicing medicine, he later became the chief rabbi. Among his many works is *Magen Avot*, a philosophical commentary on Tractate Avot.

V. LIVING WITH AWARENESS

The very nature of time is defined by its Divine flow of energy. Time is characterized by change and progress, which is a reflection of changes in the flow of Divine creative energies. This awareness imbues concrete meaning to the units into which we divide time.

It also explains why G-d created us in such a manner that we must constantly draw fresh breaths of air. With the constant arrival of new Divine creative energy—and, consequently, fresh units of time—our souls breathe in life from that fresh life-source along with the oxygen that fills our lungs.

TEXT 12

Sacred Time

Rabbi Shneur Zalman of Liadi, *Tanya, Igeret Hakodesh*, ch. 6

וְכֵן שִׁינּוּיֵי הַזְּמַנִּים בְּעָבָר הֹוֶה וְעָתִיד, וְשִׁינּוּיֵי כָּל הַקּוֹרוֹת בְּחִילוּפֵי הַזְּמַנִּים, הַכֹּל מִשִּׁינּוּיֵי צֵירוּפֵי הָאוֹתִיּוֹת, שֶׁהֵן הֵן הַמְשָׁכַת הַחַיּוּת מִמִּדּוֹתָיו יִתְבָּרַךְ שְׁמוֹ.

The distinctions between the temporal dimensions of past, present, and future, and all the variety of events throughout the progression of time, are determined by differences in the combinations of the letters [of the Divine creative speech], which symbolize the specific Divine creative force that G-d invests in creation.

FIGURE 4.1

Daily Divine Energy

Rabbi Moshe ben Nachman, Ramban, Bereshit 1:3

The world was created through the prism of the seven Divine characteristics (*sefirot*) that were the building blocks of G-d's diverse creation.

	SEFIRAH (DIVINE CHARACTER OF ENERGY)		DAY OF THE WEEK
1	*Chesed*	Kindness / Love	Sunday
2	*Gevurah*	Restraint / Fear	Monday
3	*Tiferet*	Harmony / Compassion	Tuesday
4	*Netzach*	Victory / Ambition	Wednesday
5	*Hod*	Splendor / Humility	Thursday
6	*Yesod*	Connection	Friday
7	*Malchut*	Royalty / Receptiveness	Shabbat

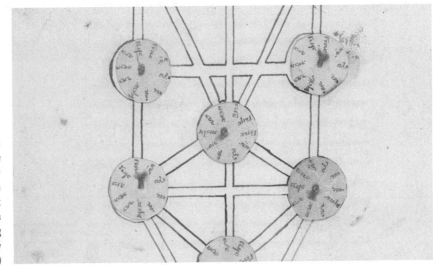

(Detail) Page from a manuscript of *Asis Rimonim*, a 16th-century kabbalistic text written by Shmuel Gallico. It contains several diagrams of the *sefirot*, including this one. (British Library [MS 27091], London)

FIGURE 4.2

Monthly and Hourly Divine Energy

Rabbi Moshe Cordevero, *Pardes Rimonim* 13:3;
Rabbi Shneur Zalman of Liadi, *Tanya, Likutei Amarim*, ch. 41;
Rabbi Yehudah Rosenberg, *Refael Hamalach*, p. 117

**The name of G-d, which symbolizes creation, has four
letters: Y-H-V-H. Each letter of this name is a code
for a different energy form. Mathematically, there
are twenty-four unique ways that these letters can
be rearranged, reflecting twenty-four unique energy
modes. Twelve of those are the root energy for the
months of the year and the daytime hours.**

	COMBINATION OF LETTERS IN DIVINE NAME		MONTH	HOUR OF DAY
1.	יהו"ה	Y-H-V-H	Nisan	1st (6–7 a.m.)
2.	יהה"ו	Y-H-H-V	Iyar	2nd (7–8 a.m.)
3.	יוה"ה	Y-V-H-H	Sivan	3rd (8–9 a.m.)
4.	הוה"י	H-V-H-Y	Tamuz	4th (9–10 a.m.)
5.	הוי"ה	H-V-Y-H	Av	5th (10–11 a.m.)
6.	ההו"י	H-H-V-Y	Elul	6th (11a.m.–12 p.m.)
7.	והי"ה	V-H-Y-H	Tishrei	7th (12–1 p.m.)
8.	והה"י	V-H-H-Y	Cheshvan	8th (1–2 p.m.)
9.	ויה"ה	V-Y-H-H	Kislev	9th (2–3 p.m.)
10.	היה"ו	H-Y-H-V	Tevet	10th (3–4 p.m.)
11.	היו"ה	H-Y-V-H	Shevat	11th (4–5 p.m.)
12.	ההי"ו	H-H-Y-V	Adar	12th (5–6 p.m.)

TEXT 13

Mystical Moments

Rabbi David Shlomo Eibeshitz, *Arvei Nachal*, Bereshit

רַק הָעִנְיָן, נוֹדַע כִּי בְּנֵי יִשָּׂשכָר חִלְּקוּ הַשָּׁעָה לְתתר"ף חֲלָקִים
בְּכַוָּנָה . . . כִּי שֵׁם הוי"ה בָּרוּךְ הוּא מִתְגַּלְגֵּל לְתתר"ף צֵרוּפִים, וּבְכָל
רֶגַע מֵאֵלּוּ הָרְגָעִים מִתְפַּשֵּׁט חַיּוּת חָדָשׁ מִן צֵרוּף חָדָשׁ לְכָל הָעוֹלָמוֹת.

It is known that the sages of the tribe of Issachar
divided the hour into 1,080 parts based on
their awareness . . . that G-d's sacred name can
be combined in 1,080 unique combinations.
In each of these hourly fractions, a new energy
emerges from another of these combinations to
provide creative energy to the entire cosmos.

RABBI DAVID SHLOMO EIBESHITZ 1755–1814

Russian-born author and rabbi. After serving numerous rabbinical posts in Europe, Rabbi Eibeshitz moved to Safed, Israel. His most noted works are *Arvei Nachal*, a Chasidic and kabbalistic commentary on the Torah; and *Levushei Serad*, a commentary to the Code of Jewish Law.

TEXT 14

Fresh Breath of Life

Rabbi David Shlomo Eibeshitz, Ibid.

וּמֵחֲמַת זֶה מֻכְרָח שֶׁיִּהְיֶה תתר"ף נְשִׁימוֹת בְּשָׁעָה, כִּי חַיּוּת
הָעוֹלָמוֹת שֶׁנִּשְׁפַּע מֵהַשֵּׁם יִתְבָּרֵךְ מִשְׁתַּלְשֵׁל מֵעוֹלָם לְעוֹלָם, וְכָל
הַנִּמְצָאִים שׁוֹאֲבִים אוֹתוֹ הַחַיּוּת, כְּמוֹ שֶׁאָמַר הַכָּתוּב (נְחֶמְיָה ט,
ו): "וְאַתָּה מְחַיֶּה אֶת כֻּלָּם", וּבְהִשְׁתַּלְשְׁלוּת לְזֶה הָעוֹלָם נַעֲשָׂה
בָּאָדָם וּבְכָל חַי שֶׁבַּיַּבָּשָׁה רוּחַ, שֶׁהוּא נִשְׁמָה שֶׁמְּנַשֵּׁם הָאָדָם
לְקִרְבּוֹ, שֶׁזֶּהוּ חַיּוּתוֹ. וְלָכֵן, לְפִי שֶׁבְּכָל רֶגַע יֵשׁ חַיּוּת חָדָשׁ, לָכֵן
צָרִיךְ נְשִׁימָה חֲדָשָׁה שֶׁיְּקַבֵּל רוּחַ הַחַיִּים הַמִּתְפַּשֵּׁט בָּרֶגַע הַזֶּה,
כִּי לֹא יִחְיֶה בָּרֶגַע הַזֶּה עַל יְדֵי הַחַיּוּת שֶׁקִּבֵּל בָּרֶגַע הַקּוֹדֶמֶת, כִּי
עַתָּה כְּבָר נַעֲשָׂה חַיּוּת חָדָשׁ וְהַנְהָגָה חֲדָשָׁה בְּכָל הָעוֹלָמוֹת מִצֵרוּף
חָדָשׁ, כָּךְ מִתְנַהֵג כָּל יְמֵי עוֹלָם, מֵרֵאשִׁית הַבְּרִיאָה עַד סוֹף.

The reason why we must breathe constantly, at an approximate rate of 1,080 breaths an hour, is that the Divine energy pulsates throughout all the spiritual worlds and energizes everything, as the verse states [using the present, ongoing tense], "You give life to all things" (NEHEMIAH 9:6). As this energy arrives in our physical universe, it manifests within humans and within every breathing creature in the air that we breathe, which provides life as we draw it into ourselves. Because a fresh burst of Divine energy is released at each moment, we need to continuously breathe to absorb the fresh spirit of life that is now radiating forth from G-d. We cannot remain animated in the present moment with the energy of the previous moment, since the world has moved on to a new energy and a fresh dynamic that has redefined all of existence. This is the way the world operated since its creation, and this is how it will continue until the end of time.

Bereshit—"in the beginning"—is the opening word of Genesis and the account of creation. In this detail from a 14th-century parchment manuscript of the Torah from Spain, the word is artfully illuminated in gold with two crowns above it. (Braginsky Collection, Zurich)

TEXT 15

Praiseworthy Breaths

Rabbi Eliyahu de Vidas, *Reshit Chochmah*, Gate of Awe, ch. 10

**RABBI ELIYAHU DE VIDAS
1518–1592**

Born in Safed; he is
considered one of the
prominent kabbalists
of the 16th century. A
student of Rabbi Moshe
Cordovero and Rabbi
Yitzchak Luria, he is
best known as the author
of *Reshit Chochmah,* a
compendium of moral
teachings culled from
various sources in the
Talmud, Midrash,
and *Zohar*. He is
buried in Hebron.

וְעוֹד פֵּרְשׁוּ, כִּי יֵשׁ תתר"ף חֲלָקִים בְּשָׁעָה,
וּכְנֶגְדָּם שֵׁם בֶּן ד' הַמִּתְגַּלְגֵּל בְּצֵרוּף נְקוּדוֹ בְּאַלְפָּא בֵּיתָא
תתר"ף צֵרוּפִין. וְאָמַר שֶׁתתר"ף חֲלָקִים אֵלּוּ שֶׁבְּשָׁעָה, הֵם
תתר"ף נְשִׁימוֹת שֶׁאָדָם מְנַשֵּׁם, וְעַל כָּל נְשִׁימָה וּנְשִׁימָה
יֵשׁ אוֹת מִשֵּׁם בֶּן ד' הַנּוֹתֵן בּוֹ חַיּוּת הַנְּשִׁימָה הַהִיא, וְזֶהוּ
"כִּי עַל כָּל מוֹצָא פִי ה' יִחְיֶה הָאָדָם" (דְּבָרִים ח, ג).

וְכֵיָון שֶׁהַשֵּׁם יִתְבָּרַךְ הוּא הַנּוֹתֵן הַנְּשִׁימָה וְהַחַיִּים,
רָאוּי שֶׁיִּהְיוּ כָּל נְשִׁימוֹתָיו לַעֲבוֹדַת הַבּוֹרֵא. וְלָזֶה כִּוְּנוּ רַבּוֹתֵינוּ
ז"ל בִּבְרֵאשִׁית רַבָּה (פָּרָשָׁה יד) בְּפָסוּק (תְּהִלִּים קנ, ו) "כָּל
הַנְּשָׁמָה תְּהַלֵּל יָ-הּ", רַבִּי לֵוִי בְּשֵׁם רַבִּי חֲנִינָא אָמַר: עַל כָּל
נְשִׁימָה וּנְשִׁימָה שֶׁהוּא נוֹשֵׁם, צָרִיךְ לְקַלֵּס לְהַקָּדוֹשׁ בָּרוּךְ
הוּא, שֶׁנֶּאֱמַר: "כָּל הַנְּשָׁמָה תְּהַלֵּל יָ-הּ", עַד כָּאן לְשׁוֹנוֹ.

וּכְשֶׁיִּסְתַּכֵּל הָאָדָם בַּדָּבָר הַזֶּה, יִּירָא מִלַּחֲטֹא, וְיִנְהַג
בְּעַצְמוֹ עֲנָוָה וְשִׁפְלוּת; כִּי אֵיךְ יֶחֱטָא וְיָקֵל רֹאשׁוֹ בַּחַיִּים
שֶׁהַשֵּׁם יִתְבָּרַךְ מֶלֶךְ מַלְכֵי הַמְּלָכִים מַשְׁפִּיעַ בּוֹ?

It is explained that there are 1,080 parts to an
hour, which reflect the 1,080 permutations of
the Divine name. These 1,080 hour fragments
also reflect the 1,080 breaths that we breathe
each hour. With each breath, we inhale life-
giving energy from another specific element
of the Divine name, as indicated in the verse,
"From that which emerges from the mouth of
G-d a person lives" (DEUTERONOMY 8:3).

Now, seeing that it is G-d who gives us breath and life, our every breath should be directed toward serving G-d. This is the intent of the Midrash (*BERESHIT RABAH* 14), which explains the verse, "Every soul [*neshamah*] will praise You" (PSALMS 150:6), as follows: "Rabbi Levi quoted Rabbi Chaninah as having stated that with each breath [*neshimah*] that we draw in, we should praise G-d."

If we reflect on this, we will be afraid to sin, and we will conduct ourselves with humility and unpretentiousness. After all, how can we transgress or act frivolously with the life that G-d is giving us *at this very moment*?

EXERCISE 4.2

How can I apply the meditation that I discovered today in my life?

VI. TAKEAWAY

It takes consistent practice and ongoing meditation to develop this perspective and live completely invested in each moment. At the same time, every breath is another active reminder of this meditation, and an opportunity to reflect on it.

HITALUT: **ELEVATION**
Yehoshua Wiseman, Israel.

FIGURE 4.3 Mechanisms of Mindfulness

Mindfulness achieves its therapeutic effects by fostering "reperceiving": the ability to stand back, as it were, from one's thoughts and emotions and view them objectively. Once a person adopts this distanced perspective, thoughts and emotions that would otherwise be distressing are instead able to be viewed dispassionately, and decisions can be made on a reflective basis rather than as mere reactions to internal states. This allows for better self-regulation, better decision-making, and an enhanced ability to tolerate negative thoughts and emotions.[1]

Here are five self-reported processes of mindfulness that, drawing from a large pool of individuals, were described as productive in dealing with and regulating negative thoughts and emotions.

1. Shapiro, S. L., et al., "Mechanism of Mindfulness," *Journal of Clinical Psychology* 62 (2006), pp. 373–386.

The Five Facets of Mindfulness[2]

OBSERVING

Noticing subtle internal states—such as thoughts, emotions, and bodily sensations—was positively correlated with openness to new experiences, emotional intelligence, and self-compassion.

DESCRIBING

Describing one's own internal states such as beliefs, emotions, or bodily sensations was positively correlated with both emotional intelligence and the ability to recognize varying emotions in oneself and others.

ACTING WITH AWARENESS

Paying attention to one's actions while doing them made one less likely to experience (was negatively correlated with) memory disruption, absentmindedness, and unawareness of one's own internal states.

NOT JUDGING INNER EXPERIENCES

Withholding evaluative judgments about one's own thoughts and feelings reduced the likelihood of experiencing (was negatively correlated with) neuroticism, thought suppression, and difficulty regulating emotions.

NON-REACTIVITY

Noticing one's thoughts and feelings without reacting to them was positively correlated with experiencing self-compassion while suffering or experiencing painful thoughts.

2. Baer, R., et al., "Using Self-Report Assessment Methods to Explore Facets of Mindfulness," *Assessment*, 13 (2006), pp. 27–45.

KEY POINTS

1   To overcome the feeling of being scattered and unfocused, we have to slow down in life and be present in each moment.

2   The world is recreated by G-d every moment, with a fresh and unique creative energy.

3   Every moment is invested with a unique purpose and is valuable in its own right, not only as a lead-up to some future moment.

4   Being fully invested in the present moment doesn't negate our responsibilities to the past and future; whatever impact the present can have on the past and future is part of the purpose of the present and is relevant to this current moment.

5   The units that we use to divide time reflect a change in the Divine flow of creative energy.

6   We have to continuously breathe to take in life from the new creative energy that is animating the world at each moment. Each breath is an opportunity to recognize the sacred purpose that G-d is investing in that moment.

"Don't Worry— Be Happy!"
The Jewish Version

A popular antidote for anxiety is to focus intensely on the present. As mentioned in the lesson, a much-loved Jewish refrain (translated from concise Hebrew rhyme) is, "The past is no longer here. The future has yet to appear. In a blink the present will disappear. So, what case is there for fear?" That is easy to say, but it requires a fair amount of mindfulness to sufficiently live in the moment. Nevertheless, as we have learned, it is eminently doable.

The concept of focusing on the present was delivered in several formats in the homiletical explanations of Torah passages and of statements found in the Talmud and the Midrash. Several of these are presented here:

YOU CAN ONLY HOLD ON TO SO MUCH ROPE

Behold, You set my days as mere handbreadths, and my advanced age is like nothing before You. Surely all vanity is in each individual—that is their permanent condition.

(Psalms 39:6)

King David compares the human lifespan to an entity short enough to be measured with one's hands ("handbreadths"). His choice of analogy is profound, for although the many days of your life are akin to a lengthy rope, nevertheless, try as you might, you can only hold on to a single handbreadth of it at any given time. The past is over, what is yet to come is certainly not in your hands, and in reality, all that is in your hands is the present—a brief sliver of rope indeed. So, place your trust in G-d and don't worry about the rest!

—Rabbi Simchah Bunim of Peshischa, cited in Rabbi Yerachmiel Danziger, *Yismach Yisrael* (Bamidbar, section 1)

"Don't Worry—Be Happy!" *continued*

A TIMELY INTERJECTION

And now, do not be depressed or deeply disturbed at having sold me here, for it was for the sake of saving lives that G-d sent me before you.

(Genesis 45:5)

So declared Joseph to his brothers, immediately after dropping the shocking revelation that he was indeed their long lost brother. As they stood speechless, drenched in shame, Joseph addressed them nobly, insisting that they should not consider themselves guilty of selling him into slavery because it was clearly orchestrated by G-d, Who wanted Joseph brought to Egypt to save the region from starvation.

What is the significance of Joseph interrupting his flow of speech with the interjection, "And now . . ." before urging his brothers to avoid feeling depressed?

His interjection contains the secret to understanding the following words, "do not be depressed or deeply disturbed." The way to avoid sadness—even when it seems an appropriate response—is to focus exclusively on the "now."

—Rabbi Shaul Brauch, cited in Rabbi Aharon Perlow (ed.), *Otzrotoheim Shel Tzadikim al Hatorah*, Vayigash, p. 125

CHASING TOMORROW

The misery of those who hurry [to worship an] alternative [deity] will increase.

(Psalms 16:4)

The Hebrew term *acher*, "alternative," can also be read *achar*, "that which comes after," leaving us with the following message: Who is sure to experience an increase in misery and despondency? Those who "hurry after"—they mentally run ahead, worrying about what might happen after the present time has elapsed. By contrast, those who live in the present and avoid fretting over what might come "after" are happier and free of sorrow.

—Rabbi Yisrael of Ruzhin, cited in Rabbi David Yehoshua Rosenwald (ed.), *Imrot Tehorot, Tehilim*, p. 63

LESSON FOUR **143**

I AM ALIVE

You who cleave to the L-rd your G-d are alive, all of you, this day.

(Deuteronomy 4:4)

This verse offers direction for successfully cleaving to G-d and living free of worry. It urges us to focus on the blessed reality that we "are alive … this day." We cannot know what tomorrow will bring, but today we are alive—and must focus on living today.

—Rabbi Yosef Waknin, *U'le Yosef Amar*, vol. 1, Va'etchanan, p. 304

ABUSING THE MOMENT

For they do not speak peace, and against the crushed people of the earth they think words of deceit.

(Psalms 35:20)

The verse employs a rare Hebrew adjective for "crushed"—*rig'ei eretz* ("the crushed of the earth"). The root of *rig'ei* is *raga* which also means "a moment" (*rega*), allowing for the following interpretation: An individual who pursues strife and deceit is failing to appreciate the immense value of the present moment.

So many waste so much of their lives wheeling and dealing, conniving their passage from one stage to the next. In truth, they act out of fear for their futures, but they fail to comprehend that there is no cause for concern—all that is relevant is the present moment. Why try so hard to manipulate a future that in truth is beyond reach?

—Rabbi Baruch of Mezhibuzh, cited in Rabbi Yosef Reuven Zlatopler (ed.), *Zechuyot Yosef*, p. 68

KNOW THIS DAY

You shall know this day and consider it in your heart, that the L-rd He is G-d in Heaven above, and upon the earth below—there is none else.

(Deuteronomy 4:39)

The first step toward knowing G-d and trusting Him is to set your focus exclusively on "this day"—today. The rest flows from there.

—Rabbi Moshe Leib of Sassov, cited in Rabbi Yehudah Treitel Samet (ed.), *Tov Lehodot*, ch. 15, p. 400

JACOB'S BLESSING

Jacob blessed them—on that day—saying: With you, Israel will bless [their children], saying: May G-d make you like Ephraim and like Manasseh!

(Genesis 48:20)

It seems unnecessary for the Torah to emphasize that Jacob's blessings were delivered "on that day"—unless the phrase "on that day" is also part of Jacob's blessing: He invested Ephraim and Manasseh with the ability to develop their trust in G-d to the extent that on each day of their lives, their focus would be exclusively "on that day," so that they would invest themselves fully in the present.

—Rabbi Moshe Leib of Sassov, *Likutei Ramal, Parshat Vayechi, s.v. "Ve'yevarech"*

THE JOY OF NOW

Then Moses and the Children of Israel sang this song to the L-rd, and they spoke, saying: I will sing to the L-rd, for very exalted is He; a horse and its rider He cast into the sea!

(Exodus 15:1)

The Midrash observes that the Hebrew word *az* ("then") always indicates joy (Midrash, *Shemot Rabah* 23:4). However, the Midrash fails to explain the association between the adverb "then" and human happiness.

We can suggest that joy stems from focusing on the present, to the exclusion of reliving past concerns or fretting over future worries. If we focus on "then"—at that time, in whichever moment in question we happen to find ourselves—we will experience joy.

—Rabbi Shlomo Yehudah Tabak, *Erech Shai*, Pesach, p. 108

MIND YOUR BUSINESS
Reframing the Routine

Most of us dispense the majority of our time on the mundane grind of daily living. That sounds antithetical to spiritual living, but this lesson demonstrates that meditation can reframe every part of life and inject profound spiritual meaning into the most mundane activities. With the proper mindset and intention, simple behaviors like working, eating, and sleeping are transformed into purposeful and spiritually significant acts.

I. JEWISH MINDFULNESS: CHANGE YOUR LIFE

In previous lessons we explored spiritual ideas that are accessible through meditation. This lesson moves from thought and feeling to practical living, discovering ways of bringing the Divine fruits of our meditation to bear in mundane arenas such as eating, sleeping, and working.

TEXT 1A

Know G-d Everywhere

Proverbs 3:6

בְּכָל דְּרָכֶיךָ דָעֵהוּ,
וְהוּא יְיַשֵּׁר אֹרְחֹתֶיךָ.

Know G-d in all your ways,
and He will direct your paths.

PROVERBS

Biblical book. The book of Proverbs appears in the "Writings" section of the Bible and contains the wise teachings, aphorisms, and parables of King Solomon, who lived in the 9th century BCE. The ethical teachings of Proverbs give counsel about overcoming temptation, extol the value of hard work, laud the pursuit of knowledge, and emphasize loyalty to G-d and His commandments as the foundation of true wisdom.

JEWISH LIFE IN SHTETL
Alex Levin, oil on canvas

TEXT 1B

A Fundamental Principle

Talmud, Berachot 63a

דָּרַשׁ בַּר קַפָּרָא: אֵיזוֹהִי פָּרָשָׁה קְטַנָּה שֶׁכָּל גּוּפֵי תוֹרָה תְּלוּיִין בָּהּ? "בְּכָל דְּרָכֶיךָ דָעֵהוּ, וְהוּא יְיַשֵּׁר אֹרְחֹתֶיךָ" (מִשְׁלֵי ג, ו).

Bar Kapara taught: "Which is a brief passage upon which all fundamental principles of Torah are dependent? 'Know G-d in all your ways, and He will direct your paths'" (PROVERBS 3:6).

BABYLONIAN TALMUD

A literary work of monumental proportions that draws upon the legal, spiritual, intellectual, ethical, and historical traditions of Judaism. The 37 tractates of the Babylonian Talmud contain the teachings of the Jewish sages from the period after the destruction of the 2nd Temple through the 5th century CE. It has served as the primary vehicle for the transmission of the Oral Law and the education of Jews over the centuries; it is the entry point for all subsequent legal, ethical, and theological Jewish scholarship.

Page from the Munich Codex Hebraicus 95, a manuscript of the Babylonian Talmud copied in 1342. This page is the beginning of Tractate Brachot. (Bavarian State Library)

TEXT 2

The Totality of Your Behavior

Maimonides, *Mishneh Torah*, Laws of Character Development 3:2

**RABBI MOSHE
BEN MAIMON
(MAIMONIDES, RAMBAM)
1135–1204**

צָרִיךְ הָאָדָם שֶׁיְכַוֵּן לִבּוֹ וְכָל מַעֲשָׂיו כֻּלָּם לֵידַע אֶת הַשֵּׁם בָּרוּךְ
הוּא בִּלְבַד, וְיִהְיֶה שִׁבְתּוֹ וְקוּמוֹ וְדִבּוּרוֹ - הַכֹּל לְעֻמַּת זֶה הַדָּבָר.

כֵּיצַד? כְּשֶׁיִּשָּׂא וְיִתֵּן אוֹ יַעֲשֶׂה מְלָאכָה לִטֹל שָׂכָר, לֹא יִהְיֶה בְּלִבּוֹ
לִקְבֹּץ מָמוֹן בִּלְבַד, אֶלָּא יַעֲשֶׂה דְבָרִים הָאֵלּוּ כְּדֵי שֶׁיִּמְצָא דְבָרִים
שֶׁהַגּוּף צָרִיךְ לָהֶם, מֵאֲכִילָה וּשְׁתִיָּה, וִישִׁיבַת בַּיִת וּנְשִׂיאַת אִשָּׁה.

וְכֵן כְּשֶׁיֹּאכַל וְיִשְׁתֶּה וְיִבְעַל, לֹא יָשִׂים עַל לִבּוֹ לַעֲשׂוֹת דְּבָרִים
הַלָּלוּ כְּדֵי לֵהָנוֹת בִּלְבַד, עַד שֶׁנִּמְצָא שֶׁאֵינוֹ אוֹכֵל וְשׁוֹתֶה
אֶלָּא הַמָּתוֹק לַחֵךְ וְיִבְעַל כְּדֵי לֵהָנוֹת, אֶלָּא יָשִׂים עַל לִבּוֹ
כְּשֶׁיֹּאכַל וְיִשְׁתֶּה כְּדֵי לְהַבְרוֹת גּוּפוֹ וְאֵבָרָיו בִּלְבַד.

לְפִיכָךְ לֹא יֹאכַל כָּל שֶׁהַחֵךְ מִתְאַוֶּה כְּמוֹ הַכֶּלֶב וְהַחֲמוֹר,
אֶלָּא יֹאכַל דְּבָרִים הַמּוֹעִילִין לוֹ, אִם מָרִים אִם מְתוּקִים. וְלֹא
יֹאכַל דְּבָרִים הָרָעִים לַגּוּף, אַף עַל פִּי שֶׁהֵן מְתוּקִין לַחֵךְ.

We should direct our hearts and the totality of our behavior to one goal: becoming aware of G-d, blessed be He. The way we rest, rise, and converse should all be directed to this end.

For example, when involved in business dealings or while working for a wage, we should not think solely of amassing wealth. Rather, we should engage in such activities for the sake of being in a position to obtain that which our body needs—food, drink, shelter, and a spouse.

Then, when we eat, drink, or engage in intimate relations, we should not intend to do these things

Halachist, philosopher, author, and physician. Maimonides was born in Córdoba, Spain. After the conquest of Córdoba by the Almohads, he fled Spain and eventually settled in Cairo, Egypt. There, he became the leader of the Jewish community and served as court physician to the vizier of Egypt. He is most noted for authoring the *Mishneh Torah*, an encyclopedic arrangement of Jewish law; and for his philosophical work, *Guide for the Perplexed*. His rulings on Jewish law are integral to the formation of halachic consensus.

solely for pleasure—to the point that we eat and
drink only that which is sweet and tasty, and we
engage in intimacy for pleasure. Rather, we should
focus our minds while eating and drinking on the
exclusive benefit of maintaining a fully healthy body.

Therefore, we should not eat whatever the
palate desires—which would put us on par with
animals—but rather, we should select foods that
are beneficial for the body, whether they are bitter
or sweet. And we should avoid substances that are
harmful to the body, even if they taste delicious.

Introduction to Maimonides's *Mishneh Torah* (Detail).
This manuscript, one of the most elaborate copies
of the *Mishneh Torah*, is believed to have been
written in Spain or Southern France in the first half
of the fourteenth century, with the artwork done in
Spain and Italy. (From the collection of the National
Library of Israel [MS. HEB. 4*1193], Jerusalem)

II. EAT

The banal act of consuming food seems to be a mostly mindless and purely carnal experience. By being mindful of the G-dly energy within food while consuming it, we can successfully transform each act of consumption into a spiritual exercise.

EXERCISE 5.1

Jot down your preferred food for each of the following:

Breakfast yogurt, oatmeal, & fruit

Dinner Date fish & potato & toast salad

Snack toast

Comfort Food mac n cheese

Dessert ice cream

You are stuck on a deserted island, without a clue as to when you might be rescued. Identify the one food that you want to have with you:

yogurt

TEXT 3

Fingers on the Bread

Rabbi Yaakov ben Asher, *Arbaah Turim, Orach Chayim* 167

**RABBI
YAAKOV BEN ASHER
(*TUR*, BAAL HATURIM)
C. 1269 – C. 1343**

 Halachic authority and codifier. Rabbi Yaakov was born in Germany and moved to Toledo, Spain, with his father, the noted halachist Rabbi Asher, to escape persecution. He wrote *Arbaah Turim ("Tur"),* an ingeniously organized and highly influential code of Jewish law. He is considered one of the greatest authorities on Halachah.

יִתֵּן שְׁתֵּי יָדָיו עַל הַפַּת, שֶׁיֵּשׁ בָּהֶן י' אֶצְבָּעוֹת כְּנֶגֶד י' מִצְוֹת
הַתְּלוּיוֹת בַּפַּת: לֹא תַחֲרשׁ בְּשׁוֹר וּבַחֲמֹר, כִּלְאַיִם, לֶקֶט, שִׁכְחָה,
פֵּאָה, בִּכּוּרִים, תְּרוּמָה, מַעֲשֵׂר רִאשׁוֹן, מַעֲשֵׂר שֵׁנִי, חַלָּה.

[Before reciting the blessing over bread,] put both your hands on the bread, for your ten fingers reflect the ten *mitzvot* associated with bread making. They are: to avoid plowing with two species of animals together; to avoid growing forbidden mixtures of plant species [*kilayim*]; to leave *leket, shikchah,* and *pe'ah* [three distinct forms of overlooked harvest] for the poor to collect; to bring the first fruit [*bikurim*] to Jerusalem; to donate the *terumah* tithe to a *Kohen*; to observe the rites of the *maaser rishon* and *maaser sheni* tithes; and to donate a portion of dough [*challah*] to a *Kohen*.

The Hispano-Moresque Haggadah, from Castile, Spain, c. 1300, has many beautiful full-page miniatures, textual illustrations, and initial-word panels decorated with gold letters. Depicted here is a Passover matzah baking scene. (British Museum [OR 2737], London)

[handwritten annotations: "choke – we can't comprehend the mitzvot", "Kosher means redeemable", "we can access the spiritual energy conscious of the godly spark in the food", "we have the ability to make eating a transformative experience"]

Why We Eat

TEXT 4A

Rabbi Yisrael Baal Shem Tov, *Keter Shem Tov* 194

RABBI YISRAEL BAAL SHEM TOV (BESHT) 1698–1760

Founder of the Chasidic movement. Born in Slutsk, Belarus, the Baal Shem Tov was orphaned as a child. He served as a teacher's assistant and clay digger before founding the Chasidic movement and revolutionizing the Jewish world with his emphasis on prayer, joy, and love for every Jew, regardless of his or her level of Torah knowledge.

כְּשֶׁאָמַר "תּוֹצֵא הָאָרֶץ נֶפֶשׁ חַיָּה" (בְּרֵאשִׁית א, כד) אוֹ "תּוֹצֵא הָאָרֶץ דֶּשֶׁא . . . וְעֵץ פְּרִי" (שָׁם, יב), אוֹתוֹ הַמַּאֲמָר הָיָה מְהַוֶּה הַכֹּל, וְהַמַּאֲמָר הַזֶּה הוּא חַיּוּת פְּנִימִי לָהֶם.

וּכְשֶׁנּוֹטֵל אָדָם פְּרִי אוֹ דְּבַר מַאֲכָל וּמְבָרֵךְ עָלָיו בְּכַוָּנָה וְאוֹמֵר "בָּרוּךְ אַתָּה ה'", כְּשֶׁמַּזְכִּיר אֶת הַשֵּׁם, מִתְעוֹרֵר אוֹתוֹ הַחַיּוּת שֶׁעַל יָדוֹ נִבְרָא הַפְּרִי הַהוּא, כִּי נִבְרָא הַכֹּל עַל יְדֵי הַשֵּׁם, וּמוֹצֵא מִין אֶת מִינוֹ וְנֵעוֹר. וְזֶה הַחַיּוּת הוּא מָזוֹן הַנְּשָׁמָה.

וְכָל זֶה בַּמַּאֲכָלִים הַמֻּתָּרִים וּכְשֵׁרִים, שֶׁצִּוָּה הַקָּדוֹשׁ בָּרוּךְ הוּא לְהַעֲלוֹתָן מִגַּשְׁמִיּוּת לְרוּחָנִיּוּת . . .

וְזֶהוּ שֶׁכָּתוּב . . . "כִּי לֹא עַל הַלֶּחֶם לְבַדּוֹ יִחְיֶה הָאָדָם, כִּי עַל כָּל מוֹצָא פִי ה' יִחְיֶה הָאָדָם" (דְּבָרִים ח, ג): פֵּרוּשׁ כְּשֶׁאַתָּה מוֹצִיא הַשֵּׁם בְּכַוָּנָה עַל יְדֵי הַבְּרָכָה שֶׁבֵּרַכְתָּ עָלָיו, שֶׁעַל יְדֵי זֶה מִתְעוֹרֵר בּוֹ הָרוּחָנִיּוּת - מִזֶּה יִחְיֶה הָאָדָם, שֶׁהִיא הַנְּשָׁמָה, נִזּוֹנֵית מֵרוּחָנִיּוּת הַמַּאֲכָלִים.

When G-d declared, "Let the earth give forth living souls!" or "Let the earth produce vegetation and fruit trees!" (GENESIS 1:24, 12)—those very words created everything. And those same utterances *continue* to function as the inner life of that which was created through them.

When we take a fruit or any food and recite a blessing over it with proper intent, articulating the words, "Blessed are you, G-d"—mentioning G-d's sacred Name—the spiritual energy responsible for bringing that fruit into existence is activated. This occurs because everything was created through the Divine Name, and our articulation of G-d's Name in the blessing awakens the Divine energy that flows from G-d's Name within the fruit. Then, the awakened energy within the fruit provides spiritual sustenance for our own soul.

This can only work with kosher food— substances that G-d Himself directed us to sublimate from mundane to Divine. . . .

This is the deeper significance of the verse . . . "Know that a person does not live by bread alone, but rather by whatever comes forth from the mouth of G-d does a person live" (DEUTERONOMY 8:3). It is not the physical bread alone that supports life. Rather, when we utter G-d's Name in a blessing and activate the spiritual energy, that is what gives life to "a person," or more precisely, to the soul that animates us.

This drawing is from a book of Birkat Hamazon (Grace after Meals) and other blessings written and decorated on parchment by Samuel ben Zwi Hirsch Dresnitz, Nikolsburg (today Czech Republic), in 1725. The blessing recited on fruits is depicted. (Braginsky Collection, Zurich)

Finding the Lost Gem

Rabbi Yisrael Baal Shem Tov, Ibid.

וְהַמָּשָׁל לְמֶלֶךְ שֶׁנֶּאֶבְדָה לוֹ אֶבֶן טוֹב מִתּוֹךְ טַבַּעְתּוֹ . . . כִּי רָצָה לְזַכּוֹת אֶת בְּנוֹ חֲבִיבוֹ, וּכְדֵי שֶׁיִּקָּרֵא הַמְצִיאָה עַל שְׁמוֹ. וְלֹא עוֹד, אֶלָּא גַם רָמַז לִבְנוֹ חֲבִיבוֹ בְּכַמָּה רְמָזִים מְקוֹם מְצִיאוּתוֹ, כִּי מִתְּחִלָּה הָיְתָה הָאֲבֵדָה מִדַּעַת הַמֶּלֶךְ אֶת מְקוֹמָהּ, וְעָשָׂה הַכֹּל רַק לְמַעַן לְזַכּוֹת אֶת בְּנוֹ חֲבִיבוֹ, וּכְדֵי שֶׁיַּגִּיעַ גַם לְהַמֶּלֶךְ מִזֶּה גֹדֶל שַׁעֲשׁוּעַ וְהִתְפָּאֲרוּת מִבְּנוֹ, לֵאמֹר: רְאוּ כִּי שׁוּם בֶּן אָדָם בָּעוֹלָם לֹא הָיָה יָכוֹל לַחֲפֹשׂ וְלִמְצֹא זוּלַת בְּנוֹ חֲבִיבוֹ.

וְהַנִּמְשָׁל מוּבָן, שֶׁתְּחִלַּת בְּרִיאַת הָעוֹלָמוֹת הָיָה כְּדֵי לְבָרֵר הַנִּצוֹצִין קַדִּישִׁין עַל יְדֵי אֻמָּה יִשְׂרְאֵלִית, כְּמוֹ שֶׁנֶּאֱמַר "בִּשְׁבִיל יִשְׂרָאֵל שֶׁנִּקְרְאוּ רֵאשִׁית", שֶׁעַל יָדָם יְבָרְרוּ מִמַּאֲכָלִים מֻתָּרִים וּכְשֵׁרִים.

וְזֶהוּ שֶׁאָמַר ר' יִשְׂרָאֵל בַּעַל שֵׁם עַל פָּסוּק "רְעֵבִים גַם צְמֵאִים, נַפְשָׁם בָּהֶם תִּתְעַטָּף" (תְּהִלִּים קז, ה), פֵּרוּשׁ, בְּכָאן סוֹד גָּדוֹל [וְנוֹרָא], וְהוּא: לָמָּה בָּרָא הַקָּדוֹשׁ בָּרוּךְ הוּא דְּבָרֵי מַאֲכָל וּמַשְׁקֶה שֶׁאָדָם תָּאֵב לָהֶם [לֶאֱכֹל וְלִשְׁתּוֹת]?

וְהַטַּעַם שֶׁהֵם [מַמָּשׁ נִיצוֹצוֹת אָדָם הָרִאשׁוֹן שֶׁהֵם] מִתְלַבְּשִׁים בְּדוֹמֵם צוֹמֵחַ חַי מְדַבֵּר, וְיֵשׁ לָהֶם חֵשֶׁק לְהִדָּבֵק בִּקְדֻשָּׁה, וְהֵם מְעוֹרְרִים מַיִן נוּקְבִין בְּסוֹד "אֵין טִפָּה יוֹרְדָה מִלְמַעְלָה שֶׁאֵין טִפַּיִם עוֹלִים כְּנֶגְדָּהּ". וְכָל אֲכִילָה [וּשְׁתִיָּה] שֶׁאָדָם אֹכֵל וְשׁוֹתֶה, הִיא מַמָּשׁ חֵלֶק נִיצוֹצוֹת שֶׁלּוֹ שֶׁהוּא צָרִיךְ לְתַקֵּן. וְזֶהוּ שֶׁכָּתוּב "רְעֵבִים גַם צְמֵאִים", כְּשֶׁאָדָם רָעֵב וְצָמֵא לָהֶם, לָמָּה זֶה? [וְזֶהוּ שֶׁכָּתוּב] "נַפְשָׁם בָּהֶם תִּתְעַטָּף", בְּסוֹד גָּלוּת [בִּלְבוּשֵׁי זָרִים], "וַיַּחְשְׁבֶהָ לְזוֹנָה כִּי כִסְּתָה פָּנֶיהָ" (בְּרֵאשִׁית לח, טו), וְכָל הַדְּבָרִים שֶׁהֵם מְשַׁמְּשִׁין לָאָדָם הֵם מַמָּשׁ בְּסוֹד הַבָּנִים שֶׁלּוֹ שֶׁהִלְבִּישׁוֹ, וְהָבֵן.

וְהַשֵּׁם יִתְבָּרַךְ רָמַז לָהֶם לְיִשְׂרָאֵל בְּכַמָּה רְמָזִים שֶׁיִּמְצְאוּ הָאֲבֵדָה וְיַחְזְרוּ לְבַעֲלֵיהֶם, לַאֲבִיהֶם שֶׁבַּשָּׁמַיִם. וְלֹא צִוָּה כֵן לַמַּלְאָכִים וּשְׂרָפִים וְאוֹפַנִּים, וְהָאֲבֵדָה הַהוּא מִדַּעַת הָיְתָה, כְּמַאֲמַר רַבּוֹתֵינוּ ז"ל שֶׁהָיָה בּוֹנֶה עוֹלָמוֹת וּמַחֲרִיבָן.

An analogy: A king once lost a precious gem
... and wished his beloved son to have the great
honor of being the one to successfully locate the
gem. In truth, the gem was not lost; the king knew
where it had been concealed, but engineered
the ploy to give his beloved son the opportunity
of earning it. The king also wanted the distinct
pleasure of witnessing his son's hard-earned
success. . . . The king went so far as to drop his
son a hint as to where the stone could be found.

The analog is clear: The entire purpose for
which G-d created this world is to enable us to
retrieve the Divine sparks that are lost within
materiality—for we are empowered to sublimate
all kosher and permissible food items.

On this theme, the Baal Shem Tov revealed a
fascinating mystical truth embedded in the
verse, "Hungry as well as thirsty, their soul
enwraps itself in them" (PSALMS 107:5). These
words come to answer the question, "Why
did G-d create us with a craving for food and
make our survival dependent on eating?"

The answer is that there are Divine sparks
trapped in material entities. These sparks long
to cleave to holiness; they call out for assistance,
and our souls hear their call and respond to their
plight. Whenever we eat or drink, we sublimate

the Divine sparks in the food or drink that have called out to us to achieve spiritual elevation through us. Thus, the mystical meaning of the verse is this: "Hungry as well as thirsty"—Why do we experience hunger or thirst?—"Their soul enwraps itself in them"—because the soul [Divine spark] is trapped within them [the food], in a state of exile, and seeks liberation.

G-d leaves hints for the Jewish people, indicating the various ways through which we will discover the lost entities [Divine sparks] and return them to their rightful Owner, our Father in Heaven.

THE FEAST OF THE REJOICING OF THE LAW AT THE SYNAGOGUE IN LEGHORN, ITALY
Solomon Alexander Hart (1806–1881), oil on canvas, 1850, England. The first Jewish member of the Royal Academy, Hart portrays the intricacy and beauty of the Italian Jewish culture in this painting of The Torah being paraded by exotically dressed Jews in the lavish synagogue in Leghorn, (Livorno), Italy, on the holiday of Simchat Torah. (The Jewish Museum, New York)

TEXT 5

Eating Like a Sacrifice

Rabbi Shneur Zalman of Liadi, *Tanya*, *Likutei Amarim*, ch. 7

**RABBI SHNEUR
ZALMAN OF LIADI
(ALTER REBBE)
1745–1812**

 Chasidic
rebbe, halachic
authority, and founder of
the Chabad movement.
The Alter Rebbe was
born in Liozna, Belarus,
and was among the
principal students of the
Magid of Mezeritch. His
numerous works include
the *Tanya*, an early
classic containing the
fundamentals of Chabad
Chasidism; and *Shulchan
Aruch Harav*, an
expanded and reworked
code of Jewish law.

הָאוֹכֵל בְּשָׂרָא שְׁמֵנָא דְתוֹרָא וְשׁוֹתֶה יַיִן מְבֻשָּׂם לְהַרְחִיב
דַּעְתּוֹ לַה' וּלְתוֹרָתוֹ, כִּדְאָמַר רָבָא: "חַמְרָא וְרֵיחָא כוּ'", אוֹ
בִּשְׁבִיל כְּדֵי לְקַיֵּם מִצְוַת עֹנֶג שַׁבָּת וְיוֹם טוֹב - אֲזַי נִתְבָּרֵר
חַיּוּת הַבָּשָׂר וְהַיַּיִן . . . וְעוֹלָה לַה' כְּעוֹלָה וּכְקָרְבָּן.

אַךְ מִי שֶׁהוּא בְּזוֹלְלֵי בָשָׂר וְסוֹבְאֵי יַיִן לְמַלְּאֹת תַּאֲוַת גּוּפוֹ
וְנַפְשׁוֹ הַבַּהֲמִית . . . הִנֵּה עַל יְדֵי זֶה יוֹרֵד חַיּוּת הַבָּשָׂר
וְהַיַּיִן שֶׁבְּקִרְבּוֹ, וְנִכְלַל לְפִי שָׁעָה בְּרַע גָּמוּר.

There's a way to position eating as an act akin
to offering a sacrifice to G-d. For example, you
can eat marbled beef and drink fragrant wine
for the sake of broadening your mind to better
understand G-d and His Torah—or to fulfill the
mitzvah of enjoying Shabbat and the festivals with
good foods and beverages. When eaten in such
a way, the meat and wine are sublimated. . . .

Conversely, if you eat meat gluttonously,
simply for corporeal pleasure . . . the energy
you derive from that food or beverage is
temporarily dragged down into the clutches
of negative energy that obstruct G-d.

A 60-second explainer on
how the soul is affected by
what we put in our body:
myjli.com/meditation

Eat Like It's Shabbat

The Rebbe, Rabbi Menachem Mendel Schneerson,
Likutei Sichot 3, p. 907

RABBI MENACHEM
MENDEL SCHNEERSON
1902–1994

דֶער תַּכְלִית הָעֲבוֹדָה אִיז אָבֶּער, אַז אִין דֶעם טָאן פֿון מִסְחָר
זָאל זִיךְ הֶערן און זֶעהֶען אֱלֹוקוּת. און נִיט נָאר אַז דֶער מִסְחָר
זָאל זַיין לְשֵׁם שָׁמַיִם, אַז דִי גַשְׁמִיּוּת זָאל עֶר נוּצְן צוּלִיב קְדֻשָׁה,
נָאר אַז דֶער גַשְׁמִיּוּת אַלֵיין זָאל וֶוערֶען קְדֻשָׁה . . .וָואס דָאס
אִיז דֶער פְּשַׁט פֿון "בְּכָל דְּרָכֶיךָ דָעֵהוּ" (מִשְׁלֵי ג, ו),
אִין אַלֶע זַיינֶער וֶועגְן זָאל זַיין "דָעֵהוּ". נִיט נָאר אַז דַיינֶע
וֶועגְן זָאל זַיין צוּלִיב דָעֵהוּ, נָאר אִין זֵיי אַלֵיין - "דָעֵהוּ".

עַל דֶּרֶךְ וִוי דֶער אֲכִילָה פֿון שַׁבָּת, וָואס דֶער אֲכִילָה
אַלֵיין אִיז אַ מִצְוָה, פָּאדֶערְט זִיךְ עַל דֶּרֶךְ זֶה אוֹיךְ אִין
אֲכִילַת חוֹל און אִין אַלֶע דִבְרֵי הָרְשׁוּת, אַז יֶעדֶער
זַאךְ וָואס מֶען עֶסְט, זָאל גֶעטָאן וֶוערְן נִיט נָאר לְשֵׁם
שָׁמַיִם, נָאר אוֹיךְ אִין אִיר גוּפָא זָאל זַיין דָעֵהוּ.

The ideal mode of serving G-d is that you should be able to sense the Divine within the business you conduct and within your field of mundane employment. This requires more than engaging in labor or commerce for the sake of Heaven, which lends a spiritual *goal* to otherwise mundane activities. Rather, beyond that, you should strive to sanctify the mundane activities themselves. This is the true meaning of the verse "In all your ways, know G-d" (PROVERBS 3:6). Not only should your activities be oriented toward

The towering Jewish leader of the 20th century, known as "the Lubavitcher Rebbe," or simply as "the Rebbe." Born in southern Ukraine, the Rebbe escaped Nazi-occupied Europe, arriving in the U.S. in June 1941. The Rebbe inspired and guided the revival of traditional Judaism after the European devastation, impacting virtually every Jewish community the world over. The Rebbe often emphasized that the performance of just one additional good deed could usher in the era of Mashiach. The Rebbe's scholarly talks and writings have been printed in more than 200 volumes.

Divine awareness, but there should be a Divine awareness within the activities themselves.

A paradigm for this is eating on Shabbat, whereby the physical act of eating is itself a fulfillment of a Divine instruction.

Similarly, our weekday food consumption and, for that matter, all mundane activities should be conducted not only for the sake of *subsequent* sacred goals, but also as *immediate* methods of experiencing Divine awareness.

The Charlotte Von Rothschild Haggadah is the only known Hebrew manuscript illuminated by a woman. Instructed by Moritz Daniel Oppenheim (1800–1882), the artist created this Haggadah as a gift for her uncle Amschel Meir Rothschild. The Haggadah was copied by Eliezer Sussman Mezeritsch, and decorated by Charlotte von Rothschild in 1842. Her initials can be found on the back of a chair in this scene of a family enjoying the traditional Passover *seder* meal. (Braginsky Collection, Zurich)

III. SLEEP

The plain act of sleeping can also be infused with purpose and meaning. With proper intention, instead of something we do simply to get rest, our time spent sleeping can be an opportunity to tap into the spiritual energy our soul receives as it is recharged.

EXERCISE 5.2

Imagine you are offered a magical pill that enables you to function endlessly, without any sleep at all. Would you take it? Explain your position.

THE SHEMA PRAYER
Parchment manuscript from the 15th century. The Shema is recited before going to sleep at night. (British Museum [MS 26971], London)

TEXT 7

Morning Blessing

Rabbi Shneur Zalman of Liadi, *Shulchan Aruch Harav*,
Orach Chayim 6:1

נָהֲגוּ הָעוֹלָם לְבָרֵךְ בְּכָל שַׁחֲרִית . . . בִּרְכַּת "אֲשֶׁר יָצַר",
לְפִי שֶׁבְּכָל יוֹם נַעֲשָׂה הָאָדָם בְּרִיָּה חֲדָשָׁה, לָכֵן שַׁיָּךְ לְבָרֵךְ
בְּכָל יוֹם וָיוֹם "אֲשֶׁר יָצַר אֶת הָאָדָם בְּחָכְמָה".

It is customary to recite the blessing of *asher
yatzar* . . . each morning, because at the start of
each day we are like freshly created beings. It is
therefore appropriate to praise G-d daily "for
having created humans with [His] wisdom."

TEXT 8

Evening Accounting

Zohar, vol. 3, p. 178a

דִּבְכָל לֵילְיָא וְלֵילְיָא, עַד לֹא יִשְׁכַּב וְעַד לֹא נָאִים, בָּעֵי
בַּר נַשׁ לְמֶעְבַּד חוּשְׁבְּנָא מֵעוֹבָדוֹי דְּעָבַד כָּל הַהוּא
יוֹמָא. וִיתוּב מִנַּיְיהוּ, וְיִבְעֵי עֲלַיְהוּ רַחֲמֵי.

Before lying down to sleep each night, we should
take stock of our deeds throughout that day.
We should repent for whatever we did wrong
and ask G-d for compassionate forgiveness.

ZOHAR

The seminal work of
kabbalah, Jewish
mysticism. The *Zohar* is a
mystical commentary on
the Torah, written in
Aramaic and Hebrew.
According to the Arizal,
the *Zohar* contains the
teachings of Rabbi
Shimon bar Yocha'i, who
lived in the Land of Israel
during the 2nd century.
The *Zohar* has become
one of the indispensable
texts of traditional
Judaism, alongside and
nearly equal in stature to
the Mishnah and Talmud.

TEXT 9

Depositing for a Spiritual Charge

Rabbi Yosef Yitzchak Schneersohn,
Sefer Hamaamarim 5702, p. 137

RABBI YOSEF YITZCHAK
SCHNEERSOHN
(RAYATZ, FRIERDIKER
REBBE, PREVIOUS REBBE)
1880–1950

Chasidic rebbe, prolific writer, and Jewish activist. Rabbi Yosef Yitzchak, the sixth leader of the Chabad movement, actively promoted Jewish religious practice in Soviet Russia and was arrested for these activities. After his release from prison and exile, he settled in Warsaw, Poland, from where he fled Nazi occupation and arrived in New York in 1940. Settling in Brooklyn, Rabbi Schneersohn worked to revitalize American Jewish life. His son-in-law Rabbi Menachem Mendel Schneerson succeeded him as the leader of the Chabad movement.

וְתִקְּנוּ לוֹמַר פָּסוּק "בְּיָדְךָ אַפְקִיד רוּחִי" (תְּהִלִּים לא, ו)
קֹדֶם הַשֵּׁנָה בִּקְרִיאַת שְׁמַע שֶׁעַל הַמִּטָּה, וְהַיְנוּ שֶׁיִּתְבּוֹנֵן
שֶׁנּוֹתֵן נַפְשׁוֹ בְּפִקָּדוֹן, וְיִתְבּוֹנֵן לְמִי נוֹתֵן אֶת הַפִּקָּדוֹן . . .
וַאֲזַי שׁוֹאֶבֶת חַיִּים מִלְמַעְלָה . . . הַיְנוּ חַיִּים רוּחָנִיִּים.

Our sages instituted the practice of reciting the verse, "I deposit my spirit into Your hand. . . ." (PSALMS 31:6) each night before going to sleep, just after reciting the bedtime Shema. We should meditate on the idea that we are depositing our souls, as if on loan, and consider to Whom we are providing the deposit. . . . Our souls then draw life from on High . . . that is, spiritual life.

Shema inscription on the Knesset Menorah in Jerusalem.

IV. WORK

Work encompasses, or swallows, the majority of our lives—at least the seemingly mundane and ordinary part of our energies and investments. If we can be cognizant of the Divinity that pervades every area of material existence and focus on that in whichever field of work we labor in, our entire life, including our workspace, can become spiritual and even Divine.

EXERCISE 5.3

Why do you work?

1

2

3

4

EXERCISE 5.4

If you won the lottery jackpot tomorrow, you would never have to worry about making a living again. Would you choose to work nonetheless?

 Yes ⬤ No

TEXT 10

G-d Loves Work

Midrash Tana'im, 5:14

MIDRASH TANA'IM

Halachic midrash on the book of Deuteronomy. Midrash is the designation of a particular genre of rabbinic literature usually forming a running commentary on specific books of the Bible. One of the important *midrashim* is *Mechilta* on the book of Exodus, attributed to the school of Rabbi Yishmael ben Elisha, and a commentary from the same school on the book of Deuteronomy was lost. *Midrash Tanaim* is an attempted reconstruction of the lost *Mechilta* to Deuteronomy, based on remnants from manuscripts and quotes found in other works, published by Rabbi David Tzvi Hoffman (1843–1921).

חֲבִיבָה הִיא הַמְּלָאכָה, שֶׁכָּל הַנְּבִיאִים נִתְעַסְּקוּ בָּהּ. בְּיַעֲקֹב אָבִינוּ הוּא אוֹמֵר: "אָשׁוּבָה אֶרְעֶה צֹאנְךָ אֶשְׁמֹר" (בְּרֵאשִׁית ל, לא). בְּמֹשֶׁה הוּא אוֹמֵר: "וּמֹשֶׁה הָיָה רֹעֶה" (שְׁמוֹת ג, א). בְּדָוִד הוּא אוֹמֵר: "וַיִּקָּחֵהוּ מִמִּכְלְאֹת צֹאן" (תְּהִלִּים עח, ע). בְּעָמוֹס הוּא אוֹמֵר: "כִּי בוֹקֵר אָנֹכִי וּבוֹלֵס שִׁקְמִים, וַיִּקָּחֵנִי ה' מֵאַחֲרֵי הַצֹּאן" (עָמוֹס ז, יד-טו).

חֲבִיבָה הִיא הַמְּלָאכָה, שֶׁלֹּא שָׁרַת רוּחַ הַקֹּדֶשׁ עַל אֱלִישָׁע בֶּן שָׁפָט אֶלָּא מִתּוֹךְ הַמְּלָאכָה, שֶׁנֶּאֱמַר: "וַיֵּלֶךְ וַיִּמְצָא אֶת אֱלִישָׁע בֶּן שָׁפָט וְהוּא חֹרֵשׁ" (מְלָכִים א יט, יט). וּמָה אֵלִיָּהוּ אוֹמֵר לוֹ? "לֵךְ שׁוּב כִּי מֶה עָשִׂיתִי לָךְ" (שָׁם, כ), שֶׁלֹּא לְבַטְּלָךְ.

Work is precious. All the prophets made a point of performing labor. Jacob requested, "Let me go back to tending and guarding your sheep" (GENESIS 30:31). Moses was described as a shepherd—"Moses was a shepherd" (EXODUS 3:1). Regarding David, it is stated, "G-d took David from the sheep pen" (PSALMS 78:70). The prophet Amos declared, "I am a cattle herder and an inspector of sycamores, but G-d took me from following the flock" (AMOS 7:14–15).

Work is precious. G-d only rested His spirit upon Elisha the son of Shafat while he was busy at work, as it is stated, "[Elijah] went from there and found Elisha the son of Shafat as he was plowing" (I KINGS 19:19). What did Elijah tell him? "Go back [to work]. What did I do to you?" (IBID., 19:20)—meaning, "I did not intend to interrupt your work."

Rabbi Simon Jacobson explores an uplifting perspective on work: myjli.com/meditation

TEXT 11

Working Is a Mitzvah

Avot DeRabbi Natan 11:1

יְהֵא אָדָם אוֹהֵב אֶת הַמְּלָאכָה, וְאַל יִהְיֶה [אָדָם] שׂוֹנֵא אֶת הַמְּלָאכָה. שֶׁכְּשֵׁם שֶׁהַתּוֹרָה נִתְּנָה בִּבְרִית, כָּךְ הַמְּלָאכָה נִתְּנָה בִּבְרִית, שֶׁנֶּאֱמַר: "שֵׁשֶׁת יָמִים תַּעֲבֹד וְעָשִׂיתָ כָּל מְלַאכְתֶּךָ, וְיוֹם הַשְּׁבִיעִי שַׁבָּת לַה' אֱלֹקֶיךָ" (שְׁמוֹת כ, ח-ט).

Love work; do not despise it. Just as G-d gave us the Torah along with a Divine covenant regarding its observance, so did G-d give us a covenant regarding our mundane work, as the Torah states, "Six days you shall work and perform all your labor, and the seventh day is a Sabbath to G-d" (EXODUS 20:8–9).

AVOT DERABBI NATAN

A commentary on, and an elaboration of, the Mishnaic tractate Avot, bearing the name of Rabbi Natan, one of the sages of the Mishnah. The work exists in two very different versions, one of which appears in many editions of the Talmud.

THE COBBLER
Issachar Ber Ryback (1897–1935), Berlin, ca. 1924, oil on canvas (Ryback Museum, Bat Yam, Israel)

TEXT 12

Earning Your Keep

Talmud, Bava Metzi'a 38a

אָדָם רוֹצֶה בְּקַב שֶׁלּוֹ מִתִּשְׁעָה קַבִּים שֶׁל חֲבֵרוֹ.
(חֲבִיבָה עָלָיו עַל יְדֵי שֶׁעָמַל בָּהֶן. - רַשִׁ"י).

A person prefers a single measure of their own labor rather than a gift of nine measures of someone else's labor. (It is dearer to the person because they have worked hard for it.—Rashi)

TEXT 13

Working Faithfully

Talmud, Shabbat 31a

אָמַר רָבָא: בְּשָׁעָה שֶׁמַּכְנִיסִין אָדָם לַדִּין, אוֹמְרִים לוֹ: "נָשָׂאתָ
וְנָתַתָּ בֶּאֱמוּנָה? קָבַעְתָּ עִתִּים לַתּוֹרָה? עָסַקְתָּ בִּפְרִיָּה וּרְבִיָּה?
צִפִּיתָ לִישׁוּעָה? פִּלְפַּלְתָּ בְּחָכְמָה? הֵבַנְתָּ דָּבָר מִתּוֹךְ דָּבָר?"

Rava taught: "When we depart this world and must face Heaven's judgment, each of us is asked: 'Did you conduct business faithfully? Did you designate times for Torah study? Did you engage in procreation? Did you long for the Final Redemption? Did you engage in the dialectics of Torah wisdom or attempt to extract a fresh concept from an existing one?'"

TEXT 14

Faithful Working

The Rebbe, Rabbi Menachem Mendel Schneerson,
Sefer Hasichot 5750:2, p. 646, fn. 48

וּבְבֵאוּר תֹּכֶן הַשְּׁאֵלָה "נָשָׂאתָ וְנָתַתָּ בֶּאֱמוּנָה", יֵשׁ לוֹמַר
(נוֹסָף עַל הַפֵּרוּשׁ הַפָּשׁוּט), שֶׁהַשְּׁאֵלָה הִיא (גַם) אִם עֲבוֹדָתוֹ
בְּעִנְיְנֵי הָעוֹלָם (מַשָׂא וּמַתָּן) הָיְתָה חֲדוּרָה בֶּאֱמוּנַת ה'.

The way the Talmud phrases Heaven's inquiry—
"Did you conduct business faithfully?"—allows for
an alternative understanding. Not only does it
include an inquiry regarding our honesty and
integrity ("faithfully"), but also about our *spiritual
approach* (full of faith): "Was your mundane and
material work saturated with faith in G-d?"

THE MARKET
Illustration by Meir Akselrod
(1902–1970), from the
book of poems by I. Harik,
Moscow, 1924 (Yachalevich
Family Collection, Maale
Adumim, Israel)

All in a Day's Work

The Rebbe, Rabbi Menachem Mendel Schneerson,
Sefer Hasichot 5750:2, p. 646

וְהַבֵּאוּר בָּזֶה - עַל פִּי הַיָּדוּעַ שֶׁתַּכְלִית בְּרִיאַת הָעוֹלָם . . . הוּא שֶׁנִּתְאַוָּה הַקָּדוֹשׁ בָּרוּךְ הוּא לִהְיוֹת לוֹ יִתְבָּרֵךְ דִּירָה בַּתַּחְתּוֹנִים, עַד בְּתַחְתּוֹן שֶׁאֵין תַּחְתּוֹן לְמַטָּה מִמֶּנּוּ. וְלָכֵן, עִקַּר וְרֹב הָעֲבוֹדָה הִיא (לֹא בְּעִנְיָנֵי קְדֻשָּׁה כְּשֶׁלְעַצְמָם, עַל דֶּרֶךְ וּבְדֻגְמַת עֲבוֹדַת הַנְּשָׁמָה לִפְנֵי וּלְאַחֲרֵי יְרִידָתָהּ לְמַטָּה לְהִתְלַבֵּשׁ בְּגוּף, אֶלָּא) בְּעִנְיָנֵי הָעוֹלָם דַּוְקָא, "שֵׁשׁ שָׁנִים תִּזְרַע שָׂדֶךָ וְגוֹ'" (וַיִּקְרָא כה, ג), שֶׁגַּם בְּ"שָׂדֶה" (תַּחְתּוֹן בְּיוֹתֵר) תִּהְיֶה הַמְשָׁכַת קְדֻשָּׁה וֶאֱלֹקוּת, דִּירָה לוֹ יִתְבָּרֵךְ בְּתַחְתּוֹנִים.

The entire purpose of Creation . . . is to create a home for G-d within this material world—a realm of existence that sits at the bottom of all Creation, beyond which there is no lower dimension of existence. For that reason, our primary work and the overwhelming majority of our pursuits are not in sacred matters per se, for that would be similar to the spiritual service of a soul in Heaven that has yet to descend to earth, or that has already departed from earth. Rather, our primary engagement is to engage with mundane and material entities. As the Torah instructs us, "Six years you shall sow your *field*" (LEVITICUS 25:3), indicating that we should introduce holiness and Divinity even to the soil of a field, the lowest dimension of existence, thereby creating a home for G-d in the lowest of realms.

FIGURE 5.1

Victor Frankl's Logotherapy Method

Viktor Frankl was a pioneering psychiatrist and psychotherapist who believed that humans are motivated by a "will to meaning"—a desire to find meaning in life.[1] He argued that life can have meaning even in the most challenging or tragic of circumstances,[2] and that our most primal motivation for remaining alive is tied to that pursuit of meaning.

Frankl named his approach "logotherapy." It directly addresses the lack of meaning, assists individuals in identifying meaning, and reduces their feelings of angst.[3]

It has been demonstrated that pursuing meaning in life positively correlates with overall quality of life, happiness, hope, and life satisfaction.[4] A sense of meaning is associated with positive emotional functioning, including coping with grief, and post-traumatic growth.[5] Preserving meaning is a protective factor that reduces the likelihood of depression, anxiety,[6] and suicidal thoughts.[7]

The following excerpts from Viktor Frankl's works express some of logotherapy's core principles.

The Will to Meaning

Let me explain why I have employed the term "logotherapy" as the name for my theory. *Logos* is a Greek word which denotes "meaning." Logotherapy, or, as it has been called by some authors, "The Third Viennese School of Psychotherapy," focuses on the meaning of human existence as well as on man's search for such a meaning. According to logotherapy, this striving to find a meaning in one's life is the primary motivational force in man. . . . Man's search for meaning is the primary motivation in his life and not a "secondary rationalization" of instinctual drives. This meaning is unique and specific in that it must and can be fulfilled by him alone; only then does it achieve a significance which will satisfy his own *will* to meaning.

Man's Search for Meaning, p. 121

Unique Meaning

One should not search for an abstract meaning of life. Everyone has his own specific vocation or mission in life to carry out a concrete assignment which demands fulfillment. Therein he cannot be replaced, nor can his life be repeated. Thus, everyone's task is as unique as is his specific opportunity to implement it.

Man's Search for Meaning, p. 131

Meaning Can Always Be Found

We must never forget that we may also find meaning in life even when confronted with a hopeless situation, when facing a fate that cannot be changed. For what then matters is to bear witness to the uniquely human potential at its best, which is to transform a personal tragedy into a triumph, to turn one's predicament into a human achievement. When we are no longer able to change a situation—just think of an incurable disease such as inoperable cancer—we are challenged to change ourselves.

Man's Search for Meaning, p. 135

Freedom and Responsibility

Man is capable of detaching himself not only from a situation but also from himself. He is capable of choosing his attitude toward himself. By so doing he really takes a stand toward his own somatic and psychic conditions and determinants. . . . Seen in this light, a person is free to shape his own character, and man is responsible for what he may have made out of himself. What matters is not the features of our character or the drives and instincts per se, but rather the stand we take toward them. And the capacity to take such a stand is what makes us human beings.

The Will to Meaning, p. 17

Meaning and Psychological Well-Being

If man can find and fulfill a meaning in his life he becomes happy but also able and capable of coping with suffering. If he can see a meaning he is even prepared to give his life. On the other hand, if he cannot see a meaning he is equally inclined to take his life even in the midst, and in spite, of all the welfare and affluence surrounding him. . . . I do not intend to say that most of the suicides are undertaken out of a feeling of meaninglessness; but I am convinced that people would have overcome the impulse to kill themselves if they had seen a meaning in their lives. Meanwhile, people have the means to live but no meaning to live for.

The Doctor and the Soul, p. 296

Frustrated Meaning

Man's will to meaning can also be frustrated, in which case logotherapy speaks of "existential frustration." . . . Existential frustration can also result in neuroses. For this type of neuroses, logotherapy has coined the term "noögenic neuroses" in contrast to neuroses in the traditional sense of the word, i.e., psychogenic neuroses. Noögenic neuroses have their origin not in the psychological but rather in the "noölogical" (from the Greek *noös* meaning mind) dimension of human existence. This is another logotherapeutic term which denotes anything pertaining to the specifically human dimension.

Man's Search for Meaning, p. 123

Full citation information for the books by Frankl quoted above:

Frankl, E. Viktor, *Man's Search for Meaning* (New York: Washington Square Publishing, 1959).

Frankl, E. Viktor, *The Will to Meaning: Foundations and Applications of Logotherapy*, Expanded Edition (New York: Meridian Books, 1988).

Frankl, E. Viktor, *The Doctor and the Soul: From Psychotherapy to Logotherapy* (New York: Knopf Doubleday Publishing Group, 2019).

1. Stege, M. F, et al., "Understanding the search for meaning in life: personality, cognitive style, and the dynamic between seeking and experiencing meaning," *Journal of Personality*, 2008 Apr;76(2): 199–228.

2. Boyraz, G., et al., "Accepting death as part of life: Meaning in life as a means for dealing with loss among bereaved individuals," *Death Studies*, 39(1), 2015: 39(1), 2015, 1–11.

3. Robatmilli, S., et al. "The effect of group logotherapy on meaning in life and depression levels of Iranian students.," *International Journal for the Advancement of Counseling*, 37(1), 2015, 54–62.

4. Park, N., et al., "When is the search for meaning related to life satisfaction?" *Applied Psychology: Health and Well-Being*, 2(1), 2010, 1–13

5. Linley, P. A., and Joseph, S., Meaning in Life and posttraumatic growth. *Journal of Loss and Trauma*, 16(2), 2011, 150–159

6. Haugan, G. "Meaning-in-life in nursing home patients: a correlate with physical and emotional symptoms," *Journal in Clinical Nursing*, 23(7–8), 2014a, 1030–43.

7. Armstrong, L. L. and Manion, L. G., "Meaningful youth engagement as a protective factor for youth suicidal ideation," *Journal on Research on Adolescence*, 25(1), 2013, 20–27

KEY POINTS

1   Jewish meditation is action-oriented, designed to deliver practical results in both physical and spiritual well-being.

2   "Know G-d in all you do" is a major axiom of the Jewish value system. It speaks to the notion that everything we do—not only the overtly spiritual and religious—can be an expression of G-dliness.

3   Eating can be transformed into a mindful, spiritual act: On a simple level, this can be achieved by being conscious of the complex journey from our food's origins to our tables. Making a blessing prior to eating brings that mindfulness into focus.

4   On a deeper level, all food possesses Divine energy. Being conscious of that, and eating only for positive purposes, allows us to release that Divine energy from the food and transform a mundane act into a Divine experience. This, too, is brought into focus while reciting the blessing prior to eating.

5   Sleep is an opportunity to reboot and refresh. We can imbue it with profound significance if we take stock of the expiring day, resolve to perform better tomorrow, and use our nocturnal rejuvenation to break free of past toxicity.

6   Work is not simply a means to an end; humans choose to work even when they do not require the money. Rather, work satisfies a basic human need to earn our own success. With proper meditation, we can find G-d in the mundanity of our daily work routines.

Chanoch the Shoemaker

Humans are empowered to perceive Divinity in everything, including mundane items and experiences, such as the food we eat, a night's sleep, and our routine work.

This idea is expressed in a cryptic midrashic tale about an early enigmatic character named Chanoch the Shoemaker. The teaching has been treated in multiple Jewish disciplines of thought in varying ways. The Chasidic lens that highlights the pursuit of Divinity in all activities is brought into sharper focus by contrasting it with several alternative and equally fascinating insights into Chanoch.

The midrashic teaching relates to a lonely verse in Genesis (5:24). There, after establishing Chanoch's place in the early human family tree and reporting his age at his passing, the Torah offers a puzzling observation: "Chanoch walked with G-d, and he was no longer, for G-d took him." The Midrash fills in some of the backstory, and includes the following description:

Chanoch would sew shoes to bind together the worlds. For every knot he would tie, he would say, "Blessed be the name of His glorious kingdom for all eternity!" for these words contain the unification and connection of all the upper chambers.

—Rabbi Eliyahu Cohen, *Midrash Talpiyot*, entry for "Chanoch"

KABBALAH	Rabbi Yitzchak of Acco, 1250–1340

📖 *Me'irat Einayim*, end of *Parshat Lech Lecha*

I questioned my teacher, Rabbi Yehudah Darshan (Ashkenazi): How did Chanoch merit to achieve such spiritual greatness? . . .

He replied that Chanoch was an *ushkaf*—a shoemaker. For each stitch he sewed into the leather used to fashion shoes, he blessed G-d with a full heart and perfect intention. His praises elicited blessings to the supernal Divine force known as *Matatron*. He never failed to bless G-d, not even for a single stitch. He continued in this manner until his immense love for G-d swelled to the point that "he was no longer, for G-d took him." He thereby merited to be called *Matatron*, and he remains at an exceedingly supernal degree of Divinity.

The teachings of kabbalah are devoted to exploring the mystical and Divine. They therefore view Chanoch with a strictly mystical lens, through which Chanoch was constantly engaged in a *spiritual* exercise, which earned him the description of "walking with G-d." Even while engaged in a mundane occupation, his mind was elsewhere, in the spiritual realms. He effectuated the union of tremendous spiritual energies ("worlds") and facilitated fresh Divine revelations within the spiritual realms of existence.

In other words, his main activities were spiritual and their achievements were not felt in the material world, but only in the heavens. Indeed, even his physical occupation (stitching materials together) only reflected his spiritual pursuit (uniting spiritual forces).

CLASSICAL CHASIDUS	Rabbi Yaakov Yosef of Polonye, 1695-1781

📖 *Toldot Yaakov Yosef*, beginning of *Parshat Vayera*

I heard in the name of my master the Baal Shem Tov . . . an explanation for the notion that Chanoch received the title *Matatron* for engaging in the unification of the Divine manifestations referred to as *Kudesha Berich Hu* ("Holy One, blessed be He") and *Shechinah* (Divine Presence) over each stitch he would make: Cognition is associated with the Divinity referred to as **Ein Sof** (Infinite) and the four-letter name *Havayah*, whereas action is associated with the Divinity referred to as *Shechinah*. When we marry our thoughts to our actions, then, while performing the action, we effectuate the unification of *Kudesha Berich Hu* and *Shechinah*.

The teachings of Chasidism brought esoteric kabbalistic ideas to bear in the religious experience of each Jewish individual. Accordingly, Classic Chasidism views Chanoch as engaged in esoteric achievements (effectuating supernal unifications, as described in kabbalah), but it introduces a fresh layer to the story: Chanoch is *our* story. Each of *us* can replicate Chanoch's praiseworthy feat to some degree through our own tangible activities, through consciously performing our mundane activities with a spiritual purpose in mind.

Chanoch the Shoemaker *continued*

LITVISH (LITHUANIAN JEWISH) PHILOSOPHY

Rabbi Chaim of Volozhin, 1749-1821	Cited in Rabbi Asher Hakohen, *Keter Rosh*, ch. 132

Once the Torah was given, we cannot deviate from it and its *mitzvot* to the slightest degree, and we must not rely on ideas supplied by our evil inclination.

The Midrash reports that Chanoch would sew shoes, and that with each stitch he sewed, he mentally effected spiritual unifications in the upper realms. Indeed, our Patriarchs operated in this manner, producing spiritual achievements with all of their activities, including their physical engagements—a concept similar to that expressed in the directive, "Know G-d in all your ways."

However, this was appropriate prior to the Giving of the Torah, and it remains appropriate today for non-Jews. In either case, individuals are granted permission to serve G-d in any way they choose, provided that their worship is directed exclusively to G-d, and that it remains within the parameters of the Seven Noachide Laws.

Not so for us, the Jewish people! G-d has given us the Torah, which sets clear boundaries for everything; each deed or activity is embraced by either a *mitzvah* or by a prohibition. We direct our intention to G-d through approaching each activity in a manner compliant with the Torah. True piety means being extremely scrupulous to observe all that we are commanded and to keep extremely distant from all that is forbidden. It includes being scrupulous with all the enactments of our sages and similar precautions that were introduced from the day the Torah was commanded to us.

A primary feature of this school of thought, particularly as it contrasts to its counterpart of Chasidic thought (that arose at the same time), is strict adherence to traditional Torah and *mitzvot*, to the absolute exclusion of all else. For a student of this tradition, the notion that a Jew can achieve anything spiritual through sewing shoes is untenable—for G-d did not explicitly command us to sew shoes. G-d is accessible only where He placed Himself, within the Torah and *mitzvot* that He gave us. So the only explanation as to how someone like Chanoch was successful in doing so, is that Chanoch predated the Giving of the Torah on Mount Sinai, but such a method of religious experience is no longer accessible for us. In fact, to think otherwise is the seduction of our evil inclination that seeks to divert our attention from our genuine obligations—the *mitzvot*.

| MUSAR (ETHICS) | Rabbi Eliyahu Dessler, 1892-1953 |

Michtav Me'Eliyahu, vol. 1, p. 34, *kuntres hachesed*

I heard a beautiful explanation for this Midrash, quoted in the name of our teacher, Rabbi Yisrael of Salant [the father of the musar movement]:

We cannot suggest that while Chanoch was busy sewing shoes he was intensely focused on lofty spiritual thoughts. Surely, that would violate the [Torah's] law! After all, how could he permit himself to be distracted while performing labor for which others are paying him? [The quality of production would suffer, and it would be immoral to sell sloppily stitched shoes.]

Rather, the unifications to which our sages refer are to be understood in a plain sense: Chanoch was intensely focused *on his craft*. He was scrupulous with each and every stitch, ensuring that it should be strong and tight, so that the shoe would be of the highest quality. His intention was to provide his customers with the maximum benefit, and his motivation for such superior labor was to actively emulate the traits of his Creator. In this way, Chanoch "effectuated unifications," for he desired nothing in life other than to constantly unite with G-d through emulating his Creator's traits.

Another advantage of his scrupulous performance was that he avoided all traces of evil, ensuring that he would not be tainted by unintentional dishonesty caused by taking more than was due for his services.

The musar movement places profound emphasis on personal ethics and immaculate conduct. Discipline, order, and extreme integrity in all personal affairs are of primary concern. When presented with a Midrash that depicts a saintly individual obsessed with each stitch of the shoes he produces, the musar-oriented mind immediately notices strains of perfectionism, and seeks to read the story as a personally applicable ethical message: Chanoch stitched actual shoes, and did so very well indeed, reflecting profound integrity, and as a means of connecting with G-d through a matter of integrity.

This is an obvious contrast to almost every other stream of thought that immediately understands this Midrash as metaphorical.

Chanoch the Shoemaker *continued*

CHABAD *CHASIDUT*	The Rebbe, Rabbi Menachem Mendel Schneerson, 1902-1994

📖 *Torat Menachem 5742:1, pp. 304-305*

The Midrash is puzzling: Why does it find it necessary to highlight that *Matatron* was [originally] a shoemaker [in the form of Chanoch]? How is such a description appropriate for the enormous exaltedness of *Matatron*, the angel referred to as G-d's Interior Minister? We find the Torah invested considerable effort to avoid a negative description of even an animal, so surely this Torah teaching could have found a better description for *Matatron* than an individual who sewed shoes! At least, it could have referred to his *spiritual* accomplishments [such as "unifier of upper chambers"] instead of offering an unqualified epitaph of "shoemaker"!

There's a deep message here vis-à-vis every Jew's religious life: You may work as a cobbler, sewing shoes in the literal sense, but there is a higher purpose to your material toil. You must remain aware that G-d arranged for you to engage in this labor for the sake of achieving tremendous spiritual feats ("supernal unifications").

Indeed, one of the great tannaic sages of the Mishnah is referred to as Rabbi Yochanan the Shoemaker. Spiritual insights aside, he also served as a shoemaker in reality. At the same time as he sewed shoes, he served as a *tanna*, an eminent mishnaic sage.

In line with the central theme explored in this lesson, the Chabad Chasidic approach does not limit Divinity to spiritual or religious areas of life. Rather, we are tasked specifically with finding Divinity—"exposing sparks"—in *all* areas of life, including our mundane workplaces. It is therefore deliberate and informative that such a remarkably saintly individual as Chanoch is described as engaged in the labor of stitching leather together to shape shoes, for even in such menial labor—more precisely, *especially* within mundane, menial labor—G-d can and should be found.

Simultaneously, Chanoch manually stitched strips of leather and mentally stitched spiritual forces. These activities are not in contradiction; they are in perfect harmony, because the occupation exists not only as a reflection of its spiritual counterpart, but *for the sake of* inspiring it, and it therefore remains *integral* to that spiritual service.

MIND AND MATTER

The Influences of Meditation on Practice, and of Practice on Meditation

In Judaism, meditation is not just an ascetic practice; rather, it is directly harnessed to the real world through practical mitzvot. *This lesson explores the fascinating two-way relationship between* mitzvot *and meditation: meditation and intention lend purpose to the* mitzvot, *but* mitzvot *also elicit meditative effects and are themselves a form of meditation.*

MEDITATION VS. ACTION

The meditations that we have explored until this point were largely mind exercises.

In this lesson, we explore the meditative quality of the active *mitzvot* and discover that they are practices imbued with meditation—and that, in addition, they generate active meditations of their own, as will be explained.

EXERCISE 6.1

On a scale of 1–5, estimate the centrality of each of the following to Judaism:

Action

1	2	3	4	5

Values

1	2	3	4	5

Faith

1	2	3	4	5

Mindful Awareness

1	2	3	4	5

TEXT 1

Deed over Creed

Mishnah, Avot 1:17

לֹא הַמִּדְרָשׁ עִקָּר, אֶלָּא הַמַּעֲשֶׂה.

The essential thing is not study, but deed.

ETHICS OF THE FATHERS
(*PIRKEI AVOT*)

A 6-chapter work on
Jewish ethics that is
studied widely by Jewish
communities, especially
during the summer. The
first 5 chapters are from
the Mishnah, tractate
Avot. Avot differs from
the rest of the Mishnah in
that it does not focus on
legal subjects; it is a
collection of the sages'
wisdom on topics related
to character
development, ethics,
healthy living, piety, and
the study of Torah.

The end of Pirkei
Avot, (chapter 1,) in an
illuminated manuscript
from the 14th or 15th
century. This collection
of liturgy for Shabbat
afternoons and Shavuot
is copied according to
the Sephardic rite and
is likely from Spain.
(Jewish Theological
Seminary Library, New
York [MS 4363])

II. MEDITATIVE ACTS

Jewish law requires that the performance of *mitzvot* be accompanied with intent. This requirement demonstrates that there is far more to the *mitzvot* than utilitarian achievement. In fact, with the meditative awareness of the function of *mitzvot*—that they are the link that connects us with G-d—the physical activities are transformed into profound spiritual experiences. Traditionally, a blessing is recited before the performance of many of the *mitzvot*, and this blessing serves to highlight the meditation.

QUESTION

It is a mitzvah for a Jew to hear the shofar sounded on Rosh Hashanah, but a particular Jewish couple are unaware of this obligation and intend simply to go for a stroll. They happen to pass a synagogue, and by a stroke of providence, the shofar is sounded just at that moment. Its plaintive wail is heard by the couple on the street.

Have they fulfilled the mitzvah of hearing the shofar?

 Yes   No

TEXT 2

Intent Required

Rabbi Shneur Zalman of Liadi, *Shulchan Aruch Harav,*
Orach Chayim 60:5

**RABBI SHNEUR
ZALMAN OF LIADI
(ALTER REBBE)
1745–1812**

Chasidic rebbe, halachic authority, and founder of the Chabad movement. The Alter Rebbe was born in Liozna, Belarus, and was among the principal students of the Magid of Mezeritch. His numerous works include the *Tanya,* an early classic containing the fundamentals of Chabad Chasidism; and *Shulchan Aruch Harav,* an expanded and reworked code of Jewish law.

כָּל הַמִּצְוֹת צְרִיכוֹת כַּוָּנָה לָצֵאת יְדֵי חוֹבָה בַּעֲשִׂיַּת אוֹתָהּ מִצְוָה. וְאִם עֲשָׂאָהּ בְּלֹא כַּוָּנָה לָצֵאת יְדֵי חוֹבָתוֹ אֶלָּא כְּמִתְעַסֵּק בְּעָלְמָא, אוֹ לְכַוָּנָה אַחֶרֶת וְלֹא לְשֵׁם אוֹתָהּ מִצְוָה - לֹא יָצָא יְדֵי חוֹבָתוֹ מִן הַתּוֹרָה. וְיֵשׁ אוֹמְרִים שֶׁמִּצְוֹות אֵין צְרִיכוֹת כַּוָּנָה, וְאַף הַמִּתְעַסֵּק יָצָא בְּדִיעֲבַד. וַהֲלָכָה כַּסְּבָרָא הָרִאשׁוֹנָה.

To fulfill a mitzvah obligation, we must actively intend to observe that mitzvah. Therefore, if we observe a mitzvah unwittingly or for a purpose other than to perform a mitzvah, we have not fulfilled the mitzvah at all. Some Torah authorities disagree and opine that *mitzvot* do not require intent and are fulfilled even when performed unwittingly. However, the final law sides with the former opinion.

SUKKOT
Jewish men inspect their *lulav* and *etrog*—the plants ritually used on the holiday of Sukkot. Leopold Pilichowski (1869–1933), oil on canvas, 1894–5, Poland (The Jewish Museum, New York)

Rabbi Manis Friedman
explores the most accurate way to translate "mitzvah":
myjli.com/meditation

EXERCISE 6.2

Identify two *mitzvot* that you recently performed:
an interpersonal mitzvah, and a ritual one.

In the chart below, describe the motivation
that propelled you to perform these *mitzvot*.
What were you trying to accomplish?

	MITZVAH	INTENTION
1		
2		

TEXT 3

Bonding Behaviors

Rabbi Yosef Yitzchak Schneersohn,
cited in *Hayom Yom*, 8 Cheshvan

מִצְוָה לָשׁוֹן צַוְתָּא וְחִבּוּר. וְהָעוֹשֶׂה מִצְוָה מִתְחַבֵּר עִם
הָעַצְמוּת בָּרוּךְ הוּא, שֶׁהוּא הַמְצַוֶּה אֶת הַצִּוּוּי הַהוּא.

וְזֶהוּ "שְׂכַר מִצְוָה מִצְוָה" (אָבוֹת ד, ב), דְּזֶה מַה שֶּׁנִּתְחַבֵּר
עִם עַצְמוּת אוֹר אֵין סוֹף מִצְוָה הַצִּוּוּי – זֶהוּ שְׂכָרוֹ.

The word "mitzvah" means "a connection," as in
the [Aramaic] term *tzavta* [attach, join]. One
who performs a mitzvah bonds with G-d's very
Self—for G-d is the Issuer of that commandment.

This is the significance of our sages' statement, "The reward of a mitzvah is the mitzvah" (MISHNAH, AVOT 2:4): the bonding [of the mortal who performs the commandment] with the Infinite G-d Who issued the commandment is itself the [greatest] reward.

TEXT 4

Divine Intimacy

Rabbi Shneur Zalman of Liadi, *Tanya, Likutei Amarim*, ch. 46

וְזֶהוּ שֶׁאוֹמְרִים: "אֲשֶׁר קִדְּשָׁנוּ בְּמִצְוֹתָיו", כְּאָדָם הַמְקַדֵּשׁ אִשָּׁה לִהְיוֹת מְיוּחֶדֶת עִמּוֹ בְּיִחוּד גָּמוּר, כְּמוֹ שֶׁכָּתוּב: "וְדָבַק בְּאִשְׁתּוֹ וְהָיוּ לְבָשָׂר אֶחָד" (בְּרֵאשִׁית ב, כד).

כָּכָה מַמָּשׁ, וְיֶתֶר עַל כֵּן לְאֵין קֵץ, הוּא יִחוּד נֶפֶשׁ הָאֱלֹקִית הָעוֹסֶקֶת בַּתּוֹרָה וּמִצְוֹת וְנֶפֶשׁ הַחִיּוּנִית וּלְבוּשֵׁיהֶן, הַנִּזְכָּרִים לְעֵיל, בְּאוֹר אֵין סוֹף בָּרוּךְ הוּא.

This is the inner significance of the blessing recited prior to performing a mitzvah: "Blessed are You . . . Who sanctified us [*kideshanu*] with His *mitzvot*." [In Hebrew, the term *kiddush* means both "sanctification" and "betrothal."] Through performing a mitzvah, we are bound to G-d like a man betrothing his wife for the sake of being intimately united with each other, as the Torah states [regarding the bonding of the first

RABBI YOSEF YITZCHAK SCHNEERSOHN (RAYATZ, FRIERDIKER REBBE, PREVIOUS REBBE) 1880–1950

Chasidic rebbe, prolific writer, and Jewish activist. Rabbi Yosef Yitzchak, the sixth leader of the Chabad movement, actively promoted Jewish religious practice in Soviet Russia and was arrested for these activities. After his release from prison and exile, he settled in Warsaw, Poland, from where he fled Nazi occupation and arrived in New York in 1940. Settling in Brooklyn, Rabbi Schneersohn worked to revitalize American Jewish life. His son-in-law Rabbi Menachem Mendel Schneerson succeeded him as the leader of the Chabad movement.

human couple], "He shall cleave to his wife, and they shall become one flesh" (GENESIS 2:24).

When we study the Torah or perform a commandment we achieve a similar—indeed, an infinitely deeper and truer—unity between our soul, along with all of its elements, and G-d's absolutely infinite light.

THERE'S MORE...

For a detailed meditation on the magnitude of a mitzvah's effect vis-à-vis our relationship with G-d, see Appendix (page 204).

A woman lighting candles for Shabbat. Drawing beneath the text of part of the blessing recited over the candles. From a book of selected prayers likely created as a wedding gift, by Yaakov ben Yehudah Leib Shamash in Hamburg, 1741. (Braginsky Collection, Zurich)

III. ACTIVE MEDITATIONS

Everything in Judaism, flowing as it does from Divine wisdom, embraces multiple layers. Another layer to the function of *mitzvot* is the individual benefit that they provide to the person who performs them, in terms of self-improvement.

Judaism urges us to recognize the influence our behavior wields over our attitudes. Each mitzvah is designed to guide us to proper moral and spiritual perspectives. In this sense, *mitzvot* are forms of active meditations—the act of the mitzvah focuses our minds, shapes our thoughts, and forms our attitudes. Each mitzvah is unique and projects a meditation that reflects its specific content.

TEXT 5

Acts of Refinement

Rabbi Moshe ben Nachman, Deuteronomy 22:6

"לֹא נִתְּנוּ הַמִּצְוֹת אֶלָּא לְצָרֵף בָּהֶם אֶת הַבְּרִיּוֹת" (בְּרֵאשִׁית רַבָּה מד, א)... שֶׁאֵין הַתּוֹעֶלֶת בַּמִּצְוֹת לְהַקָּדוֹשׁ בָּרוּךְ הוּא בְּעַצְמוֹ יִתְעַלֶּה, אֲבָל הַתּוֹעֶלֶת בָּאָדָם עַצְמוֹ לִמְנוֹעַ מִמֶּנּוּ נֶזֶק, אוֹ אֱמוּנָה רָעָה אוֹ מִדָּה מְגוּנָה, אוֹ לִזְכּוֹר הַנִּסִּים וְנִפְלָאוֹת הַבּוֹרֵא יִתְבָּרַךְ, וְלָדַעַת אֶת הַשֵּׁם.

וְזֶהוּ "לְצָרֵף בָּהֶן", שֶׁיִּהְיוּ כְּכֶסֶף צָרוּף, כִּי הַצּוֹרֵף הַכֶּסֶף אֵין מַעֲשֵׂהוּ בְּלֹא טַעַם, אֲבָל לְהוֹצִיא מִמֶּנּוּ כָּל סִיג, וְכֵן הַמִּצְוֹת לְהוֹצִיא מִלִּבֵּנוּ כָּל אֱמוּנָה רָעָה, וּלְהוֹדִיעֵנוּ הָאֱמֶת וּלְזוֹכְרוֹ תָּמִיד.

Our sages state that "the *mitzvot* were given only to refine the person" (MIDRASH, *BERESHIT RABAH* 44:1).... The purpose of the *mitzvot* is not to benefit G-d but, rather, to benefit humankind—to keep them safe from harm, to

RABBI MOSHE BEN NACHMAN (NACHMANIDES, RAMBAN) 1194–1270

Scholar, philosopher, author, and physician. Nachmanides was born in Spain and served as leader of Iberian Jewry. In 1263, he was summoned by King James of Aragon to a public disputation with Pablo Cristiani, a Jewish apostate. Though Nachmanides was the clear victor of the debate, he had to flee Spain because of the resulting persecution. He moved to Israel and helped reestablish communal life in Jerusalem. He authored a classic commentary on the Pentateuch and a commentary on the Talmud.

shield them from negative beliefs and base character traits, to remind them of the miracles and wonders of the Creator, and to help them know G-d.

The Midrash employs the term *tzareif* for "refining," which usually refers to refining silver. This informs us that the *mitzvot* refine mortals in a similar way to the way a silversmith refines silver. Silver refinement is a purposeful task, done for the sake of removing all impurities. Similarly, the *mitzvot* are designed to remove every harmful belief from our hearts, to inform us of the truth, and to enable us to be constantly mindful of the truth.

TEXT 6

Communicating Ideals

Maimonides, *Guide for the Perplexed* 3:31

שֶׁכָּל מִצְוָה מֵאֵלּוּ הַתַּרְיַ"ג מִצְוֹת הִיא, אִם לִנְתִינַת דַּעַת אֲמִתִּי, אוֹ לְהָסִיר דַּעַת רַע, אוֹ לִנְתִינַת סֵדֶר יָשָׁר, אוֹ לְהָסִיר עָוֶל, אוֹ לְהִתְלַמֵּד בְּמִדּוֹת טוֹבוֹת, אוֹ לְהַזְהִיר מִמִּדּוֹת רָעוֹת.

Each of the six hundred and thirteen commandments exists either to communicate a correct view or to dismiss an unhealthy view; to communicate a rule of justice or to ward off an injustice; to endow people with a noble moral quality or to warn them against a negative moral quality.

TEXT 7

Actions Influence Attitude

Sefer Hachinuch, Mitzvah 16

וְעַתָּה בְּנִי . . . אֲלַמֶּדְךָ לְהוֹעִיל בַּתּוֹרָה וּבַמִצְוֹת. דַּע כִּי
הָאָדָם נִפְעַל כְּפִי פְּעֻלוֹתָיו, וְלִבּוֹ וְכָל מַחְשְׁבֹתָיו תָּמִיד
אַחַר מַעֲשָׂיו שֶׁהוּא עוֹסֵק בָּהֶם, אִם טוֹב וְאִם רָע . . .

וּבְכֹחַ מַעֲשָׂיו יָמִית הַיֵּצֶר הָרַע, כִּי אַחֲרֵי הַפְּעֻלוֹת נִמְשָׁכִים הַלְּבָבוֹת.

And now my child . . . I will enlighten you to appreciate the Torah and its precepts. You are influenced by your behavior, and your feelings and thoughts consistently follow your actions, whether for the positive or the negative. . . .

Your actions have the power to overcome the negative inclination within you, since the attitudes of your heart are influenced by your behaviors.

SEFER HACHINUCH

A work on the biblical commandments. Four aspects of every mitzvah are discussed in this work: the definition of the mitzvah; ethical lessons that can be deduced from the mitzvah; basic laws pertaining to the observance of the mitzvah; and who is obligated to perform the mitzvah, and when. The work was composed in the 13th century by an anonymous author who refers to himself as "the Levite of Barcelona." It has been widely thought that this referred to Rabbi Aharon Halevi of Barcelona (Re'ah); however, this view has been contested.

EXERCISE 6.3

▶ Slouch your shoulders and frown for 10 seconds. How do you feel?

▶ Stand tall and straight, with a wide smile and arms open wide for 10 seconds. How do you feel?

Dr. Amy Cuddy
explains the power of your body language to shape your mood:
myjli.com/meditation

TEXT 8

Side Effects

The Rebbe, Rabbi Menachem Mendel Schneerson,
Likutei Sichot, vol. 17, p. 440

RABBI MENACHEM MENDEL SCHNEERSON 1902–1994

מְקַיֵּם זַיְן דִי מִצְוֹת בְּפֹעַל, וָארוּם מַעֲשֶׂה הוּא הָעִקָּר. צוּזַאמֶען דֶערמִיט וְוִירְקְט יֶעדֶע עֲשִׂיָּה עַל פִּי תּוֹרָה אוֹיף דֶעם מַהֲלַךְ הַנֶּפֶשׁ פוּן דֶעם לוֹמֵד תּוֹרָה וּמְקַיֵּם הַמִּצְוֹת, אוּן אֵיידְלְט אִים אוֹיס סַיי אִין שֵׂכֶל אוּן סַיי אִין מִדּוֹת, וְוִי דֶער רַמְבַּ״ם, דֶער מוֹרֵה הַנְּבוֹכִים פוּן זַיְן דוֹר אוּן פוּן אַלֶע שְׁפֶּעטֶערְדִיקֶע דוֹרוֹת, אִיז דָאס מַדְגִּישׁ אִין מֶערֶערֶע עֶרטֶער.

The main focus within Judaism is action, which entails practically fulfilling the *mitzvot*. At the same time, each Torah-based action has an effect on the person's character. Learning Torah and fulfilling *mitzvot* refine the mind and emotions, as repeatedly emphasized in the works of Maimonides, who served as a guide for the perplexed of his generation and continues to serve as a guide for truth seekers in all subsequent eras.

The towering Jewish leader of the 20th century, known as "the Lubavitcher Rebbe," or simply as "the Rebbe." Born in southern Ukraine, the Rebbe escaped Nazi-occupied Europe, arriving in the U.S. in June 1941. The Rebbe inspired and guided the revival of traditional Judaism after the European devastation, impacting virtually every Jewish community the world over. The Rebbe often emphasized that the performance of just one additional good deed could usher in the era of Mashiach. The Rebbe's scholarly talks and writings have been printed in more than 200 volumes.

M. Oppenheim fec.   Verlag von Louis Lamm, Berlin C.2.

BAR-MITZWA-VORTRAG.
THE BAR-MITZVA-DISCOURSE.   DISCOURS DE BAR MITZVA.

THE BAR MITZVA DISCOURSE
From the famous cycle *Scenes from Traditional Jewish Family Life* by Moritz Daniel Oppenheim (1800–1882) of Frankfurt am Main. This page is from a beautiful gift edition of the prints put together by Louis Lamm, a Bavarian publisher, who was murdered in Auschwitz in 1943.

Rabbi Simon Jacobson
explores an uplifting perspective on work:
myjli.com/meditation

In the chart below, record what you might consider the meditative agenda of the listed *mitzvot*.

MITZVAH	PROPOSED MEDITATIVE AGENDA
Charity	
Honor Parents	
Observe Shabbat	
Tefilin	
Mezuzah	

Then read Texts 9–13. After reading the Text readings, return to this chart and record the traditional meditation of each mitzvah.

MITZVAH	TRADITIONAL MEDITATIVE AGENDA
Charity	
Honor Parents	
Observe Shabbat	
Tefilin	
Mezuzah	

TEXT 9

Charity Meditation

Sefer Hachinuch, Mitzvah 66

מִצְוַת הַלְוָאָה לְעָנִי . . . שֹׁרֶשׁ הַמִּצְוָה, שֶׁרָצָה הָקֵל לִהְיוֹת בְּרוּאָיו
מְלָמָּדִים וּמְרְגָּלִים בְּמִדַּת הַחֶסֶד וְהָרַחֲמִים, כִּי הִיא מִדָּה מְשֻׁבַּחַת,
וּמִתּוֹךְ הֶכְשֵׁר גּוּפָם בַּמִּדּוֹת הַטּוֹבוֹת יִהְיוּ רְאוּיִים לְקַבָּלַת הַטּוֹבָה, כְּמוֹ
שֶׁאָמַרְנוּ שֶׁחָלוֹת הַטּוֹב וְהַבְּרָכָה לְעוֹלָם עַל הַטּוֹב לֹא בְּהֶפְכּוֹ . . .

וְאִם לָאו, מִצַּד שֹׁרֶשׁ זֶה, הֲלֹא הוּא בָּרוּךְ הוּא יַסְפִּיק לָעָנִי דֵּי מַחְסֹרוֹ
זוּלָתֵנוּ, אֶלָּא שֶׁהָיָה מֵחַסְדּוֹ בָּרוּךְ הוּא שֶׁנַּעֲשֵׂינוּ שְׁלוּחִים לוֹ לִזַכּוֹתֵנוּ.

The root of the mitzvah to lend to the poor
. . . is that G-d desired that His creatures
become accustomed and train themselves in
the characteristics of kindness and mercy, for
these are praiseworthy characteristics. And
through training their bodies to act according to
positive traits, they will be worthy of receiving
goodness. For, as we have explained, goodness
and blessing fall exclusively on the good. . . .

If it were not for this benefit, G-d could
provide the poor with their needs without
us. Rather, out of sheer kindness, the blessed
G-d made us His messengers so that we can
become meritorious through the process.

Rabbi Lord Jonathan Sacks on how we should understand the reason of *mitzvot*: myjli.com/meditation

TEXT 10

Honoring Parents Meditation

Sefer Hachinuch, Mitzvah 33

מִצְוַת כִּבּוּד אָב וָאֵם . . . מִשָּׁרְשֵׁי מִצְוָה זוֹ, שֶׁרָאוּי לוֹ לָאָדָם שֶׁיַּכִּיר
וְיִגְמֹל חֶסֶד לְמִי שֶׁעָשָׂה עִמּוֹ טוֹבָה, וְלֹא יִהְיֶה נָבָל וּמִתְנַכֵּר וּכְפוּי
טוֹבָה, שֶׁזּוֹ מִדָּה רָעָה וּמְאוּסָה בְּתַכְלִית לִפְנֵי אֱלֹקִים וַאֲנָשִׁים.

וְשֶׁיִּתֵּן אֶל לִבּוֹ כִּי הָאָב וְהָאֵם הֵם סִבַּת הֱיוֹתוֹ בָּעוֹלָם, וְעַל כֵּן
בֶּאֱמֶת רָאוּי לוֹ לַעֲשׂוֹת לָהֶם כָּל כָּבוֹד וְכָל תּוֹעֶלֶת שֶׁיּוּכַל, כִּי
הֵם הֱבִיאוּהוּ לָעוֹלָם, וְגַם יָגְעוּ בּוֹ כַּמָּה יְגִיעוֹת בְּקַטְנוּתוֹ.

The root of the commandment for an individual to honor their father and mother . . . is that it is fitting for a person to acknowledge and return kindness to those who provided goodness, and to avoid becoming a selfish ingrate—an evil and repulsive attribute in the eyes of G-d and mortals alike.

The mitzvah is designed to spur us to contemplate that our parents are the material cause of our existence in this world. It is therefore truly fitting to honor them in every way and to provide them with every benefit that is within our ability, for they brought us into the world and also toiled on our behalf in numerous ways when we were young.

TEXT 11

Shabbat Meditation

Sefer Hachinuch, Mitzvah 32

שֶׁלֹּא לַעֲשׂוֹת מְלָאכָה בְּשַׁבָּת . . . מִשָּׁרְשֵׁי מִצְוָה זוֹ, שֶׁנִּהְיֶה פְּנוּיִים מֵעֲסָקֵינוּ לִכְבוֹד הַיּוֹם, לִקְבּוֹעַ בְּנַפְשׁוֹתֵינוּ אֱמוּנַת חִדּוּשׁ הָעוֹלָם, שֶׁהִיא חֶבֶל הַמּוֹשֶׁכֶת כָּל יְסוֹדֵי הַדָּת.

The root of this commandment to abstain from work on Shabbat . . . is that we should free ourselves from our occupations to honor the day of Shabbat, thereby instilling within ourselves belief in G-d's creation of the universe. For this belief is the cord to which every foundation of our religion is attached.

TEXT 12

Tefilin Meditation

Sefer Hachinuch, Mitzvah 324

וּמִכְּלַל הַמִּצְוֹת שֶׁצִּוָּנוּ לְהַתְפִּישׂ מַחְשַׁבְתֵּנוּ בַּעֲבוֹדָתוֹ בְּטָהֳרָה, הִיא מִצְוַת הַתְּפִלִּין, לִהְיוֹתָן מֻנָּחוֹת כְּנֶגֶד אֶבְרֵי הָאָדָם הַיְדוּעִים בּוֹ לְמִשְׁכַּן הַשֵּׂכֶל, וְהֵם הַלֵּב וְהַמֹּחַ. וּמִתּוֹךְ פָּעֳלוֹ זֶה, תָּמִיד יְיַחֵד כָּל מַחְשְׁבוֹתָיו לְטוֹב, וְיִזְכֹּר וְיִזָּהֵר תָּמִיד כָּל הַיּוֹם לְכַוֵּן כָּל מַעֲשָׂיו בְּיֹשֶׁר וּבְצֶדֶק.

Among those commandments from G-d that are for the sake of molding thoughts in order to serve Him in purity is the commandment of *tefilin*.

Tefilin are to be placed on the body in locations corresponding to the brain and the heart—organs that are referred to as the seats of intellect and perception. Laying *tefilin* and contemplating their purpose leads to dedicating all thoughts to the good, and leads to constantly remembering to be careful to calibrate all deeds in righteousness and justice.

TEXT 13

Mezuzah **Meditation**

Maimonides, *Mishneh Torah*, Laws of *Tefilin*, *Mezuzah*, and *Sefer Torah* 6:13

חַיָּב אָדָם לְהִזָּהֵר בִּמְזוּזָה, מִפְּנֵי שֶׁהִיא חוֹבַת הַכֹּל תָּמִיד.

וְכָל זְמַן שֶׁיִּכָּנֵס וְיֵצֵא, יִפְגַּע בְּיִחוּד הַשֵּׁם - שְׁמוֹ שֶׁל הַקָּדוֹשׁ בָּרוּךְ הוּא, וְיִזְכֹּר אַהֲבָתוֹ וְיֵעוֹר מִשְּׁנָתוֹ וְשִׁגְיוֹתָיו בְּהַבְלֵי הַזְּמַן. וְיֵדַע שֶׁאֵין דָּבָר הָעוֹמֵד לְעוֹלָם וּלְעוֹלְמֵי עוֹלָמִים אֶלָּא יְדִיעַת צוּר הָעוֹלָם. וּמִיָּד הוּא חוֹזֵר לְדַעְתּוֹ, וְהוֹלֵךְ בְּדַרְכֵי מֵישָׁרִים.

We must be careful to observe the mitzvah of *mezuzah*, for it is an obligation that is constantly incumbent upon everyone.

Through observing this precept, whenever we enter or leave [our homes], we encounter the symbol of G-d's unity and recall our love for Him. This activity shakes us awake from our spiritual slumber—our obsession with material vanities—so that we recognize that nothing we gain lasts forever except knowledge of the Creator of the universe. This will spur us to regain proper mindful awareness and make upright decisions.

IV. TAKEAWAY

This fresh perspective on *mitzvot*, gained through highlighting their meditative elements, is of mutual benefit to ourselves and the *mitzvot*: Now that we can appreciate them in this way, we are moved to enhance the way we perform them. And we are now equipped to allow them to enhance our perspectives, characters, and life choices.

EXERCISE 6.5

What can I do or contemplate before I perform a mitzvah that will help me tune into the mitzvah's meditative power?

A young man kisses the *mezuzah* as he walks through a doorway. Postcard of Moritz Daniel Oppenheim's painting *Der Dorfgeher*–The Village Walker, from the portfolio Pictures from *Old Jewish Family Life*, Frankfurt am Main. Approximately 1882. Watercolor on board. (Jewish Museum Berlin)

FIGURE 6.1

Jewish Mindful Awareness Practices

Much of our decision-making and behavior is done unconsciously, disconnected from our true intention. Mindful awareness practices help us align our reactions with our core values and our greater purpose. Bringing these primary motivations to the front of our minds makes it more likely that our words, actions, and responses, particularly during challenging moments, are consistent with our principles and in line with our goals.

Studies show that mindful awareness practices impact health, well-being and capacity for learning.[1]

Many Jewish religious practices also serve the role of focusing us on our greater purpose and core values in life. The following texts highlight some of these practices.

1. Yamada, K. and Victor, T. L., "The Impact of Mindful Awareness Practices on College Student Health, Well-Being, and Capacity for Learning: A Pilot Study," *Psychology Learning and Teaching* 11(2), 2012, pp. 139–145.

Modeh Ani:
First Thing in the Morning

In Jewish practice, we begin our day by reciting the Modeh Ani immediately upon awakening. While we sleep at night, Judaism teaches that our soul leaves the body and ascends to Heaven for spiritual rejuvenation. Sleep is, therefore, akin to partial demise, and our awakening is a restoration of life.

In the brief Modeh Ani prayer, we express our gratitude for being granted the opportunity of a new day. Contemplating the meaning of this prayer, and acknowledging every day as a gift given to us for a purpose, can serve as an anchor for our entire day, keeping it aligned with our core principles and beliefs.

The prayer concludes with "Your faithfulness is great," alluding to G-d's confidence in us to fulfill the mission he has entrusted us with – to make our corner of the world a better place.

The following is the transliteration and translation of Modeh Ani:

Modeh ani lefanecha, Melech chai vekayam, shehechezarta bi nishmati bechemla, rabah emunatecha.

I thank You, living and eternal King, for You have graciously restored my soul within me; Your faithfulness is great.

The Rebbe, Rabbi Menachem Mendel Schneerson, 1902-1994, *Likutei Sichot*, vol. 3, pp. 940–941

We engage in a range of activities in the course of the day. Some are associated with our corporeal needs, and others with our spiritual pursuits. However, G-d's Divine light is not discernable within our daily preoccupations . . . and they can even lead us to veer from the straight path to the extent that we might act contrary to G-d's wishes.

It is therefore necessary to mobilize ourselves preemptively, at the very start of our day—well before approaching our various routine activities—and to first and foremost express our absolute dedication to G-d.

This is the significance of our reciting Modeh Ani immediately upon awakening. We thank G-d for restoring our soul—and at the same time, we acknowledge that G-d is our King. The latter is necessary because in a relationship between a genuine monarch and a subject, the individual is entirely dedicated, heart and soul, to the monarch's will and interests.

We similarly dedicate ourselves completely to our King, and we do so at the very start of our day, so that this approach can influence each subsequent hour of the day—including time spent on personal needs and pursuits. Our Modeh Ani echoes through those activities as well, ensuring that they are imbued with a sense of dedication to our King, our Creator. As a natural consequence of this approach, G-d responds in kind, imbuing our everyday affairs with His own blessings and influence.

The Afternoon Prayer

In Judaism, we pray three times a day: morning, afternoon, and night. The Morning Prayer service is the most comprehensive, while the afternoon and evening services are brief.

The afternoon prayer, known as Minchah, is recited anytime from early afternoon until sunset, usually necessitating an interruption of the workday. The service consists of four parts. It begins with Ashrei (Psalms 145), followed by the Amidah, recited while standing and facing Jerusalem. The service concludes with Tachanun, a confessional prayer; and Aleinu, a song of praise for G-d.

Minchah thus provides an excellent opportunity to pause momentarily in the throes of our routine engagements for a moment of reflection, facilitating a realignment of our daily endeavors with our life's purpose.

Rabbi Yaakov ben Asher, 1269-1343, *Arbaah Turim, Orach Chayim* 232

Rabbi Chelbo quoted Rabbi Huna as teaching that we should always be careful to recite the afternoon Minchah service, for the prophet Elijah was answered specifically at the Minchah service, as it is stated (I Kings 18:36), "It happened at the time of the Minchah that Elijah the prophet came near" (Talmud, Berachot 6b).

The reason for the extra significance of the afternoon prayer is due to its timing. The morning service is scheduled for early morning; immediately upon rising from sleep, we ready ourselves for prayer—before we become engrossed in other concerns. Similarly, the evening service is scheduled for after we return home from work in the evenings, when we are no longer busy with our affairs. By contrast, the afternoon service arrives in the middle of the day, interrupting our work. We are required to set everything aside and focus sincerely on our prayers. If we actually do so, our reward in great indeed.

Nighttime Shema

The brief prayer recited before retiring for the night is a deeply personal, individualized, and particularly private ritual. Its main feature is the Shema ("Hear, O Israel") passages, supplemented with additional prayers and requests for forgiveness and protection.

Just before reciting Shema, we make an honest self-accounting in our minds and hearts of our conduct throughout the day that has ended. We meditate on our purpose in life and compare it to our thoughts, speech, emotions, and behaviors that day. We identify flaws that require work and successes to be repeated and amplified. Thus we set goals and chart a path for the next day, in sync with our purpose and spiritual goals.

Rabbi Yosef Yitzchak Schneersohn, 1880-1950, *Sefer Hamaamarim* 5702, pp. 92–93

The primary service of the Shema recited before retiring at night is the introspective review that must accompany it. When we recite the Shema, we should contemplate the mission for which G-d sent us to this world, and evaluate how we are fulfilling our individual purpose. We need to analyze the way we spent our day to determine whether it was conducted in the manner that the Torah expects:

Our first thought and spoken words upon awakening should be dedicated to G-d's service. For that reason, we recite the Modeh Ani prayer, which serves as an all-inclusive expression of gratitude to G-d for His tremendous kindness in restoring our souls. This is uttered immediately upon regaining consciousness after sleep, even before we wash our hands.

After rising, we must engage in actual Divine service—each individual according to their capability. Those who spend their days in the study of Torah must now engage in its study. Those unable to study Torah should recite Tehilim [Psalms], and pray the morning service with a congregation at an unhurried pace.

Before starting the service, we should accept upon ourselves to fulfill the mitzvah of loving our fellow Jews. Then, during the prayers, we must plead with G-d to give us the merit of fulfilling the mitzvah of loving our fellow Jews in actual practice and in a beautiful way.

Following the service, we must engage in our work honestly. We must also maintain scheduled times for Torah study each day. The afternoon and evening services must be recited with a congregation, and we must conduct ourselves in a good and refined manner throughout the day.

Such is the general order of daily conduct that the Torah expects of each individual, and every night we should evaluate the extent to which our past day indeed reflected this.

KEY POINTS

1   Although Judaism emphasizes action over all else, the active performance of the *mitzvot* have a meditative quality too.

2   *Mitzvot,* as acts of service to G-d, bridge the divide between mortal mankind and the infinite G-d, and *mitzvot* serve to establish a relationship with G-d.

3   This meditative intent that motivates mitzvah performance is what makes them meaningful.

4   *Mitzvot* also personally benefit the person performing them.

5   Our actions and behaviors shape our mindsets and attitudes.

6   Each mitzvah serves a meditative function to shape our moral and spiritual perspectives and to develop positive attitudes.

APPENDIX

TEXT 14

Divine Embrace

Rabbi Shneur Zalman of Liadi, *Tanya*, *Likutei Amarim*, chapter 46

וְהוּא, כַּאֲשֶׁר יָשִׂים אֶל לִבּוֹ מַה שֶׁאָמַר הַכָּתוּב: "כַּמַּיִם הַפָּנִים לַפָּנִים,
כֵּן לֵב הָאָדָם אֶל הָאָדָם" (מִשְׁלֵי כז, יט). פֵּרוּשׁ, כְּמוֹ שֶׁכִּדְמוּת
וְצוּרַת הַפָּנִים שֶׁהָאָדָם מַרְאֶה בַּמַּיִם - כֵּן נִרְאֶה לוֹ שָׁם בַּמַּיִם אוֹתָהּ
צוּרָה עַצְמָהּ, כָּכָה מַמָּשׁ לֵב הָאָדָם הַנֶּאֱמָן בְּאַהֲבָתוֹ לְאִישׁ אַחֵר
- הֲרֵי הָאַהֲבָה זוֹ מְעוֹרֶרֶת אַהֲבָה בְּלֵב חֲבֵרוֹ אֵלָיו גַּם כֵּן, לִהְיוֹת
אוֹהֲבִים נֶאֱמָנִים זֶה לָזֶה, בִּפְרָט כְּשֶׁרוֹאֶה אַהֲבַת חֲבֵרוֹ אֵלָיו. וְהִנֵּה
זֶהוּ טֶבַע הַנָּהוּג בְּמִדַּת כָּל אָדָם, אַף אִם שְׁנֵיהֶם שָׁוִים בְּמַעֲלָה.

וְעַל אַחַת כַּמָּה וְכַמָּה אִם מֶלֶךְ גָּדוֹל וְרַב מַרְאֶה אַהֲבָתוֹ הַגְּדוֹלָה
וְהָעֲצוּמָה לְאִישׁ הֶדְיוֹט וְנִבְזֶה וּשְׁפַל אֲנָשִׁים וּמְנֻוָל הַמֻּטָּל בָּאַשְׁפָּה,
וְיוֹרֵד אֵלָיו מִמְּקוֹם כְּבוֹדוֹ עִם כָּל שָׂרָיו יַחְדָּו, וּמְקִימוֹ וּמְרִימוֹ
מֵאַשְׁפָּתוֹ, וּמַכְנִיסוֹ לְהֵיכָלוֹ הֵיכַל הַמֶּלֶךְ חֶדֶר לִפְנִים מֵחֶדֶר, מָקוֹם
שֶׁאֵין כָּל עֶבֶד וְשַׂר נִכְנָס לְשָׁם, וּמִתְיַחֵד עִמּוֹ שָׁם בְּיִחוּד וְקֵרוּב
אֲמִתִּי וְחִבּוּק וְנִשּׁוּק, וְאִתְדַּבְּקוּת רוּחָא בְּרוּחָא בְּכָל לֵב וָנֶפֶשׁ -

עַל אַחַת כַּמָּה וְכַמָּה שֶׁתִּתְעוֹרֵר מִמֵּילָא הָאַהֲבָה כְּפוּלָה
וּמְכֻפֶּלֶת בְּלֵב הַהֶדְיוֹט וּשְׁפַל אֲנָשִׁים הַזֶּה אֶל נֶפֶשׁ הַמֶּלֶךְ,
בְּהִתְקַשְׁרוּת הַנֶּפֶשׁ מַמָּשׁ מִלֵּב וָנֶפֶשׁ, מֵעֻמְקָא דְלִבָּא לְאֵין
קֵץ. וְאַף אִם לִבּוֹ כְּלֵב הָאֶבֶן - הֵמֵס יִמַּס וְהָיָה לְמָיִם, וְתִשְׁתַּפֵּךְ
נַפְשׁוֹ כַּמַּיִם בִּכְלוֹת הַנֶּפֶשׁ מַמָּשׁ לְאַהֲבַת הַמֶּלֶךְ.

וְהִנֵּה כָּל הַדְּבָרִים הָאֵלֶּה וּכְכָל הַחִזָּיוֹן הַזֶּה, וְגָדוֹל יָתֵר מְאֹד
בְּכִפְלֵי כִפְלַיִם לְאֵין קֵץ עָשָׂה לָנוּ אֱלֹקֵינוּ, כִּי לִגְדֻלָּתוֹ אֵין
חֵקֶר, וְאִיהוּ מְמַלֵּא כָּל עָלְמִין וְסוֹבֵב כָּל עָלְמִין . . .

כִּי הִנִּיחַ הַקָּדוֹשׁ בָּרוּךְ הוּא אֶת הָעֶלְיוֹנִים וְאֶת הַתַּחְתּוֹנִים, וְלֹא
בָחַר בְּכֻלָּם כִּי אִם בְּיִשְׂרָאֵל עַמּוֹ, וְהוֹצִיאָם מִמִּצְרַיִם עֶרְוַת
הָאָרֶץ, מְקוֹם הַזֻּהֲמָא וְהַטֻּמְאָה, לֹא עַל יְדֵי מַלְאָךְ וְלֹא עַל

יְדֵי וְכוּ', אֶלָּא הַקָּדוֹשׁ בָּרוּךְ הוּא בִּכְבוֹדוֹ וּבְעַצְמוֹ יָרַד לְשָׁם,
כְּמוֹ שֶׁכָּתוּב: "וָאֵרֵד לְהַצִּילוֹ וְגו'" (שְׁמוֹת ג, ח), כְּדֵי לְקָרְבָם
אֵלָיו בְּקֵרוּב וְיִחוּד אֲמִתִּי, בְּהִתְקַשְּׁרוּת הַנֶּפֶשׁ מַמָּשׁ.

בִּבְחִינַת:

נְשִׁיקִין פֶּה לְפֶה, לְדַבֵּר דְּבַר ה' זוֹ הֲלָכָה.

וְאִתְדַּבְּקוּת רוּחָא בְּרוּחָא, הִיא הַשָּׂגַת הַתּוֹרָה
וִידִיעַת רְצוֹנוֹ וְחָכְמָתוֹ, דְּכָלָּא חַד מַמָּשׁ.

וְגַם בִּבְחִינַת חִבּוּק, הוּא קִיּוּם הַמִּצְוֹת מַעֲשִׂיּוֹת בְּרַמַ"ח אֵבָרִים,
דְּרַמַ"ח פִּקּוּדִין הֵן רַמַ"ח אֵבָרִין דְּמַלְכָּא, כַּנִּזְכָּר לְעֵיל.

[One way to arrive at a love for G-d is to] take to heart the verse: "As water reflects a face, so does the heart of man reflect another heart" (PROVERBS 27:19). This means that just as water reflects the very image and features that a person presents before it, so too, a heart that is loyal in its love for another awakens a corresponding loving response, cementing the mutual love and loyalty. This is especially true when the love is observable. This is a universal law of human nature that applies even if the two people involved are equal.

How much more so this law applies if a great and mighty king shows immense love for a commoner, who is scorned, lowly, covered in filth, and lying in a dunghill. [Imagine the king] leaving his [royal palace] and, accompanied by his entire retinue of ministers, he approaches the commoner. The king extracts him from the dunghill and brings him into the innermost chamber of his royal palace, a room where no servant or minister is permitted entry. There the king embraces and kisses him and shares with him the closest of friendships, a spiritual attachment of the heart and soul.

How great will be the love of this commoner and lowly individual for the king? He will most certainly be attached to the king with heart and soul, with infinite heartfelt sincerity. Even if his heart is made of stone, it will surely melt and become water, and it will pour with soulful longing for the love of the king.

Now, all of this precisely, exactly as described, G-d has done with us. But it is infinitely greater because His greatness defies comprehension, and He pervades all worlds and transcends all worlds. . . .

G-d disregarded the higher and lower worlds and their inhabitants, and He chose none else but Israel, His nation. He brought them out of Egypt—the most decadent place on earth, a place of spiritual filth and impurity. He did not send an angel to take them out; rather, He alone in His majesty and glory descended there, as G-d said: "I have come down to rescue them. . . ." (EXODUS 3:8). He took them out to bring them near to Him with true closeness and unity, to share with them a soul connection.

This connection includes:

— Kisses, mouth to mouth, which occurs when we speak the word of G‑d, namely, the Halachah;

— The fusion of spirits, which occurs when we comprehend the Torah and know His will and wisdom, all of which is truly one with G‑d;

— And also embracing, which occurs when we use our 248 limbs to fulfill the 248 *mitzvot* of the Torah, which symbolize G‑d's "organs" [and thus when fulfilling them, we embrace G‑d's "body"].

The decorated initial word of the book of Proverbs in the North French Hebrew Miscellany. Detail, last quarter of the 13th century. (British Museum [MS 11639], London)

COURSE CONCLUSION

LESSON 1

LESSON 2

LESSON 3

LESSON 4

LESSON 5

LESSON 6

A Mitzvah Blessing Meditation

The observance of a mitzvah is usually preceded with the recital of a blessing, praising G-d for directing us to perform this specific duty. The standard formulation for these blessings is, "Blessed are You G-d, our L-rd, Ruler of the universe, Who has sanctified us with His commandments and commanded us . . ." The blessing's conclusion is personalized for the specific mitzvah under consideration.

In the teachings of *Chasidut*, multiple layers of profound meaning are revealed within the standard blessing formulation— including the following classic meditation:

בָּרוּךְ
Baruch   Blessed

The Hebrew term for blessing, *baruch*, is etymologically related to the verb for layering a grapevine, *mavri'ach*. The layering process entails channeling a branch of a vine downward through the soil, for the purpose of sprouting another vine in a different place. In the context of the blessing, *baruch* refers to drawing down Divine energy—from its spiritual origin into our world.

אַתָּה
Atah   [Are] You

"You" is the most direct form of address, used when our audience is present before us. In the context of a blessing, we request that G-d's light be drawn down and revealed to us overtly—to the extent that it is as directly present and obvious as someone we can address directly as "you."

אֲשֶׁר
asher   Who has

The Hebrew word *asher* is etymologically related to the word *ashreinu*, "we are fortunate." When reciting a blessing we are proclaiming how fortunate we are that G-d has sanctified us with his commandments.

קִדְּשָׁנוּ
kideshanu   sanctified us

The word *kideshanu*, "sanctified us" (from the root: *k-d-sh*) is also used to refer to the matrimonial bond that unites husband and wife as one. G-d not only bestows sanctity upon us, but intimately bonds with us in the process of that bestowal.

ה׳
Ado-nai   **G-d**

This pronunciation of G-d's name (*Ado-nai*) is used as a substitute for G-d's most personal, ineffable name (which is from the root: *Y-H-V-H*) that refers to G-d's absolutely infinite Divinity that transcends everything that exists.

אֱ-לֹהֵינוּ
Elo-heinu   **our L-rd**

This Divine name, *Elokim*, (L-rd) refers to G-d as He relates to His creations. Moreover, we describe G-d as "*our L- rd*," meaning that G-d is the source of our personal strength and vitality. When reciting a blessing, we are asking G-d to express His infinite Divine light (*Ado-nai*) overtly, within our tangible reality (*Elo-heinu*).

מֶלֶךְ
melech   **ruler**

Referring to G-d as the Ruler of the universe and all its affairs.

הָעוֹלָם
ha'olam   **of the universe**

The Hebrew term for universe or world is *olam*, etymologically related to the word *he'elem*, "concealment," because our world conceals G-d's presence. When reciting a blessing, we ask for G-d's rule (*Melech*)—to be revealed within this world of concealment (*olam*).

בְּמִצְוֹתָיו
bemitzvotav   **with His commandments**

Through His commandments, G-d sanctifies and bonds with us, in the sense that we unite with The One Whose will we are implementing through the performance of a mitzvah.

וְצִוָּנוּ
vetzivanu   **and commanded us**

"Mitzvah" means "commandment," and also "attachment." With each mitzvah, G-d provides us with another channel through which to bond with Him. And with the full array of *mitzvot*, we become bonded to Him to the extent that we are His holy nation—holy as He is.

Sources: *Torah Or*, Miketz 37c; *Likutei Torah, Derushim Leyom Hakipurim* 68c; *Tanya, Likutei Amarim*, ch. 46; *Maamarei Admur Ha'emtza'i, Neviim Uketuvim*, p. 278; *Torat Shmuel* 5639:1, p. 216.

The Purpose of *Mitzvot*

The following texts present a range of
perspectives about the purpose of *mitzvot*.

THE LOGIC OF *MITZVOT*

📖 Maimonides, 1135-1204, *Guide for the Perplexed* 3:27

The overall object of the Torah is twofold: that we obtain the well-being of the soul and the well-being of the body.

The well-being of the soul is promoted by correct opinions communicated to people according to their capacity. Some of these opinions are therefore imparted in plain form, others allegorically, because certain opinions in their plain form are too strong for the capacity of the common people.

The well-being of the body is established by a proper management of human relations. This is obtained through two things: first by removing all violence from our midst. That is to say, that we disallow an environment where people do as they please, as they desire, and as they are able to do. Rather, we promote a society in which everyone contributes toward the common welfare. Secondly, by teaching us good morals that are necessary to produce a good social state. . . .

The true Torah of Moses, aside from which there is no other Torah, has come to give us this twofold perfection. It aims first at the establishment of good mutual relations among people by removing injustice and creating the noblest feelings, so that the people in every land live with stability and acquire the first perfection. Secondly, it seeks to train us in faith, and to impart correct and true opinions when the intellect is sufficiently developed.

Scripture clearly mentions both of these perfections and tells us that their acquisition is the object of all the Divine commandments. "G-d commanded us to obey all these decrees and to be in awe of Him, for our good always, so that He will preserve us as is the case today" (Deuteronomy 6:24). Here the second perfection is mentioned first because it is of greater importance, being, as we have shown, the ultimate aim of our existence.

MULTILAYERED *MITZVOT*

The Rebbe, Rabbi Menachem Mendel Schneerson, 1902-1994, *Likutei Sichot* 32, p. 178, fn. 34 and marginal note

Maimonides rejected the opinion that *mitzvot* are an expression of G-d's will. However, it can be argued that Maimonides does agree that the *original* source of *mitzvot* is in G-d's will that transcends reason. He only intended to reject the possibility that *mitzvot* are exclusively an expression of will, without any reason at all.

In *Guide for the Perplexed*, Maimonides provides reasons for the *mitzvot*, which can be appreciated on the most rudimentary level of human logic. Beyond this, however, there are multiple degrees of profundity to the rationale behind the *mitzvot*. There are the reasons that exist within G-d's own wisdom, which are far beyond the grasp of mortal perception, and there are insights that have descended into lower forms of wisdom, the lowest of which is basic human logic.

G-D'S DESIRE

Rabbi Yehudah Halevi, 1075-1141, *Kuzari* 1:98–99, 2:26

Man can only merit to achieve closeness to G-d through G-dly matters, namely, through performing the actions commanded by G-d. . . . G-d is not served through human reason, logical deduction, or intellectual inquiry. Were this to be the way to serve Him, philosophers would attain greater closeness to G-d through their wisdom and intellectual inquiry than the Jewish people do [through performance of the *mitzvot*]. . . .

The greatest and most exalted way to perform the commandments is to do so because they are G-d's instructions. One who accepts this completely without intellectual speculation is greater than one that speculates and ponders them.

The Purpose of *Mitzvot* continued

ACTIONS SHAPE CHARACTER

📖 *Sefer Hachinuch*, 13th Century, Mitzvah 16

Now, my child, "If you have understanding" (Job 34:16), "incline your ear and hear" (Proverbs 22:17), and I will teach you properly about Torah and *mitzvot*.

You must know that humans are influenced by their actions; our hearts and thoughts are always influenced by our actions, for the good or for the bad. Even complete sinners whose desires are only for evil, if they will have the good sense to occupy themselves with Torah and *mitzvot*—even if not for the sake of Heaven—they will immediately become inclined toward good. And from performing actions for ulterior motives they will eventually come to perform them for their own sake, because hearts are drawn after actions.

On the other hand, even if people are perfectly righteous and their hearts are straight and innocent and they desire Torah and *mitzvot*, if they constantly deal with improper things—like those forced by the king to work a wicked craft—they will become wicked if they occupy themselves with it constantly. For it is known and true that people are influenced by their actions, as we have said.

The sages of blessed memory said about this: "G-d wished to make Israel meritorious and therefore gave them an abundance of Torah and *mitzvot*" (Mishnah, Makot 3:16). The object of the many *mitzvot* is to occupy all of our thoughts so that we can become better people, because we are positively influenced by our good actions, and through this we will merit eternal life.

ABUNDANT *MITZVOT*

📖 *Rabbi Moshe Alshich, 1508-1600 , Psalms 119:4*

Why did G-d give us 613 *mitzvot* to fulfill? Is it not sufficient to guard ourselves from wrongdoing? . . .

It is with this question in mind that Rabbi Chananyah ben Akashya taught (Talmud, Makot 23b), "G-d wished to make Israel meritorious and therefore gave them an abundance of Torah and *mitzvot*. As it is written (Isaiah 42:21), 'G-d desired, for the sake of Israel's righteousness, to make the Torah extensive and glorious.'"

Rabbi Chananyah's teaching was motivated by the following concern: the Talmud teaches (Kidushin 39b) that those who do a single mitzvah and guard themselves from sin inherit the World to Come. Why, then, did G-d give us such an extensive Torah and so many *mitzvot*?

Rabbi Chananyah's solution, as per his teaching, is that G-d wished to make us meritorious—He gave us Torah and *mitzvot* in abundant measure in order that we should be able to increase our merit by observing more *mitzvot*.

Additionally, providing us with an abundance of commandments guarantees that we will always have the opportunity to fulfill a mitzvah. This would not have been the case if we only had a few *mitzvot*.

MITZVAH REVELATION

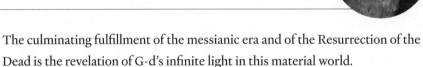

Rabbi Shneur Zalman of Liadi, 1745-1812, *Tanya, Likutei Amarim*, ch. 37

The culminating fulfillment of the messianic era and of the Resurrection of the Dead is the revelation of G-d's infinite light in this material world.

This revelation depends on our actions throughout the duration of the exile. For the reward of a mitzvah is the direct outcome of the mitzvah itself. That is, by virtue of performing a commandment, a person suffuses a flood of infinite Divine light from above downward, to be clothed in the corporeality of the world, in something that was previously under the dominion of impure forces and from which it had received its vitality.

This occurs when we utilize things, in a proper way, to perform a mitzvah. For example, when we take the hides of kosher animals to produce a pair of *tefilin*, a *mezuzah*, or a Torah scroll. Or when we utilize an *etrog* not subject to the prohibition of *orlah* to fulfill the mitzvah of *lulav* and *etrog*. Or when we donate money that has not been acquired through theft to charity. And other similar examples.

When a person performs the commandment by means of utilizing these permissible items, their vitality ascends and is absorbed into the light of G-d, and on this level, there is no concealment of G-d's light. . . .

Active mitzvah performance is our entire purpose and the reason we were created—to turn the darkness of this lowly world into light, so that the Divine Presence should become apparent throughout the entire physical world, with the emphasis on *physical*, and "All flesh shall see it together" (Isaiah 40:5), as has been discussed earlier.

Acknowledgments

We are grateful to the following individuals for their contributions to this course:

Flagship Director
RABBI SHMULY KARP

Curriculum Coordinator
RIVKI MOCKIN

Flagship Administrator
NAOMI HEBER

Author
RABBI MENASHE WOLF

Curriculum Team
RABBI MORDECHAI DINERMAN
RABBI AHRELE LOSCHAK
RABBI SHMUEL SUPER

Instructor Advisory Board
RABBI YANKIE DENBURG
RABBI MENACHEM FELDMAN
RABBI MICHOEL GOURARIE
RABBI YOSEF LEVIN
RABBI MENDEL LIFSHITZ
RABBI MORDECHAI NEWMAN

Research
RABBI YAKOV GERSHON

Copywriter
RABBI YAAKOV PALEY

Proofreading
RACHEL MUSICANTE
YA'AKOVAH WEBER

Hebrew Punctuation
RABBI MOSHE WOLFF

Instructor Support
RABBI ISAAC ABELSKY
RABBI MENDEL ABELSKY

Design and Layout Administrator
ROCHEL KARP

Textbook and Marketing Design
CHAYA MUSHKA KANNER
RABBI LEVI WEINGARTEN

Textbook Layout
RIVKY FIELDSTEEL
SHAYNA GROSH
RABBI ZALMAN KORF

Permissions
SHULAMIS NADLER

Imagery
SARA ROSENBLUM

Publication and Distribution
RABBI LEVI GOLDSHMID
RABBI MENDEL SIROTA

Branding and Marketing
RABBI MENDEL JACOBSON

PowerPoint Presentations
CHANIE DENBURG
MUSHKA DRUK
MUSHKA GOLDFARB
BAILA GOLDSTEIN
CHAYA MINTZ

Course Videos
GETZY RASKIN
MOSHE RASKIN

Key Points Videos
RABBI MOTTI KLEIN

We are immensely grateful for the encouragement of JLI's visionary chairman, the vice-chairman of *Merkos L'Inyonei Chinuch*—Lubavitch World Headquarters, **Rabbi Moshe Kotlarsky**. Rabbi Kotlarsky has been highly instrumental in building the infrastructure for the expansion of Chabad's international network and is also the architect of scores of initiatives and services to help Chabad representatives across the globe succeed in their mission.

We are blessed to have the unwavering support of JLI's principal benefactor, **Mr. George Rohr**, who is fully invested in our work, continues to be instrumental in JLI's monumental growth and expansion, and is largely responsible for the Jewish renaissance that is being spearheaded by JLI and its affiliates across the globe.

The commitment and sage direction of JLI's dedicated Executive Board—**Rabbis Chaim Block**, **Hesh Epstein**, **Ronnie Fine**, **Yosef Gansburg**, **Shmuel Kaplan**, **Yisrael Rice**, and **Avrohom Sternberg**—and the countless hours they devote to the development of JLI are what drive the vision, growth, and tremendous success of the organization.

Finally, JLI represents an incredible partnership of more than 1,600 *shluchim* and *shluchot* in more than 1,000 locations across the globe, who contribute their time and talent to further Jewish adult education. We thank them for generously sharing feedback and making suggestions that steer JLI's development and growth.

Inspired by the call of the **Lubavitcher Rebbe**, of righteous memory, it is the mandate of the Rohr JLI to provide a community of learning for all Jews throughout the world where they can participate in their precious heritage of Torah learning and experience its rewards. May this course succeed in fulfilling this sacred charge!

On behalf of the Rohr Jewish Learning Institute,

RABBI EFRAIM MINTZ
Executive Director

RABBI YISRAEL RICE
Chairman, Editorial Board

5 Teves, 5782

The Rohr Jewish Learning Institute

CURRICULUM DEVELOPMENT
Rabbi Mordechai Dinerman
Rabbi Naftali Silberberg
EDITORS IN CHIEF

Rabbi Shmuel Klatzkin, PhD
ACADEMIC CONSULTANT

Rabbi Yanki Tauber
COURSE DESIGNER

Rabbi Chaim Fieldsteel
Rabbi Eliezer Gurkow
Rabbi Shmuel Super
Rabbi Menashe Wolf
CURRICULUM AUTHORS

Rabbi Yaakov Paley
Rabbi Boruch Werdiger
WRITERS

Rabbi Ahrele Loschak
EDITOR, TORAH STUDIES

Rabbi Mendel Glazman
Mrs. Mushka Grossbaum
Rabbi Zalman Margolin
Rabbi Moshe Wolff
EDITORIAL SUPPORT

Rabbi Shmuel Gomes
Rabbi Yakov Gershon
RESEARCH

Rabbi Michoel Lipskier
Rabbi Mendel Rubin
EXPERIENTIAL LEARNING

Mrs. Rivki Mockin
CONTENT COORDINATOR

MARKETING AND BRANDING
Rabbi Zalman Abraham
DIRECTOR

Avi Webb
BRAND COPYWRITER

Ms. Rochel Karp
DESIGN ADMINISTRATOR

Mrs. Chaya Mushka Kanner
Ms. Estie Ravnoy
Mrs. Shifra Tauber
Rabbi Levi Weingarten
GRAPHIC DESIGN

Mrs. Rivky Fieldsteel
Mrs. Shayna Grosh
Rabbi Motti Klein
Rabbi Zalman Korf
Rabbi Moshe Wolff
PUBLICATION DESIGN

Lazer Cohen
Yosef Feigelstock
Menachem Klein
Mrs. Basya Stevenson
SOCIAL MEDIA

Rabbi Yaakov Paley
WRITER

Rabbi Yossi Grossbaum
Rabbi Mendel Lifshitz
Rabbi Shraga Sherman
Rabbi Ari Sollish
Rabbi Mendel Teldon
MARKETING COMMITTEE

MARKETING CONSULTANTS
Alan Rosenspan
ALAN ROSENSPAN & ASSOCIATES
Sharon, MA

Gary Wexler
PASSION MARKETING
Los Angeles, CA

JLI CENTRAL
Rabbi Isaac Abelsky
Rabbi Mendel Abelsky
Mrs. Adina Lerman
Ms. Mimi Rabinowitz
Mrs. Aliza Scheinfeld
ADMINISTRATION

Ms. Liba Leah Gutnick
Rabbi Motti Klein
Mrs. Sara Rosenblum
Rabbi Shlomie Tenenbaum
Rabbi Chaim Zippel
PROJECT MANAGERS

Mrs. Mindy Wallach
AFFILIATE ORIENTATION

Mrs. Bunia Chazan
Mrs. Chanie Denburg
Mrs. Mushka Druk
Mrs. Mushka Goldfarb
Mrs. Baila Goldstein
Rabbi Motti Klein
Getzy Raskin
Moshe Raskin
MULTIMEDIA DEVELOPMENT

Rabbi Mendel Ashkenazi
Yoni Ben-Oni
Rabbi Mendy Elishevitz
Mendel Grossbaum
Ms. Mushkie Lent
Rabbi Aron Liberow
Mrs. Chana Weinbaum
ONLINE DIVISION

Mrs. Ya'akovah Weber
LEAD PROOFREADER

Mrs. Rachel Musicante
PROOFREADER

Rabbi Levi Goldshmid
Rabbi Mendel Sirota
PRINTING AND DISTRIBUTION

Mrs. Musie Liberow
Mrs. Shaina B. Mintz
Mrs. Shulamis Nadler
ACCOUNTING

Ms. Chaya Mintz
Mrs. Shulamis Nadler
Mrs. Mindy Wallach
CONTINUING EDUCATION

JLI FLAGSHIP
Rabbi Yisrael Rice
CHAIRMAN

Rabbi Shmuly Karp
DIRECTOR

Mrs. Naomi Heber
PROJECT MANAGER

CLINICAL ADVISORY BOARD

Sigrid Frandsen-Pechenik, PSY.D.
CLINICAL DIRECTOR

Kammarauche Asuzu, M.D., M.H.S.
Ryan G. Beale, MA, TLLP
David A. Brent, M.D.
Gittel Francis, LMSW
Jill Harkavy-Friedman, PhD
Madelyn S. Gould, PhD, M.P.H.
Lisa Jacobs, M.D., MBA
Thomas Joiner, PhD
E. David Klonsky, PhD
Bella Schanzer, M.D.
Jonathan Singer, PhD, LCSW
Casey Skvorc, PhD, JD
Darcy Wallen, LCSW, PC

JLI INTERNATIONAL

Rabbi Avrohom Sternberg
CHAIRMAN

Rabbi Dubi Rabinowitz
DIRECTOR

Rabbi Berry Piekarski
ADMINISTRATOR

Rabbi Eli Wolf
ADMINISTRATOR, JLI IN THE CIS
In Partnership with the Federation
of Jewish Communities of the CIS

Rabbi Shevach Zlatopolsky
EDITOR, JLI IN THE CIS

Rabbi Nochum Schapiro
REGIONAL REPRESENTATIVE, AUSTRALIA

Rabbi Avraham Golovacheov
REGIONAL REPRESENTATIVE, GERMANY

Rabbi Shmuel Katzman
REGIONAL REPRESENTATIVE, NETHERLANDS

Rabbi Avrohom Steinmetz
REGIONAL REPRESENTATIVE, BRAZIL

Rabbi Bentzi Sudak
REGIONAL REPRESENTATIVE,
UNITED KINGDOM

Rabbi Shlomo Cohen
FRENCH COORDINATOR,
REGIONAL REPRESENTATIVE

NATIONAL JEWISH RETREAT

Rabbi Hesh Epstein
CHAIRMAN

Mrs. Shaina B. Mintz
DIRECTOR

Bruce Backman
HOTEL LIAISON

Rabbi Menachem Klein
PROGRAM COORDINATOR

Rabbi Shmuly Karp
Rabbi Chaim Zippel
SHLUCHIM LIAISON

Rabbi Mendel Rosenfeld
LOGISTICS COORDINATOR

Ms. Rochel Karp
Mrs. Aliza Scheinfeld
SERVICE AND SUPPORT

JLI LAND & SPIRIT
Israel Experience

Rabbi Shmuly Karp
DIRECTOR

Rabbi Levi Goldshmid
SHLUCHIM LIAISON

Mrs. Shaina B. Mintz
ADMINISTRATOR

Rabbi Yechiel Baitelman
Rabbi Dovid Flinkenstein
Rabbi Chanoch Kaplan
Rabbi Levi Klein
Rabbi Mendy Mangel
Rabbi Sholom Raichik
STEERING COMMITTEE

SHABBAT IN THE HEIGHTS

Rabbi Shmuly Karp
DIRECTOR

Mrs. Shulamis Nadler
SERVICE AND SUPPORT

Rabbi Chaim Hanoka
CHAIRMAN

Rabbi Mordechai Dinerman
Rabbi Zalman Marcus
STEERING COMMITTEE

MYSHIUR
Advanced Learning Initiative

Rabbi Shmuel Kaplan
CHAIRMAN

Rabbi Shlomie Tenenbaum
ADMINISTRATOR

TORAHCAFE.COM
Online Learning

Rabbi Mendy Elishevitz
WEBSITE DEVELOPMENT

Moshe Levin
CONTENT MANAGER

Mendel Laine
FILMING

MACHON SHMUEL
The Sami Rohr Research Institute

Rabbi Zalman Korf
ADMINISTRATOR

Rabbi Moshe Miller
Rabbi Gedalya Oberlander
Rabbi Chaim Rapoport
Rabbi Levi Yitzchak Raskin
Rabbi Chaim Schapiro
RABBINIC ADVISORY BOARD

Rabbi Yakov Gershon
RESEARCH FELLOW

FOUNDING DEPARTMENT HEADS

Rabbi Mendel Bell
Rabbi Zalman Charytan
Rabbi Mendel Druk
Rabbi Menachem Gansburg
Rabbi Meir Hecht
Rabbi Levi Kaplan
Rabbi Yoni Katz
Rabbi Chaim Zalman Levy
Rabbi Benny Rapoport
Dr. Chana Silberstein
Rabbi Elchonon Tenenbaum
Rabbi Mendy Weg

JLI Chapter Directory

ALABAMA

BIRMINGHAM
Rabbi Yossi Friedman 205.970.0100

MOBILE
Rabbi Yosef Goldwasser 251.265.1213

ALASKA

ANCHORAGE
Rabbi Yosef Greenberg
Rabbi Mendy Greenberg 907.357.8770

ARIZONA

CHANDLER
Rabbi Mendy Deitsch 480.855.4333

FLAGSTAFF
Rabbi Dovie Shapiro 928.255.5756

FOUNTAIN HILLS
Rabbi Mendy Lipskier 480.776.4763

ORO VALLEY
Rabbi Ephraim Zimmerman 520.477.8672

PARADISE VALLEY
Rabbi Shlomo Levertov 480.788.9310

PHOENIX
Rabbi Dovber Dechter 347.410.0785
Rabbi Zalman Levertov
Rabbi Yossi Friedman 602.944.2753

SCOTTSDALE
Rabbi Yossi Levertov 480.998.1410

SEDONA
Rabbi Mendel Kessler 928.985.0667

TUCSON
Rabbi Yehuda Ceitlin 520.881.7956

ARKANSAS

LITTLE ROCK
Rabbi Pinchus Ciment 501.217.0053

CALIFORNIA

AGOURA HILLS
Rabbi Moshe Bryski 818.516.0444

ALAMEDA
Rabbi Meir Shmotkin 510.640.2590

BAKERSFIELD
Rabbi Shmuli Schlanger 661.834.1512

BEL AIR
Rabbi Chaim Mentz 310.475.5311

BURBANK
Rabbi Shmuly Kornfeld 818.954.0070

CARLSBAD
Rabbi Yeruchem Eilfort
Mrs. Nechama Eilfort 760.943.8891

CHATSWORTH
Rabbi Yossi Spritzer 818.307.9907

CONCORD
Rabbi Berel Kesselman 925.326.1613

CONTRA COSTA
Rabbi Dovber Berkowitz 925.937.4101

DANA POINT
Rabbi Eli Goorevitch 949.290.0628

DANVILLE
Rabbi Shmuli Raitman 213.447.6694

EMERYVILLE
Rabbi Menachem Blank 510.859.8808

ENCINO
Rabbi Aryeh Herzog 818.784.9986
Chapter founded by Rabbi Joshua Gordon, OBM

FOLSOM
Rabbi Yossi Grossbaum 916.608.9811

FREMONT
Rabbi Moshe Fuss 510.300.4090

GLENDALE
Rabbi Simcha Backman 818.240.2750

HOLLYWOOD
Rabbi Zalman Partouche 818.964.9428

HUNTINGTON BEACH
Rabbi Aron David Berkowitz 714.846.2285

LAGUNA NIGUEL
Rabbi Mendy Paltiel 949.831.7701

LA JOLLA
Rabbi Baruch Shalom Ezagui 858.455.5433

LAKE BALBOA
Rabbi Eli Gurary 347.403.6734

LOMITA
Rabbi Sholom Pinson 310.326.8234

LONG BEACH
Rabbi Abba Perelmuter 562.773.1350

LOS ANGELES
Rabbi Yossi Elifort 310.515.5310
Rabbi Leibel Korf 323.660.5177
Rabbi Zalmy Labkowsky 213.618.9486
Rabbi Mendel Zajac 310.770.9051

MALIBU
Rabbi Levi Cunin 310.456.6588

MARINA DEL REY
Rabbi Danny Yiftach-Hashem
Rabbi Dovid Yiftach 310.859.0770

MAR VISTA
Rabbi Shimon Simpson 646.401.2354

NEWHALL
Rabbi Choni Marosov 661.254.3434

NORTHRIDGE
Rabbi Eli Rivkin 818.368.3937

OJAI
Rabbi Mordechai Nemtzov 805.613.7181

PACIFIC PALISADES
Rabbi Zushe Cunin 310.454.7783

PALO ALTO
Rabbi Menachem Landa 415.418.4768
Rabbi Yosef Levin
Rabbi Ber Rosenblatt 650.424.9800

PASADENA
Rabbi Zushe Rivkin 626.788.3343

PLEASANTON
Rabbi Josh Zebberman 925.846.0700

POWAY
Rabbi Mendel Goldstein 858.208.6613

RANCHO CUCAMONGA
Rabbi Sholom Ber Harlig 909.949.4553

RANCHO MIRAGE
Rabbi Shimon H. Posner 760.770.7785

RANCHO PALOS VERDES
Rabbi Yitzchok Magalnic 310.544.5544

RANCHO S. FE
Rabbi Levi Raskin 858.756.7571

REDONDO BEACH
Rabbi Yossi Mintz
Rabbi Zalman Gordon 310.214.4999

RIVERSIDE
Rabbi Shmuel Fuss 951.329.2747

S. CLEMENTE
Rabbi Menachem M. Slavin 949.489.0723

S. CRUZ
Rabbi Yochanan Friedman 831.454.0101

S. DIEGO
Rabbi Rafi Andrusier 619.387.8770
Rabbi Yechiel Cagen 832.216.1534

S. FRANCISCO
Rebbetzin Mattie Pil 415.933.4310
Rabbi Gedalia Potash 415.648.8000
Rabbi Shlomo Zarchi 415.752.2866

S. MATEO
Rabbi Yossi Marcus 650.341.4510

S. RAFAEL
Rabbi Yisrael Rice 415.492.1666

SHERMAN OAKS
Rabbi Nachman Abend 818.989.9539

SONOMA
Rabbi Mendel Wolvovsky 707.292.6221

SOUTH LAKE TAHOE
Rabbi Mordechai Richler 530.539.4363

SUNNYVALE
Rabbi Yisroel Hecht 408.720.0553

TEMECULA
Rabbi Yonason Abrams 951.234.4196

TUSTIN
Rabbi Yehoshua Eliezrie...............714.508.2150

VACAVILLE
Rabbi Chaim Zaklos...............707.592.5300

WEST HILLS
Rabbi Avi Rabin...............818.337.4544

WEST HOLLYWOOD
Rabbi Mordechai Kirschenbaum...............310.691.9988

WEST LOS ANGELES
Rabbi Mordechai Zaetz...............424.652.8742

YORBA LINDA
Rabbi Dovid Eliezrie...............714.693.0770

COLORADO

ASPEN
Rabbi Mendel Mintz...............970.544.3770

DENVER
Rabbi Yossi Serebryanski...............303.744.9699
Rabbi Mendel Popack...............720.515.4337
Rabbi Mendy Sirota...............720.940.3716

FORT COLLINS
Rabbi Yerachmiel Gorelik...............970.407.1613

HIGHLANDS RANCH
Rabbi Avraham Mintz...............303.694.9119

LONGMONT
Rabbi Yakov Borenstein...............303.678.7595

VAIL
Rabbi Dovid Mintz...............970.476.7887

WESTMINSTER
Rabbi Benjy Brackman...............303.429.5177

CONNECTICUT

FAIRFIELD
Rabbi Shlame Landa...............203.373.7551

GREENWICH
Rabbi Yossi Deren
Rabbi Menachem Feldman...............203.629.9059

HAMDEN
Rabbi Moshe Hecht...............203.635.7268

MILFORD
Rabbi Schneur Wilhelm...............203.887.7603

NEW HAVEN
Rabbi Mendy Hecht...............203.589.5375
Rabbi Chanoch Wineberg...............203.479.0313

NEW LONDON
Rabbi Avrohom Sternberg...............860.437.8000

STAMFORD
Rabbi Yisrael Deren
Rabbi Levi Mendelow...............203.3.CHABAD

WESTPORT
Rabbi Yehuda Kantor...............561.460.3758

WEST HARTFORD
Rabbi Shaya Gopin...............860.232.1116

SHELTON
Rabbi Schneur Brook...............203.364.4149

DELAWARE

WILMINGTON
Rabbi Chuni Vogel...............302.529.9900

DISTRICT OF COLUMBIA

WASHINGTON
Rabbi Levi Shemtov
Rabbi Yitzy Ceitlin...............202.332.5600

FLORIDA

ALTAMONTE SPRINGS
Rabbi Mendy Bronstein...............407.280.0535

BAL HARBOUR
Rabbi Dov Schochet...............305.868.1411

BOCA RATON
Rabbi Zalman Bukiet...............561.487.2934
Rabbi Arele Gopin...............561.994.6257
Rabbi Moishe Denburg...............561.526.5760
Rabbi Ruvi New...............561.394.9770

BONITA SPRINGS
Rabbi Mendy Greenberg...............239.949.6900

BOYNTON BEACH
Rabbi Yosef Yitzchok Raichik...............561.732.4633

BRADENTON
Rabbi Menachem Bukiet...............941.388.9656

CAPE CORAL
Rabbi Yossi Labkowski...............239.963.4770

CORAL GABLES
Rabbi Avrohom Stolik 305.490.7572

CORAL SPRINGS
Rabbi Yankie Denburg 954.471.8646

CUTLER BAY
Rabbi Yossi Wolff 305.975.6680

DAVIE
Rabbi Aryeh Schwartz 954.376.9973

DELRAY BEACH
Rabbi Yaakov Perman 561.666.2770

FISHER ISLAND
Rabbi Efraim Brody 347.325.1913

FLEMING ISLAND
Rabbi Shmuly Feldman 904.290.1017

FORT LAUDERDALE
Rabbi Yitzchok Naparstek 954.568.1190

HALLANDALE BEACH
Rabbi Mordy Feiner 954.458.1877

HOLLYWOOD
Rabbi Leibel Kudan 954.801.3367

JUPITER
Rabbi Berel Barash 561.317.0968

KENDALL
Rabbi Yossi Harlig 305.234.5654

KEY BISCAYNE
Rabbi Avremel Caroline 305.365.6744

LAUDERHILL
Rabbi Shmuel Heidingsfeld 323.877.7703

LONGWOOD
Rabbi Yanky Majesky 407.636.5994

MAITLAND
Rabbi Sholom Dubov
Rabbi Levik Dubov 470.644.2500

MARION COUNTY
Rabbi Yossi Hecht 352.330.4466

MIAMI
Rabbi Mendy Cheruty 305.219.3353
Rabbi Yakov Fellig 305.445.5444

MIAMI BEACH
Rabbi Yisroel Frankforter 305.534.3895

N. MIAMI BEACH
Rabbi Eli Laufer 305.770.4412

ORLANDO
Rabbi Yosef Konikov 407.354.3660

ORMOND BEACH
Rabbi Asher Farkash 386.672.9300

PALM CITY
Rabbi Shlomo Uminer 772.485.5501

PALM BEACH
Rabbi Zalman Levitin 561.659.3884

PALM BEACH GARDENS
Rabbi Dovid Vigler 561.624.2223

PALM HARBOR
Rabbi Pinchas Adler 727.789.0408

PARKLAND
Rabbi Mendy Gutnick 954.600.6991

PEMBROKE PINES
Rabbi Mordechai Andrusier 954.874.2280

PLANTATION
Rabbi Pinchas Taylor 954.644.9177

PONTE VEDRA BEACH
Rabbi Nochum Kurinsky 904.543.9301

ROYAL PALM BEACH
Rabbi Nachmen Zeev Schtroks 561.714.1692

S. AUGUSTINE
Rabbi Levi Vogel 904.521.8664

S. JOHNS
Rabbi Mendel Sharfstein 347.461.3765

SARASOTA
Rabbi Chaim Shaul Steinmetz 941.925.0770

SATELLITE BEACH
Rabbi Zvi Konikov 321.777.2770

SINGER ISLAND
Rabbi Berel Namdar 347.276.6985

SOUTH PALM BEACH
Rabbi Leibel Stolik 561.889.3499

SOUTH TAMPA
Rabbi Mendy Dubrowski 813.922.1723

SOUTHWEST BROWARD COUNTY
Rabbi Aryeh Schwartz 954.252.1770

SUNNY ISLES BEACH
Rabbi Alexander Kaller 305.803.5315

SURFSIDE
Rabbi Dov Schochet 305.790.8294

TAMARAC
Rabbi Kopel Silberberg 954.882.7434

VENICE
Rabbi Sholom Ber Schmerling 941.330.4477

WESLEY CHAPEL
Rabbi Mendy Yarmush
Rabbi Mendel Friedman 813.731.2977

WEST PALM BEACH
Rabbi Yoel Gancz 561.659.7770

WESTON
Rabbi Yisroel Spalter 954.349.6565

GEORGIA

ALPHARETTA
Rabbi Hirshy Minkowicz 770.410.9000

ATLANTA
Rabbi Yossi New
Rabbi Isser New 404.843.2464
Rabbi Alexander Piekarski 678.267.6418

ATLANTA: INTOWN
Rabbi Eliyahu Schusterman
Rabbi Ari Sollish 404.898.0434

CUMMING
Rabbi Levi Mentz 310.666.2218

GWINNETT
Rabbi Yossi Lerman 678.595.0196

MARIETTA
Rabbi Ephraim Silverman 770.565.4412

HAWAII

KAPA'A
Rabbi Michoel Goldman 808.647.4293

IDAHO

BOISE
Rabbi Mendel Lifshitz 208.853.9200

ILLINOIS

ARLINGTON HEIGHTS
Rabbi Yaakov Kotlarsky 224.357.7002

CHAMPAIGN
Rabbi Dovid Tiechtel 217.355.8672

CHICAGO
Rabbi Meir Hecht 312.714.4655
Rabbi Dovid Kotlarsky 773.495.7127
Rabbi Mordechai Gershon 773.412.5189
Rabbi Yosef Moscowitz 773.772.3770
Rabbi Levi Notik 773.274.5123

DES PLAINES
Rabbi Lazer Hershkovich 224.392.4442

ELGIN
Rabbi Mendel Shemtov 847.440.4486

GLENVIEW
Rabbi Yishaya Benjaminson 847.910.1738

GURNEE
Rabbi Sholom Tenenbaum 847.782.1800

HIGHLAND PARK
Mrs. Michla Schanowitz 847.266.0770

NAPERVILLE
Rabbi Mendy Goldstein 630.957.8122

NORTHBROOK
Rabbi Meir Moscowitz 847.564.8770

NORWOOD PARK
Rabbi Mendel Perlstein 312.752.8894

OAK PARK
Rabbi Yitzchok Bergstein 708.524.1530

PEORIA
Rabbi Eli Langsam 309.370.7701

SKOKIE
Rabbi Yochanan Posner 847.677.1770

VERNON HILLS
Rabbi Shimmy Susskind 718.755.5356

WILMETTE
Rabbi Dovid Flinkenstein 847.251.7707

INDIANA

INDIANAPOLIS
Rabbi Avraham Grossbaum
Rabbi Dr. Shmuel Klatzkin 317.251.5573

IOWA

BETTENDORF
Rabbi Shneur Cadaner 563.355.1065

KANSAS

OVERLAND PARK
Rabbi Mendy Wineberg 913.649.4852

KENTUCKY

LOUISVILLE
Rabbi Avrohom Litvin 502.459.1770

LOUISIANA

BATON ROUGE
Rabbi Peretz Kazen 225.267.7047

METAIRIE
Rabbi Yossie Nemes
Rabbi Mendel Ceitlin 504.454.2910

NEW ORLEANS
Rabbi Mendel Rivkin 504.302.1830

MAINE

PORTLAND
Rabbi Levi Wilansky 207.650.1783

MARYLAND

BALTIMORE
Rabbi Velvel Belinsky 410.764.5000
Classes in Russian

Rabbi Dovid Reyder 781.796.4204

BEL AIR
Rabbi Kushi Schusterman 443.353.9718

BETHESDA
Rabbi Sender Geisinsky 301.913.9777

CHEVY CHASE
Rabbi Zalman Minkowitz 301.260.5000

COLUMBIA
Rabbi Hillel Baron
Rabbi Yosef Chaim Sufrin 410.740.2424

FREDERICK
Rabbi Boruch Labkowski 301.996.3659

GAITHERSBURG
Rabbi Sholom Raichik 301.926.3632

OLNEY
Rabbi Bentzy Stolik 301.660.6770

OWINGS MILLS
Rabbi Nochum Katsenelenbogen 410.356.5156

POTOMAC
Rabbi Mendel Bluming 301.983.4200
Rabbi Mendel Kaplan 301.983.1485

ROCKVILLE
Rabbi Shlomo Beitsh 646.773.2675
Rabbi Moishe Kavka 301.836.1242

MASSACHUSETTS

ANDOVER
Rabbi Asher Bronstein 978.470.2288

ARLINGTON
Rabbi Avi Bukiet 617.909.8653

BOSTON
Rabbi Yosef Zaklos 617.297.7282

BRIGHTON
Rabbi Dan Rodkin 617.787.2200

CAPE COD
Rabbi Yekusiel Alperowitz 508.775.2324

CHESTNUT HILL
Rabbi Mendy Uminer 617.738.9770

LEXINGTON
Rabbi Yisroel New 646.248.9053

LONGMEADOW
Rabbi Yakov Wolff 413.567.8665

NEWTON
Rabbi Shalom Ber Prus 617.244.1200

PEABODY
Rabbi Nechemia Schusterman 978.977.9111

SUDBURY
Rabbi Yisroel Freeman 978.443.0110

SWAMPSCOTT
Rabbi Yossi Lipsker 781.581.3833

MICHIGAN

ANN ARBOR
Rabbi Aharon Goldstein 734.995.3276

BLOOMFIELD HILLS
Rabbi Levi Dubov 248.949.6210

GRAND RAPIDS
Rabbi Mordechai Haller 616.957.0770

TROY
Rabbi Menachem Caytak 248.873.5851

WEST BLOOMFIELD
Rabbi Shneur Silberberg 248.855.6170

MINNESOTA

MINNETONKA
Rabbi Mordechai Grossbaum
Rabbi Shmuel Silberstein 952.929.9922

S. PAUL
Rabbi Shneur Zalman Bendet 651.998.9298

MISSOURI

S. LOUIS
Rabbi Yosef Landa 314.725.0400
Rabbi Yosef Abenson 314.448.0927

MONTANA

BOZEMAN
Rabbi Chaim Shaul Bruk 406.600.4934

NEVADA

LAS VEGAS
Rabbi Yosef Rivkin 702.217.2170

SUMMERLIN
Rabbi Yisroel Schanowitz
Rabbi Tzvi Bronchtain 702.855.0770

NEW JERSEY

BASKING RIDGE
Rabbi Mendy Herson
Rabbi Mendel Shemtov 908.604.8844

CHERRY HILL
Rabbi Mendel Mangel 856.874.1500

CLINTON
Rabbi Eli Kornfeld 908.623.7000

ENGLEWOOD
Rabbi Shmuel Konikov 201.519.7343

FAIR LAWN
Rabbi Avrohom Bergstein 201.794.3770

GREATER MERCER COUNTY
Rabbi Dovid Dubov
Rabbi Yaakov Chaiton 609.213.4136

HASKELL
Rabbi Mendy Gurkov 201.696.7609

HOLMDEL
Rabbi Shmaya Galperin 732.772.1998

MADISON
Rabbi Shalom Lubin 973.377.0707

MANALAPAN
Rabbi Boruch Chazanow
Rabbi Levi Wolosow 732.972.3687

MEDFORD
Rabbi Yitzchok Kahan 609.451.3522

MOUNTAIN LAKES
Rabbi Levi Dubinsky 973.551.1898

MULLICA HILL
Rabbi Avrohom Richler 856.733.0770

OLD TAPPAN
Rabbi Mendy Lewis 201.767.4008

RED BANK
Rabbi Dovid Harrison 718.915.8748

ROCKAWAY
Rabbi Asher Herson
Rabbi Mordechai Baumgarten 973.625.1525

RUTHERFORD
Rabbi Yitzchok Lerman 347.834.7500

SCOTCH PLAINS
Rabbi Avrohom Blesofsky 908.790.0008

SHORT HILLS
Rabbi Mendel Solomon
Rabbi Avrohom Levin 973.725.7008

SOUTH BRUNSWICK
Rabbi Levi Azimov 732.398.9492

TENAFLY
Rabbi Mordechai Shain 201.871.1152

TOMS RIVER
Rabbi Moshe Gourarie 732.349.4199

WEST ORANGE
Rabbi Mendy Kasowitz 973.325.6311

WOODCLIFF LAKE
Rabbi Dov Drizin 201.476.0157

NEW MEXICO

LAS CRUCES
Rabbi Bery Schmukler 575.524.1330

NEW YORK

ALBANY
Rabbi Mordechai Rubin 518.368.7886

BAY SHORE
Rabbi Shimon Stillerman 631.913.8770

BEDFORD
Rabbi Arik Wolf 914.666.6065

BENSONHURST
Rabbi Avrohom Hertz 718.753.7768

BINGHAMTON
Mrs. Rivkah Slonim 607.797.0015

BRIGHTON BEACH
Rabbi Dovid Okonov 718.368.4490
Rabbi Moshe Winner 718.946.9833

BRONXVILLE
Rabbi Sruli Deitsch 917.755.0078

BROOKLYN
Rabbi Nissi Eber 347.677.2276
Rabbi Dovid Okonov 917.754.6942

BROOKVILLE
Rabbi Mendy Heber 516.626.0600

CEDARHURST
Rabbi Zalman Wolowik 516.295.2478

COMMACK
Rabbi Mendel Teldon 631.543.3343

DELMAR
Rabbi Zalman Simon 518.866.7658

DOBBS FERRY
Rabbi Benjy Silverman 914.693.6100

EAST HAMPTON
Rabbi Leibel Baumgarten
Rabbi Mendy Goldberg 631.329.5800

ELLENVILLE
Rabbi Shlomie Deren 845.647.4450

FOREST HILLS
Rabbi Yossi Mendelson 917.861.9726

GLEN OAKS
Rabbi Shmuel Nadler 347.388.7064

GREAT NECK
Rabbi Yoseph Geisinsky 516.487.4554

KINGSTON
Rabbi Yitzchok Hecht 845.334.9044

LARCHMONT
Rabbi Mendel Silberstein 914.834.4321

LITTLE NECK
Rabbi Eli Shifrin 718.423.1235

LONG BEACH
Rabbi Eli Goodman 516.574.3905

MANHASSET
Rabbi Mendel Paltiel 516.984.0701

MINEOLA
Rabbi Anchelle Perl 516.739.3636

MONTEBELLO
Rabbi Shmuel Gancz 845.746.1927

MELVILLE
Rabbi Yosef Raskin 631.276.4453

NEW HARTFORD
Rabbi Levi Charitonow 716.322.8692

NEW YORK
Rabbi Yakov Bankhalter 917.613.1678
Rabbi Berel Gurevitch 212.518.3122
Rabbi Daniel Kraus 917.294.5567
Rabbi Shmuel Metzger 212.758.3770

NYC TRIBECA
Rabbi Zalman Paris 212.566.6764

NYC UPPER EAST SIDE
Rabbi Uriel Vigler 212.369.7310

NYC WEST SIDE
Rabbi Shlomo Kugel 212.864.5010

OCEANSIDE
Rabbi Levi Gurkow 516.764.7385

OSSINING
Rabbi Dovid Labkowski 914.923.2522

OYSTER BAY
Rabbi Shmuel Lipszyc
Rabbi Shalom Lipszyc 347.853.9992

PARK SLOPE
Rabbi Menashe Wolf 347.957.1291

PORT WASHINGTON
Rabbi Shalom Paltiel 516.767.8672

PROSPECT HEIGHTS
Rabbi Mendy Hecht 347.622.3599

ROSLYN HEIGHTS
Rabbi Aaron Konikov 516.484.3500

ROCHESTER
Rabbi Nechemia Vogel 585.271.0330

SOUTHAMPTON
Rabbi Chaim Pape 917.627.4865

STATEN ISLAND
Rabbi Mendy Katzman 718.370.8953

STONY BROOK
Rabbi Shalom Ber Cohen 631.585.0521

SUFFERN
Rabbi Shmuel Gancz 845.368.1889

YORKTOWN HEIGHTS
Rabbi Yehuda Heber 914.962.1111

NORTH CAROLINA

CARY
Rabbi Yisroel Cotlar 919.651.9710

CHAPEL HILL
Rabbi Zalman Bluming 919.357.5904

CHARLOTTE
Rabbi Yossi Groner
Rabbi Shlomo Cohen 704.366.3984

GREENSBORO
Rabbi Yosef Plotkin 336.617.8120

RALEIGH
Rabbi Pinchas Herman
Rabbi Lev Cotlar 919.637.6950

WINSTON-SALEM
Rabbi Levi Gurevitz 336.756.9069

OHIO

BEACHWOOD
Rabbi Moshe Gancz 216.647.4884

CINCINNATI
Rabbi Yisroel Mangel 513.793.5200

COLUMBUS
Rabbi Yitzi Kaltmann 614.294.3296

DAYTON
Rabbi Nochum Mangel
Rabbi Shmuel Klatzkin 937.643.0770

OKLAHOMA

OKLAHOMA CITY
Rabbi Ovadia Goldman 405.524.4800

TULSA
Rabbi Yehuda Weg 918.492.4499

OREGON

PORTLAND
Rabbi Mordechai Wilhelm 503.977.9947

SALEM
Rabbi Avrohom Yitzchok Perlstein 503.383.9569

TIGARD
Rabbi Menachem Orenstein 971.329.6661

PENNSYLVANIA

AMBLER
Rabbi Shaya Deitsch 215.591.9310

BALA CYNWYD
Rabbi Shraga Sherman 610.660.9192

CLARKS SUMMIT
Rabbi Benny Rapoport 570.587.3300

DOYLESTOWN
Rabbi Mendel Prus 215.340.1303

GLEN MILLS
Rabbi Yehuda Gerber 484.620.4162

LAFAYETTE HILL
Rabbi Yisroel Kotlarsky 484.533.7009

LANCASTER
Rabbi Elazar Green 717.723.8783

LEWISBURG
Rabbi Yisroel Baumgarten 631.880.2801

MONROEVILLE
Rabbi Mendy Schapiro 412.372.1000

NEWTOWN
Rabbi Aryeh Weinstein 215.497.9925

PHILADELPHIA: CENTER CITY
Rabbi Yochonon Goldman 215.238.2100

PITTSBURGH
Rabbi Yisroel Altein .... 412.422.7300 EXT. 269

PITTSBURGH: SOUTH HILLS
Rabbi Mendy Rosenblum 412.278.3693

READING
Rabbi Yosef Lipsker 610.334.3218

RYDAL
Rabbi Zushe Gurevitz 267.536.5757

UNIVERSITY PARK
Rabbi Nosson Meretsky 814.863.4929

WYNNEWOOD
Rabbi Moishe Brennan 610.529.9011

PUERTO RICO

CAROLINA
Rabbi Mendel Zarchi 787.253.0894

RHODE ISLAND

WARWICK
Rabbi Yossi Laufer 401.884.7888

SOUTH CAROLINA

BLUFFTON
Rabbi Menachem Hertz 843.301.1819

COLUMBIA
Rabbi Hesh Epstein
Rabbi Levi Marrus 803.782.1831

GREENVILLE
Rabbi Leibel Kesselman 864.534.7739

TENNESSEE

KNOXVILLE
Rabbi Yossi Wilhelm 865.588.8584

MEMPHIS
Rabbi Levi Klein 901.754.0404

TEXAS

AUSTIN
Rabbi Mendy Levertov 512.905.2778

BELLAIRE
Rabbi Yossi Zaklikofsky 713.839.8887

CYPRESS
Rabbi Levi Marinovsky 832.651.6964

DALLAS
Rabbi Mendel Dubrawsky
Rabbi Moshe Naparstek 972.818.0770

EL PASO
Rabbi Levi Greenberg 347.678.9762

FORT WORTH
Rabbi Dov Mandel 817.263.7701

HOUSTON
Rabbi Dovid Goldstein
Rabbi Zally Lazarus 281.589.7188
Rabbi Moishe Traxler 713.774.0300

HOUSTON: RICE UNIVERSITY AREA
Rabbi Eliezer Lazaroff 713.522.2004

LEAGUE CITY
Rabbi Yitzchok Schmukler 281.724.1554

PLANO
Rabbi Eli Block 214.620.4083
Rabbi Mendel Block 972.596.8270

ROCKWALL
Rabbi Moshe Kalmenson 469.350.5735

ROUND ROCK
Rabbi Mendel Marasow 512.387.3171

S. ANTONIO
Rabbi Chaim Block
Rabbi Levi Teldon 210.492.1085
Rabbi Tal Shaul 210.877.4218

SOUTHLAKE
Rabbi Levi Gurevitch 817.451.1171

SUGAR LAND
Rabbi Mendel Feigenson 832.758.0685

THE WOODLANDS
Rabbi Mendel Blecher 281.865.7242

UTAH

PARK CITY
Rabbi Yehuda Steiger 435.714.8590

SALT LAKE CITY
Rabbi Benny Zippel 801.467.7777

S. GEORGE
Rabbi Mendy Cohen 862.812.6224

VERMONT

BURLINGTON
Rabbi Yitzchok Raskin 802.658.5770

VIRGINIA

ALEXANDRIA/ARLINGTON
Rabbi Mordechai Newman 703.370.2774

FAIRFAX
Rabbi Leibel Fajnland 703.426.1980

GAINESVILLE
Rabbi Shmuel Perlstein 571.445.0342

LOUDOUN COUNTY
Rabbi Chaim Cohen 248.298.9279

NORFOLK
Rabbi Aaron Margolin
Rabbi Levi Brashevitzky 757.616.0770

RICHMOND
Rabbi Shlomo Pereira 804.740.2000

WINCHESTER
Rabbi Yisahi Dinerman 540.324.9879

WASHINGTON

BAINBRIDGE ISLAND
Rabbi Mendy Goldshmid 206.397.7679

BELLINGHAM
Rabbi Yosef Truxton 360.224.9919

MERCER ISLAND
Rabbi Elazar Bogomilsky 206.527.1411
Rabbi Nissan Kornfeld 206.851.2324

OLYMPIA
Rabbi Yosef Schtroks 360.867.8804

SEATTLE
Rabbi Yoni Levitin 206.851.9831
Rabbi Shnai Levitin 347.342.2259

SPOKANE COUNTY
Rabbi Yisroel Hahn 509.443.0770

WISCONSIN

BAYSIDE
Rabbi Cheski Edelman 414.439.5041

BROOKFIELD
Rabbi Levi Brook 925.708.4203

KENOSHA
Rabbi Tzali Wilschanski 262.359.0770

MADISON
Rabbi Avremel Matusof 608.335.3777

MEQUON
Rabbi Menachem Rapoport 262.242.2235

MILWAUKEE
Rabbi Levi Emmer 414.277.8839
Rabbi Mendel Shmotkin 414.961.6100

ARGENTINA

BUENOS AIRES
Mrs. Chani Gorowitz 54.11.4865.0445
Rabbi Menachem M. Grunblatt 54.911.3574.0037
Rabbi Mendy Gurevitch 55.11.4545.7771
Rabbi Shlomo Levy 54.11.4807.2223
Rabbi Yosef Levy 54.11.4504.1908
Rabbi Mendi Mizrahi 54.11.4963.1221
Rabbi Shiele Plotka 54.11.4634.3111
Rabbi Pinhas Sudry 54.1.4822.2285
Rabbi Shloimi Setton 54.11.4982.8637

CORDOBA
Rabbi Menajem Turk 54.351.233.8250

SALTA
Rabbi Rafael Tawil 54.387.421.4947

S. MIGUEL DE TUCUMÁN
Rabbi Ariel Levy 54.381.473.6944

AUSTRALIA

NEW SOUTH WALES

BELLEVUE HILL
Mrs. Chaya Kaye 614.3342.2755

DOUBLE BAY
Rabbi Yanky Berger 612.9327.1644

DOVER HEIGHTS
Rabbi Motti Feldman 614.0400.8572

NEWTOWN
Rabbi Eli Feldman 614.0077.0613

NORTH SHORE
Rabbi Nochum Schapiro
Rebbetzin Fruma Schapiro 612.9488.9548

TASMANIA

SOUTH LAUNCESTON
Mrs Rochel Gordon 614.2055.0405

QUEENSLAND

BRISBANE
Rabbi Levi Jaffe 617.3843.6770

VICTORIA

EAST S. KILDA
Rabbi Sholem Gorelik 614.5244.8770

MOORABBIN
Rabbi Elisha Greenbaum 614.0349.0434

WESTERN AUSTRALIA

PERTH
Rabbi Shalom White 618.9275.2106

AZERBAIJAN

BAKU
Mrs. Chavi Segal 994.12.597.91.90

BELARUS

BOBRUISK
Mrs. Mina Hababo 375.29.104.3230

MINSK
Rabbi Shneur Deitsch
Mrs. Bassie Deitsch 375.29.330.6675

BELGIUM

ANTWERP
Rabbi Mendel Gurary 32.48.656.9878

BRUSSELS
Rabbi Shmuel Pinson 375.29.330.6675

BRAZIL

CURITIBA
Rabbi Mendy Labkowski 55.41.3079.1338

S. PAULO
Rabbi Avraham Steinmetz 55.11.3081.3081

CANADA

ALBERTA

CALGARY
Rabbi Mordechai Groner 403.281.3770

EDMONTON
Rabbi Ari Drelich
Rabbi Mendy Blachman 780.200.5770

BRITISH COLUMBIA

NANAIMO
Rabbi Benzti Shemtov 250.797.7877

RICHMOND
Rabbi Yechiel Baitelman 604.277.6427

VANCOUVER
Rabbi Dovid Rosenfeld 604.266.1313
Rabbi Shmuel Yeshayahu 604.738.7060

VICTORIA
Rabbi Meir Kaplan 250.595.7656

MANITOBA

WINNIPEG
Rabbi Shmuel Altein 204.339.8737

ONTARIO

BAYVIEW
Rabbi Levi Gansburg 416.551.9391

MAPLE
Rabbi Yechezkel Deren 647.883.6372

MISSISSAUGA
Rabbi Yitzchok Slavin 905.820.4432

NORTH YORK
Rabbi Sruli Steiner 647.501.5618

OTTAWA
Rabbi Menachem M. Blum 613.843.7770

RICHMOND HILL
Rabbi Mendel Bernstein 905.303.1880

THORNHILL
Rabbi Yisroel Landa 416.897.3338

GREATER TORONTO REGIONAL OFFICE & THORNHILL
Rabbi Yossi Gansburg 905.731.7000

TORONTO
Rabbi Shmuel Neft 647.966.7105
Rabbi Moshe Steiner 416.635.9606

WATERLOO
Rabbi Moshe Goldman 226.338.7770

QUEBEC

CÔTE S.-LUC
Rabbi Levi Naparstek 438.409.6770

DOLLARD-DES ORMEAUX
Rabbi Leibel Fine 514.777.4675

HAMPSTEAD
Rabbi Moshe New
Rabbi Berel Bell 514.739.0770

MONTREAL
Rabbi Ronnie Fine
Pesach Nussbaum 514.738.3434

OLD MONTREAL/GRIFFINTOWN
Rabbi Nissan Gansbourg
Rabbi Berel Bell 514.800.6966

S. LAZARE
Rabbi Nochum Labkowski 514.436.7426

TOWN OF MOUNT ROYAL
Rabbi Moshe Krasnanski
Rabbi Shneur Zalman Rader 514.342.1770

SASKATCHEWAN

SASKATOON
Rabbi Raphael Kats 306.384.4370

CAYMAN ISLANDS

GEORGE TOWN
Rabbi Berel Pewzner 717.798.1040

COLOMBIA

BOGOTA
Rabbi Chanoch Piekarski 57.1.635.8251

COSTA RICA

S. JOSÉ
Rabbi Hershel Spalter
Rabbi Moshe Bitton 506.4010.1515

CROATIA

ZAGREB
Rabbi Pinchas Zaklas 385.1.4812227

DENMARK

COPENHAGEN
Rabbi Yitzchok Loewenthal 45.3316.1850

DOMINICAN REPUBLIC

S. DOMINGO
Rabbi Shimon Pelman 829.341.2770

ESTONIA

TALLINN
Rabbi Shmuel Kot 372.662.30.50

FRANCE

BOULOGNE
Rabbi Michael Sojcher 33.1.46.99.87.85

DIJON
Rabbi Chaim Slonim 33.6.52.05.26.65

LA VARENNE-S.-HILAIRE
Rabbi Mena'hem Mendel Benelbaz 33.6.17.81.57.47

MARSEILLE
Rabbi Eliahou Altabe 33.6.11.60.03.05
Rabbi Mena'hem Mendel Assouline 33.6.64.88.25.04
Rabbi Emmanuel Taubenblatt 33.4.88.00.94.85

PARIS
Rabbi Yona Hasky 33.1.53.75.36.01
Rabbi Acher Marciano 33.6.15.15.01.02
Rabbi Avraham Barou'h Pevzner 33.6.99.64.07.70

PONTAULT-COMBAULT
Rabbi Yossi Amar 33.6.61.36.07.70

VILLIERS-SUR-MARNE
Rabbi Mena'hem Mendel Mergui 33.1.49.30.89.66

GEORGIA

TBILISI
Rabbi Meir Kozlovsky 995.32.2429770

GERMANY

BERLIN
Rabbi Yehuda Tiechtel 49.30.2128.0830

DUSSELDORF
Rabbi Chaim Barkahn 49.173.2871.770

HAMBURG
Rabbi Shlomo Bistritzky 49.40.4142.4190

HANNOVER 49.511.811.2822
Chapter founded by Rabbi Binyamin Wolff, OBM

GREECE

ATHENS
Rabbi Mendel Hendel 30.210.323.3825

GUATEMALA

GUATEMALA CITY
Rabbi Shalom Pelman 502.2485.0770

ISRAEL

ASHKELON
Rabbi Shneor Lieberman 054.977.0512

BALFURYA
Rabbi Noam Bar-Tov 054.580.4770

CAESAREA
Rabbi Chaim Meir Lieberman 054.621.2586

EVEN YEHUDA
Rabbi Menachem Noyman 054.777.0707

GANEI TIKVA
Rabbi Gershon Shnur 054.524.2358

GIV'ATAYIM
Rabbi Pinchus Bitton 052.643.8770

JERUSALEM
Rabbi Levi Diamond 055.665.7702
Rabbi Avraham Hendel 054.830.5799

KARMIEL
Rabbi Mendy Elishevitz 054.521.3073

KFAR SABA
Rabbi Yossi Baitch 054.445.5020

KIRYAT BIALIK
Rabbi Pinny Marton 050.661.1768

KIRYAT MOTZKIN
Rabbi Shimon Eizenbach 050.902.0770

KOCHAV YAIR
Rabbi Dovi Greenberg 054.332.6244

MACCABIM-RE'UT
Rabbi Yosef Yitzchak Noiman 054.977.0549

NES ZIYONA
Rabbi Menachem Feldman 054.497.7092

NETANYA
Rabbi Schneur Brod 054.579.7572

RAMAT GAN-KRINITZI
Rabbi Yisroel Gurevitz 052.743.2814

RAMAT GAN-MAROM NAVE
Rabbi Binyamin Meir Kali 050.476.0770

RAMAT YISHAI
Rabbi Shneor Zalman Wolosow 052.324.5475

RISHON LEZION
Rabbi Uri Keshet 050.722.4593

ROSH PINA
Rabbi Sholom Ber Hertzel 052.458.7600

TEL AVIV
Rabbi Shneur Piekarski 054.971.5568

JAMAICA

MONTEGO BAY
Rabbi Yaakov Raskin 876.452.3223

JAPAN

TOKYO
Rabbi Mendi Sudakevich 81.3.5789.2846

KAZAKHSTAN

ALMATY
Rabbi Shevach Zlatopolsky 7.7272.77.59.49

KYRGYZSTAN

BISHKEK
Rabbi Arye Raichman 996.312.68.19.66

LATVIA

RIGA
Rabbi Shneur Zalman Kot
Mrs. Rivka Glazman 371.6720.40.22

LITHUANIA

VILNIUS
Rabbi Sholom Ber Krinsky 370.6817.1367

LUXEMBOURG

LUXEMBOURG
Rabbi Mendel Edelman 352.2877.7079

MEXICO

S. MIGUEL DE ALLENDE
Rabbi Daniel Huebner 52.41.5181.8092

NETHERLANDS

ALMERE
Rabbi Moshe Stiefel 31.36.744.0509

AMSTERDAM
Rabbi Yanki Jacobs 31.644.988.627
Rabbi Jaacov Zwi Spiero 31.652.328.065

EINDHOVEN
Rabbi Simcha Steinberg 31.63.635.7593

HAGUE
Rabbi Shmuel Katzman 31.70.347.0222

HEEMSTEDE-HAARLEM
Rabbi Shmuel Spiero 31.23.532.0707

MAASTRICHT
Rabbi Avrohom Cohen 32.48.549.6766

NIJMEGEN
Rabbi Menachem Mendel Levine 31.621.586.575

ROTTERDAM
Rabbi Yehuda Vorst 31.10.265.5530

PANAMA

PANAMA CITY
Rabbi Ari Laine
Rabbi Gabriel Benayon 507.223.3383

RUSSIA

ASTRAKHAN
Rabbi Yisroel Melamed 7.851.239.28.24

BRYANSK
Rabbi Menachem Mendel Zaklas 7.483.264.55.15

CHELYABINSK
Rabbi Meir Kirsh 7.351.263.24.68

MOSCOW
Rabbi Aizik Rosenfeld 7.906.762.88.81
Rabbi Mordechai Weisberg 7.495.645.50.00

NIZHNY NOVGOROD
Rabbi Shimon Bergman 7.920.253.47.70

NOVOSIBIRSK
Rabbi Shneur Zalmen Zaklos 7.903.900.43.22

OMSK
Rabbi Osher Krichevsky 7.381.231.33.07

PERM
Rabbi Zalman Deutch 7.342.212.47.32

ROSTOV
Rabbi Chaim Danzinger 7.8632.99.02.68

S. PETERSBURG
Rabbi Shalom Pewzner 7.911.726.21.19
Rabbi Zvi Pinsky 7.812.713.62.09

SAMARA
Rabbi Shlomo Deutch 7.846.333.40.64

SARATOV
Rabbi Yaakov Kubitshek 7.8452.21.58.00

TOGLIATTI
Rabbi Meier Fischer 7.848.273.02.84

UFA
Rabbi Dan Krichevsky 7.347.244.55.33

VORONEZH
Rabbi Levi Stiefel 7.473.252.96.99

SINGAPORE

SINGAPORE
Rabbi Mordechai Abergel 656.337.2189
Rabbi Netanel Rivni 656.336.2127
Classes in Hebrew

SOUTH AFRICA

JOHANNESBURG
Rabbi Dovid Masinter
Rabbi Ari Kievman 27.11.440.6600

SWEDEN

STOCKHOLM
Rabbi Chaim Greisman 46.70.790.8994

SWITZERLAND

LUZERN
Rabbi Chaim Drukman 41.41.361.1770

THAILAND

BANGKOK
Rabbi Yosef C. Kantor 6681.837.7618

UKRAINE

BERDITCHEV
Mrs. Chana Thaler 380.637.70.37.70

DNEPROPETROVSK
Rabbi Dan Makagon 380.504.51.13.18

NIKOLAYEV
Rabbi Sholom Gotlieb 380.512.37.37.71

ODESSA
Rabbi Avraham Wolf
Rabbi Yaakov Neiman .... 38.048.728.0770 EXT. 280

ZAPOROZHYE
Mrs. Nechama Dina Ehrentreu 380.957.19.96.08

ZHITOMIR
Rabbi Shlomo Wilhelm 380.504.63.01.32

UNITED KINGDOM

BOURNEMOUTH
Rabbi Bentzion Alperowitz 44.749.456.7177

CHEADLE
Rabbi Peretz Chein 44.161.428.1818

ESSEX

EPPING
Rabbi Yossi Posen 44.749.650.4345

LEEDS
Rabbi Eli Pink 44.113.266.3311

LONDON
Rabbi Moshe Adler 44.771.052.4460
Rabbi Boruch Altein 44.749.612.3342
Rabbi Mechel Gancz 44.758.332.3074
Rabbi Chaim Hoch 44.753.879.9524
Rabbi Dovid Katz 44.207.625.2682
Mrs. Esther Kesselman 44.794.432.4829
Rabbi Mendy Korer 44.794.632.5444
Rabbi Eli Levin 44.754.046.1568
Mrs. Chanie Simon 44.208.458.0416
Rabbi Bentzi Sudak 44.781.211.1890
Rabbi Shneur Wineberg 44.745.628.6538

MANCHESTER
Rabbi Levi Cohen 44.161.792.6335
Rabbi Shmuli Jaffe 44.161.766.1812

RADLETT, HERTFORDSHIRE
Rabbi Alexander Sender Dubrawsky 44.794.380.8965

The Jewish Learning Multiplex

Brought to you by the Rohr Jewish Learning Institute

In fulfillment of the mandate of the Lubavitcher Rebbe, of blessed memory, whose leadership guides every step of our work, the mission of the Rohr Jewish Learning Institute is to transform Jewish life and the greater community through the study of Torah, connecting each Jew to our shared heritage of Jewish learning.

While our flagship program remains the cornerstone of our organization, JLI is proud to feature additional divisions catering to specific populations, in order to meet a wide array of educational needs.

THE ROHR JEWISH LEARNING INSTITUTE

A subsidiary of Merkos L'Inyonei Chinuch,
the adult educational arm of the Chabad-Lubavitch movement

Torah Studies provides a rich and nuanced encounter with the weekly Torah reading.

Jewish teens forge their identity as they engage in Torah study, social interaction, and serious fun.

The Rosh Chodesh Society gathers Jewish women together once a month for intensive textual study.

TorahCafe.com provides an exclusive selection of top-rated Jewish educational videos.

Participants delve into our nation's past while exploring the Holy Land's relevance and meaning today.

This yearly event rejuvenates mind, body, and spirit with a powerful synthesis of Jewish learning and community.

Equips youths facing adulthood with education and resources to address youth mental health.

Select affiliates are invited to partner with peers and noted professionals, as leaders of innovation and excellence.

MyShiur courses are designed to assist students in developing the skills needed to study Talmud independently.

This rigorous fellowship program invites select college students to explore the fundamentals of Judaism.

A crash course that teaches adults to read Hebrew in just five sessions.

Machon Shmuel is an institute providing Torah research in the service of educators worldwide.